THE NORTH STAFFORDSHIRE RAILWAY

UNIFORM WITH THIS BOOK

The Callander & Oban Railway	John Thomas
The Cambrian Railways Volume 1: 1852-1888, Volume 2: 1889-1968	Rex Christiansen and R. W. Miller
The Campbeltown & Machrihanish Light Railway	N. S. C. Macmillan
The Cavan & Leitrim Railway	Patrick J. Flanagan
The Great North of Scotland Railway	H. A. Vallance
The Highland Railway	H. A. Vallance
A History of the Narrow-gauge Railways of North East Ireland *Part One: The Ballycastle Railway* *Part Two: The Ballymena Lines*	Edward M. Patterson
A History of the Narrow-gauge Railways of North-West Ireland *Part One: The County Donegal Railways* (second edition) *Part Two: The Londonderry & Lough Swilly Railway*	Edward M. Patterson
A History of the Railways of the Forest of Dean *Part One: The Severn & Wye Railway* *Part Two: The Great Western Railway in Dean*	H. W. Paar
The Lancashire & Yorkshire Railway, Volumes 1 & 2	John Marshall
The Little Railways of South West Scotland	David L. Smith
The London & South Western Railway, Volume 1	R. A. Williams
The Lynton & Barnstaple Railway	G. A. Brown J. D. C. A. Prideaux and H. G. Radcliffe
The Midland & South Western Junction Railway	Colin G. Maggs
The North British Railway, Volume 1	John Thomas
The North Staffordshire Railway	Rex Christiansen and R. W. Miller
The Ravenglass & Eskdale Railway	W. J. K. Davies
The Royal Deeside Line	A. D. Farr
The Somerset & Dorset Railway	Robin Atthill and O. S. Nock
The West Highland Railway	John Thomas

Superheated 4—4—2T locomotive No 14 departs from Stoke-on-Trent with a Crewe to Derby express in 1912

THE NORTH STAFFORDSHIRE RAILWAY

by

REX CHRISTIANSEN

&

R. W. MILLER

DAVID & CHARLES : NEWTON ABBOT

ISBN 0 7153 5121 4

Set in Linotype Pilgrim
and printed in Great Britain
by Bristol Typesetting Company Limited
for David & Charles (Publishers) Limited
South Devon House Newton Abbot Devon

Contents

List of Illustrations

IN THE TEXT

NSR standard gauge
LMS/BR built
NSR joint line
NSR narrow gauge
other main line railway
private railway
canal
tramroad
iron/steel works
colliery
brick/tile works
other works
station/halt
tunnel

Symbols used in maps throughout the book

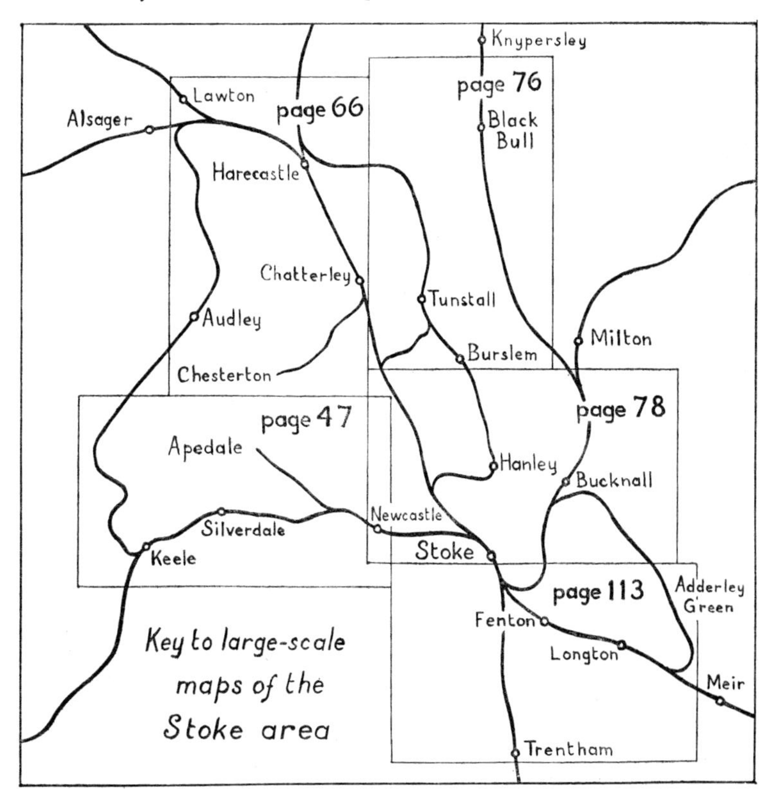

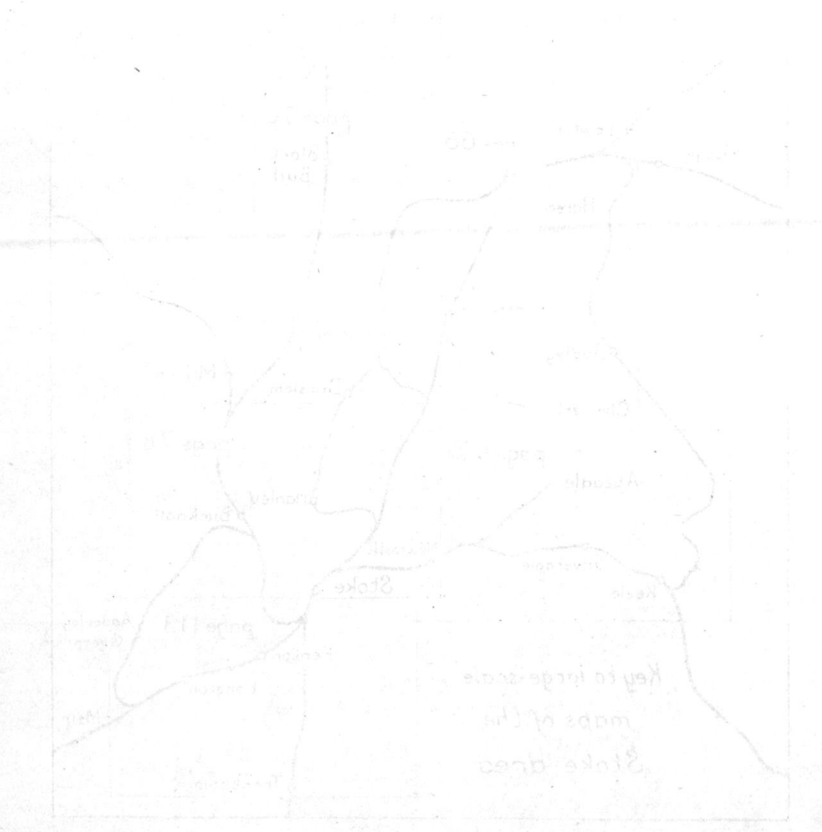

The Knotty: A Memory

Partly they form one of the ugliest industrial areas of Britain. Partly they are one of the most beautiful. For besides the pit shafts and blast furnaces, waste heaps, bottle-shaped kilns and desolate lakes, the Potteries are surrounded by hills and valleys, steep and gentle, many thickly wooded. The casual traveller of sixty years ago would have found both 'Edens' bound together by a 'small octopus' of lines operated by the North Staffordshire Railway and called The Knotty because of its emblem, the Staffordshire Knot, simple and neat, and more universally the hallmark of a proud county.

To serve the dense population at its heart the Knotty ran hundreds of local trains. On a winter's morning the system was alive long before dawn began to shape the landmarks out of darkness. Around 5 am on such a morning in 1908 a little workmen's train would come to a stand in the station at Tunstall on the Loop; a small tank at the head of a short rake of trim coaches, all in crimson lake. In the dim gaslight the engine might be recognised as one of the company's latest: an 0–4–4 tank, short and squat, belonging to a class introduced less than a year earlier.

Under a new timing announced on a yellow handbill with letters an inch high, the train was preparing to leave at 5 20 am for a thirty-six minute journey through the Potteries' heart to Normacot. For some of the passengers, checking perhaps their third class tickets printed in drab and green (an official description with which none quibbled), there was a four minute connection at Stoke for Newcastle. Nothing was tardy about the Knotty, even before dawn.

Some of the passengers were men on their way to the company's own locomotive and carriage works at Stoke. If they thought about the day's work ahead, it was only to run over details of a job in hand. They knew there was no question of having any say in management. The directors had made that perfectly clear when the men got a pay rise about a year before.

There was nothing luxurious about the trains, but workmen remember them as having been clean, well-lighted and warm. Not that they stayed in them any longer than necessary. It is related how one from Newcastle to Leycett was always half-empty by the time it reached its destination, for as it slowed down about 50 yards before Leycett, men jumped out and joined in a mad dash to the colliery lamphouse, where it was 'first come, first served'.

Long after those miners, and thousands of others, had gone down the pit, the wealthy people of that Edwardian age began thinking of the day ahead. Not always were their thoughts concerned with the need to earn a living. The same handbill that announced the re-timing of the 5 20 am workmen's, also gave details of 'hunting arrangements'. Hunting country lay in the rolling acres to the west, and well clear of the Potteries' grime. It was a popular sport and Knotty management was careful to cultivate relations with its hunters. There was a stiff upper-lip tone to a note about tickets. It stated: 'Hunting Contract Tickets (First Class only) are issued under special regulations during the Hunting Season'. The 9 27 am Stoke to Stone, it stated, would be extended to Norton Bridge or Sandon with Horse Boxes when required . . .

> In the event of a meet of Hounds in the Shallowford District on Tuesdays or Saturdays, Gentlemen should communicate with the Station Master at Stoke-on-Trent the previous night, with a view to special arrangements being made for working Horse Boxes and Passengers specially to Norton Bridge.

It was easier for the gentry to have their fun than it was for the workers and only a few months earlier, 370 shareholders had pressed for a limit on excursions run on Sundays —the only day on which the working classes could get out of the towns. As it happened the workers found a champion among the gentry—the Knotty chairman, Tonman Mosley, who replied that although he would not yield to any man in his love of the old English sabbath, he felt there was a great deal to be said for the anxiety felt by the men who worked six days a week to have an opportunity of getting out of town into the green fields and the country to enjoy themselves. The company, he declared, must take care that they did not allow prejudices of their own to interfere with the natural right and privilege of the people to enjoy fresh air.

To encourage people to enjoy the open air, the company issued its own illustrated guide. But it had also another purpose for it stated its main intention was to dispel, by facts and photographs, the notion held by many people that the Potteries were a bleak and stony area.

Expresses between London and the Potteries may have been run by the LNWR but the Knotty's sturdy hand was upon them. Often the Manchester—Euston expresses were in the hands of nothing more than a 4–4–2 tank to Stoke. But it was a Knotty tank—well able to handle twelve packed coaches including a diner. Little wonder that the Knotty lives on vividly in the minds of men nearly half a century after it was grouped into the LMS. But there were other reasons, as we shall now explain.

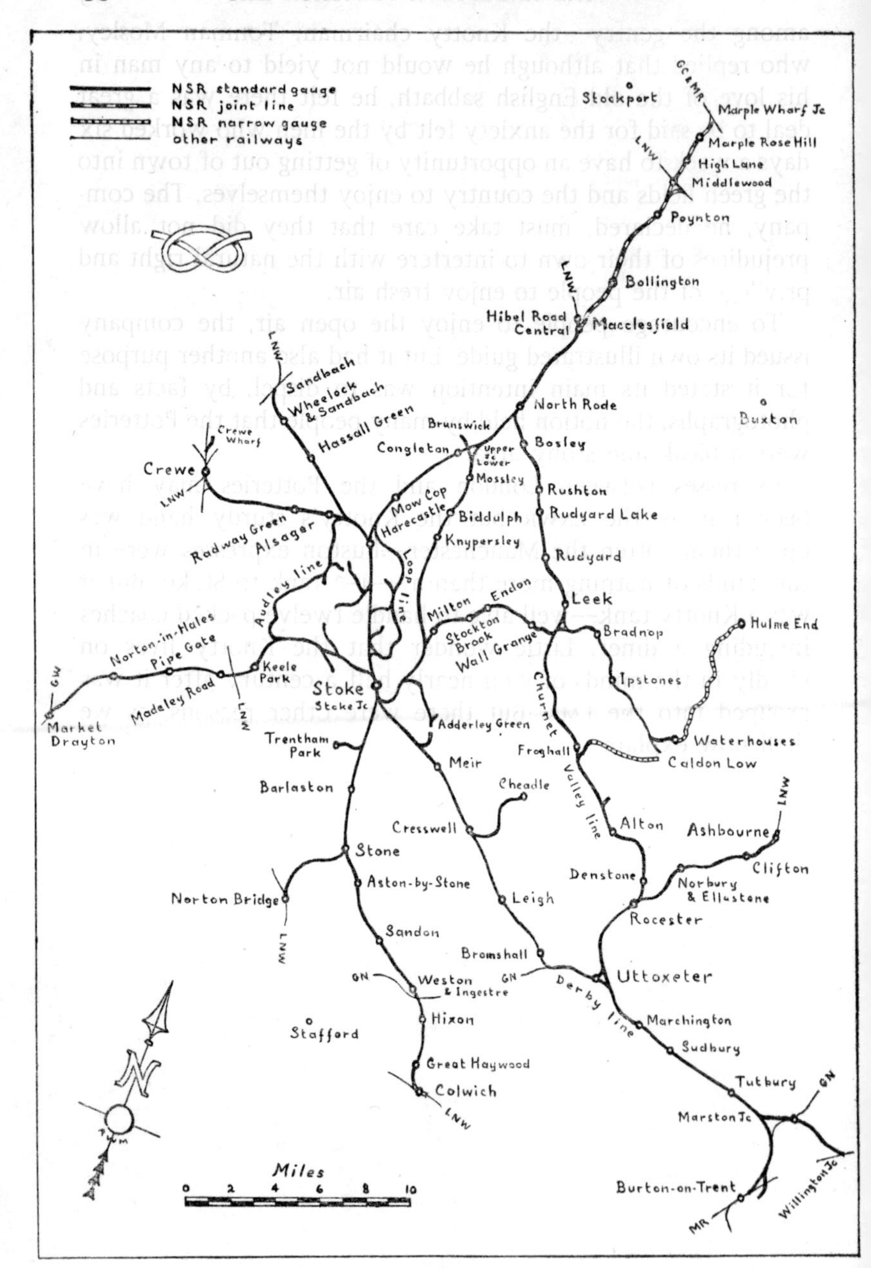

The North Staffordshire Railway 1922

CHAPTER ONE

Pause for Breath

EARLY CANALS AND TRAMROADS

The North Staffordshire may not have been a big railway. Indeed, as its title implied, it served in the main only the northern half of that county, together with south Cheshire and parts of Derbyshire. But it was an old railway which claimed an ancestry going back further than most—to the days of George III to 13 May 1776 when the proprietors of the Trent & Mersey Canal got powers to build a railway or plateway from the limestone quarries at Caldon Low down to a canal basin proposed at Froghall in the Churnet Valley 649ft below. This line of some 4 miles was opened in 1777, although its route had changed somewhat by the time the NSR acquired it through its purchase of the canal in 1847.

In George III's reign, the Potteries industry of North Staffordshire was being established in the villages and towns just east of Newcastle-under-Lyme. Newcastle was by far the largest town and the market for the area, but as the Potteries developed, so did smaller towns and six of them—Tunstall, Burslem, Hanley, Stoke, Fenton and Longton[1]—later grew to reach municipal status and eventually amalgamated as the City of Stoke-on-Trent with a quarter of a million inhabitants.

Although the Potteries lay to the east of Newcastle it was the area to the northwest—mostly in the large parish of Wolstanton—which was the centre of the coal and ironstone mines. Batteries of blast furnaces competed with the bottle-shaped kilns of the potters to pollute the atmosphere.

The area badly needed better transport to carry the bulky West Country clay brought by sea to the Mersey. James

Brindley who, with John Gilbert, had built the Bridgewater Canal near Manchester in 1761 for the Duke of Bridgewater, had surveyed a canal through the Potteries in 1758. A canal from the Mersey to the navigable Trent at Derwent Mouth (between Derby and Nottingham) was actively promoted by the leading potters, especially Josiah Wedgwood of Burslem, the Duke of Bridgewater and his brother-in-law, Earl Gower, of Trentham Hall. They got an Act for the 93 mile canal, the first trunk route to be conceived in Britain since Roman times, on 12 May 1766. It took eleven years to build being opened in May 1777 at a cost of some £300,000. Success was immediate and spectacular and dividends reached an incredible 75 per cent in 1822. The canal was still paying 30 per cent in 1845 despite the arrival of railway competition.

Other canals were soon demanded and the 17 mile Caldon branch from Etruria to Froghall was authorised in 1776 and opened in 1779. In 1795 the rival Commercial Canal was proposed from the Chester Canal at Nantwich via Newcastle, Burslem, Cheadle and Uttoxeter to the Ashby-de-la-Zouch Canal. A second proposal was one from the Peak Forest Canal at Marple, via Macclesfield, Rudyard and Leek to the Caldon branch of the T & M. To counter these threats the T & M proposed its own branches—a short one to Burslem, another from the Caldon branch to Leek with a giant reservoir at Rudyard, and a 13 mile extension from Froghall to Uttoxeter along the Churnet Valley. These were accepted and authorised in 1797—the two shorter branches and Rudyard Lake were completed in 1802-5 and the Uttoxeter extension was opened between 1808 and 1811.

Newcastle was not to be outdone. In 1775 Sir Nigel Gresley got powers to build a 3 mile canal from his ironworks and collieries at Apedale into Newcastle whilst he and other Newcastle interests got an Act in 1795 for the Newcastle-under-Lyme canal from a junction with the T & M at Stoke into Newcastle from the opposite direction. Both were opened a few years after their Acts.

As the canals terminated ¾ mile apart and at different levels, the Newcastle-under-Lyme Junction Canal was promoted in 1798 through the town to a position from which there was to be a ¼ mile inclined railway down to the Brook Street basin of the Newcastle Canal. The canal was built, but not the railway. About 1827 the Apedale and Junction canals came under the control of Robert Edenser Heathcote and are subsequently referred to as Heathcote's Canal. The NSR was to lease the Newcastle-under-Lyme Canal from 1 July 1863, but earlier, in May 1851, it paid £1,000 for about ¾ mile of Heathcote's canal and the bed was used to carry the Newcastle branch railway between Newcastle Station and Brampton.

The T & M owners built three separate tram roads, all authorised in 1802, to link the canal with the centres of Longton, Hanley and Burslem.[2] Several other private lines were also built to serve the canal.[3] The original tramway line from Froghall to the Caldon Quarries seems to have given trouble as an Act was obtained in 1783 for an alternative. A third route, authorised in 1802, allowed a double line of plateway on five inclined planes, all worked by the weight of the descending wagons. This was the line taken over by the NSR in 1847 but the new owners were still not satisfied, building a fourth route in 1849 with three inclines, the gauge of railway being 3ft 6in.[4]

The T & M Canal was a vital artery to the Potteries. In 1836 184,500 tons of goods were carried away to other waterways (chiefly to the Mersey, Manchester and London) whilst another 143,610 tons were brought into the Potteries (mainly from the Mersey).

FIRST SCHEMES

The most important early railway proposal in the area was that of 1806, to link the pits and ironworks around Newcastle with the Chester Canal at Nantwich. The plan envisaged two routes for horse-railways or tramroads; the first west from the Newcastle-under-Lyme Canal at Newcastle to the Silverdale Ironworks, where it would have turned northwest towards Audley. The second route was to have run west from the northern end of the Apedale Canal. Both lines were to have joined about a mile south-west of Audley and passed south of the villages of Crewe and Nantwich.[5] Both schemes lay dormant for nearly twenty years until the building of the Stockton & Darlington Railway stimulated fresh proposals.

Among such later schemes was one of 1825 for a link between Birmingham and Liverpool, although the terminus was to be on the opposite bank of the Mersey at Birkenhead.[6] The promoters were drawn from a wide area including the Potteries, and a branch was planned from Ravensmoor, near Nantwich, to Lane End between Fenton and Longton. The scheme was revised before being put before Parliament in 1826 and excluded the branch: local interests were delighted when the whole project was defeated.

It was followed four years later by a scheme centred on Manchester: the Central Junction Railway, which aimed to build a line between Manchester and Madeley with a branch to Chorlton Brow.[7] When a fresh group started promoting a new link between Liverpool and Birmingham, they paid lip service to the Potteries—but chose their route via Whitmore. This was one of the schemes that led to the birth of the Grand Junction Railway, and its authorisation between Birmingham and Warrington on 6 May 1833 first brought a railway within reach of the Potteries. Even so, its route was via Whitmore. The future pattern of rail connection between London, Birmingham and the North West became clearer when the GJR got authority to absorb the Warrington & Newton Railway from 12 June 1835, so as to link up with the Liverpool & Manchester at Newton Junction. This satisfied Liverpool businessmen, but those of Manchester were unhappy, and wanted a direct railway between Manchester and Birmingham which would reduce the mileage from 99 via Newton to only 82.

THE POTTERIES RAILWAY

Meanwhile a scheme was generated from within the Potteries by local interests who met at Hanley on 13 January 1835 under the chairmanship of Robert Edenser Heathcote, an influential canal owner and industrialist. They asked George Stephenson to prepare a route for the Potteries Railway. He suggested it should run from Harecastle to Norton Bridge with one branch from Etruria to Heathcote's canal at Newcastle, to give access to pits around Apedale. Stephenson felt no other branches were needed because works which had railways to canal wharves could easily extend them to form branches off the main line.

Despite opposition from canal interests, the promoters liked Stephenson's scheme and asked the GJR to support it. The request was made at an unfortunate time for the GJR was then formulating its own plans to invade the area and had instructed Joseph Locke to survey a line from Whitmore to Etruria and the coal and iron mines in the area. As a concession to local interests, Locke was also to survey a line through the Potteries in the shape of a crescent. Its purpose was to be a feeder for the GJR! Dismissing this idea, the local promoters asked Stephenson to survey an extension from his projected line at Harecastle to the GJR at Crewe. These ideas remained under consideration until 1837 when a shortage of money stopped any immediate hopes of development.

The Manchester interests, who were pressing for a direct link to the south, planned to join the GJR at Crewe or a point further south. Alternatively they considered building an independent route to London through the Potteries, which lay on the most direct line between London and Manchester. A scheme put forward by the Manchester interests in 1835 was again called the Central Junction Railway. It was projected from Manchester through Alderley and Congleton to the GJR at Madeley. It lacked more than nominal support but it was quickly followed by a crop of schemes like the Manchester & Cheshire Junction, surveyed by John U. Rastrick, one of the former engineers of the GJR, which, incidentally, appreciated its value as a feeder line. In December 1835 the GJR promised its promoters 'every assistance'. Rastrick favoured a direct route of 30 miles between Manchester and Crewe running only through rural areas and serving with branches such centres of population as Stockport, Poynton (a village in the Cheshire foothills with important collieries), Macclesfield and Congleton. Critics saw the concept of branches as the weakness of the scheme and when it was before Parliament it was debated alongside the rival Manchester South Union.[8] This was being promoted by a Manchester group dedicated to remaining independent of the GJR over the whole route to London. They appointed George Stephenson as engineer and he planned a line through Stockport, Macclesfield and Leek to a junction at Burton-on-Trent with the Birmingham & Derby, which was to build a line south to Rugby to keep traffic off GJR metals. The 'Unionists' maintained implacable resistance to joining the GJR and continued to press for an independent route between Manchester and Rugby even though both lines were to run side by side for many miles.

Under the title of the Manchester, Cheshire & Staffordshire Railway, the MCJ revised plans for a line between Manchester and Crewe, this time through Stockport and Alderley, which was to be the junction for a branch going more directly south to join the GJR at Chebsey, near Norton Bridge. The revised South Union route was also to run via Stockport and then Congleton and along the Trent Valley to Tamworth. It was also called the Manchester & Tamworth Railway. Faced with both schemes, a Parliamentary Committee forced an amalgamation and paved the way for the creation of the Manchester & Birmingham Railway on 30 June 1837. Its 45½ mile route was an amalgam of earlier plans. From Manchester it was authorised via Stockport and Congleton (as Rastrick planned) and on through the Potteries and Stone to Chebsey (per Stephenson) to join the GJR, which was also to be reached by a 16 mile branch from Alderley to Crewe.

When the GJR was opened between Birmingham and Warrington on 4 July 1837 the Potteries benefited immediately as horse omnibuses and coaches started feeder services between local towns and stations at Stafford, Norton Bridge, Whitmore, Madeley and Crewe. In 1838 *Osborne* listed coach services which included one from Stafford via Uttoxeter to Derby and Nottingham.[9]

The next major development—the opening of the London & Birmingham Railway on 17 September 1838 not only completed the link between London and the North West but it placed the GJR in a strong position and it at once opposed every move by the M & B to route its traffic via Chebsey instead of Crewe. The M & B retaliated by promoting a line from Stone to Rugby. Called the M & B Extension Railway, it deposited plans in February 1838. It was soon defeated because, among other reasons, there were 459 separate objections.

The M & B route surveyed through the Potteries was a good one and the stiffest gradient between Manchester and the summit at Harecastle was to be no more than 1 in 378. But that meant heavy engineering works including a long tunnel at Harecastle and a 42 arch viaduct over the river Dane at Congleton, 1,030 yards long and 98ft high. The foundation stone was laid by the Mayor of Congleton on 25 September 1839, but the company found costs prohibitive, even though the engineer, George Watson Buck, who had been an assistant engineer on the L & B, suggested that £50,000 might be saved if the level of the viaduct was lowered.

Ever quick to exploit a situation, the GJR approached the M & B suggesting it should abandon its line through the Potteries to Chebsey and instead join up at Crewe. Not only would this lengthen the distance over which goods would have to be routed, it would also remove the GJR's fear that any line built in the Potteries might fall into the hands of a company planning an independent London—Manchester route.

As an added incentive, it offered every facility for M & B traffic between Crewe and Birmingham. When the Pottery interests heard of the offer, public meetings were called at Congleton and Stoke and M & B directors were pressurised to complete the Potteries line. They contended that costs had risen tremendously: Rastrick's estimate of £21,000 a mile had more than doubled to £45,000, partly due to landowners making heavy demands.

The Pottery opinions were ignored and the M & B accepted the GJR offer in 1839 but managed to keep the secret for a year. Once it became known, the M & B Extension Railway was abandoned, although when shareholders met in 1841 they embarked on the planning of a new venture over much the same route: the Stafford & Rugby railway, which was to have a branch from Stafford to Stoke.

Next to be upset was the M & B when it found that the GJR refused to allow its trains to run south from Crewe. The M & B retaliated by opening its Manchester—Crewe line only as far as Sandbach, reached on 10 May 1842. The rest was not opened until 10 August and the Macclesfield branch was not completed for another three years until 24 November 1845. The total cost was about £1,890,000.

Among a number of schemes deposited in the interim years was one which Joseph Locke engineered for the GJR of a

12 mile branch from Basford, near Crewe, to Stoke.[10] It was rejected by the Commons after passing the committee stage.[11] Just a week after the Stoke scheme, the Manchester South Union interests deposited plans[12] for using Macclesfield as a spearhead for a line through the Potteries to Rugeley. Called the South Union, or Manchester & London Railway, it was also to serve Crewe.

THE RAILWAY MANIA

The Railway Mania of 1845 found the Potteries still without a railway. It was a fast growing industrial district riper than many for development, a factor reflected in no less than twenty-four lines being proposed in the area bounded by Macclesfield, Stafford, Derby and Crewe. Those which foundered will be dealt with later in the chapter for the sake of clarity.

Agitation for lines came from individuals as well as bodies: Firmstone, the owner of Madeley Colliery at Leycett, built his own railway to the GJR at Madeley, which lay within sight of the pit. The Earl of Granville also wanted to build a line into his ironworks at Etruria and was waiting to see how near a main line would be built.

Through the years of doubt, local interests kept alive the Staffordshire Potteries Railway and the men who originally backed the Stephenson project of 1835 revived it, adding a branch from Harecastle to the M & B at Macclesfield. Another scheme to link up with this branch was projected in 1844 when Stephenson and Cubitt planned a line through the Churnet Valley to Tamworth with a second outlet at Willington, near Derby. Stoke was to be served by a branch from Leek. The main purpose of this plan was a rival London—Manchester route shorter than the GJR. It was to link up with the Midland between Tamworth and Hampton, where trains would join the London & Birmingham. The Bill was rejected in Parliament.

The next tactic came from the L & B, which agreed to ultimately absorb the M & B and also, if they got Acts, the Trent company (which did) and the Churnet Valley (which failed). The scheme was also to have taken in the Staffordshire Potteries Railway.

Gradually as the L & B, M & B and GJR came to realise the futility of moves and counter moves, relations became more friendly and in 1845 they made a traffic agreement which also incorporated the Trent and Churnet schemes. Things now looked set for railways in the Potteries to be developed from outside, but the situation changed dramatically when the big three started arguing over alleged traffic poaching.

THE KNOTTY IS BORN

When it reported on the Trent and Churnet schemes, the Railway Department of the Board of Trade suggested a pause of a year 'to afford time for consideration and for maturing some more complete scheme for the accommodation of that important district'.

The Pottery interests quickly took advantage of the suggestion and formed the North Staffordshire or Churnet Valley & Trent Junction Railway, with a registered provisional capital of £235,000. The Committee of Direction was led by a man of remarkable foresight and ability, John Lewis Ricardo, MP for Stoke. In the company prospectus, issued from 1 Old Palace Yard, Westminster, on 30 April 1845, the Committee announced its intention of following the Board of Trade's suggestion and also 'to combine direct accommodation to the Manchester district with the requirements of the Potteries districts'.

It arranged, in co-operation with the L & B, to incorporate the Churnet line with the Staffordshire Potteries Railway 'with the addition of so much of the Trent Valley Railway as was destined for the service of the Potteries'. Ricardo was later to state that this agreement avoided powerful opposition or ruinous competition if both lines had been passed.

The company prospectus stated the line was to run from the M & B at Macclesfield passing near Congleton (the hilly country made it impossible to take it through the town centre, although this was not mentioned), and run via Harecastle into the Potteries 'giving the most ample accommodation to the towns of Tunstall, Burslem, Newcastle-under-Lyme, Hanley, Stoke, Fenton, Longton and Stone.' The line was to join the GJR at Colwich and there were to be branches from Harecastle to Crewe and from Stone to the GJR 'at or near' Norton Bridge.

The Churnet Valley line was seen as a direct link between Manchester and Derby and also as giving the Potteries an outlet to eastern England. This line was planned via Leek and Cheadle to Uttoxeter. The Norton Bridge branch would give a direct link between the iron districts of Staffordshire and Shropshire and provide a West of England link. Likewise, the Crewe link was seen as something far more strategic than simply a branch: it was to be the most convenient 'course' for traffic to Chester, Holyhead, Birkenhead and Liverpool. The whole system was envisaged as opening up extensive coalfields and other mineral districts. The prospectus ended by stating that the arrangement between the companies and parties united to form the undertaking would provide all the necessary capital. There was to be no call for outside help.

Under the streamlined title, the North Staffordshire Railway was incorporated in April 1845. Capital of £2,350,000 was in £20 shares. The creation of the company brought it into 'direct and complete' competition with the Trent & Mersey Canal whose shareholders were mainly influential landowners, bankers and manufacturers. As the canal interests had already defeated several attempts to form a competing railway, the NSR directors felt they must get agreement for the canal shareholders to get an income from the system under railway management. An agreement of 12 July 1845 provided for the NSR to pay £30 a share free of all deductions except income tax until the whole railway opened. After that the guaranteed minimum was to be 5 per cent or £22 10s a share. To make sure that if the railway was highly profitable the canal shareholders would benefit too, a further clause covered profits. If they rose above £5 a share on NSR capital, profit was to be shared proportionally up to a limit of £30 for each canal share. Under the agreement, signed between Ricardo and the canal pioneer, Francis Twemlow, the lease of the canal was to start from 15 January 1846. The company reckoned to save £300,000 through not having to meet opposition from the canal owners. The agreement also eliminated any danger that during such a battle, the canal owners might have linked up with an NSR competitor. The NSR was not so successful in establishing friendly relations with its neighbours, notably the GJR and its successor from 16 July 1846, the LNWR. The basic bone of contention remained through traffic between London and Manchester, the NSR feeling always that it was not getting its fair share. But there were other differences and feelings.

LIVERPOOL EXTENSION

By the time the LNWR was formed, the NSR was a seasoned campaigner having fought many earlier battles with such companies as the GJR. Ricardo was to tell shareholders how on its formation the NSR board 'at once commenced hostilities' with the GJR when it saw no prospect of conciliation over obtaining Manchester traffic. The board, stated Ricardo, decided 'frankly and fearlessly' to accept the contest. It scored an early success when the Lords rejected a GJR scheme for the branch from Basford to Stoke. The legal battle cost the NSR £1,800, and another £605 9s (shared with the canal owners), was spent on defeating a GJR project for a line from Preston Brook to Runcorn. The NSR opposed this when the GJR refused to let canal traffic use the branch on 'favourable terms'.

The NSR went a stage further with an imaginative offensive into the heart of GJR territory, surveying a route from Harecastle to Liverpool. It was to cross the Mersey at Fidler's Ferry, just west of Warrington, and run to a terminus near the north docks at Liverpool. The Committee of Direction met on 30 April 1845 and sought the backing of the canal interests. The matter then passed to the board of the newly-formed company and on 15 July it resolved that it was expedient to make a line from Harecastle, or nearby, 'in the direction of Preston Brook or Frodsham with a view to a direct link with Liverpool or Birkenhead'. The Mersey crossing was obviously presenting difficulties. There was another obstacle, for Lord Francis Egerton had a Bill before Parliament for a link from Preston Brook or Frodsham with a view to a direct link with NSR felt they needed to press for a clause to ensure the passage of traffic destined either for the canal or other railways.

On 20 August the chairman pointed to the advisability of having the co-operation of the Chester & Birkenhead promoters over the proposed line to Liverpool. The engineer's survey had been via Sandbach, Middlewich and Northwich. Six days later Stephenson and G. P. Bidder were ordered to complete the Parliamentary survey of the Liverpool extension. Capital was to be increased by £1,700,000. Bidder reported on 10 October that Parliamentary levels were being prepared between Harecastle and the Mersey, while those between Liverpool and Broadgreen (on the outskirts of the port) were nearly ready. The main difficulties were stated to be the Mersey crossing and the entrance of the line into Liverpool, where the terminus was to be at the Royal Exchange to save expense and to capture traffic from the north. Ricardo said he had arranged with what he described as 'the northern companies' to use the same terminus.

Negotiations began for land purchase and plans for the line as far as Sandbach were deposited,[13] an impressive beginning of a major scheme. It was also the end for the time was now ripe for agreement with the GJR and one of the conditions for that was the withdrawal of the Liverpool scheme. Terms were drawn up in consultation with the London & Birmingham, the latter being also engaged in talks with the GJR which were to lead to the formation of the LNWR a few months later.

The concessions were contained in two agreements of 25 November 1845, which provided for the NSR to abandon both the Liverpool plan and the line to Preston Brook: instead it was to build a branch from Harecastle as far as Sandbach. It was agreed that if the GJR ever decided to construct the abandoned lines, the NSR would find half the capital.

So much for NSR concessions. Far more important were concessions by the GJR which agreed to use 'every means in its power' to support the amalgamation of the NSR and the Derby & Crewe (a company which the GJR had supported on its formation earlier that year), which planned a line via Stoke and Uttoxeter, with a branch to Colwich. Subsequently two more branches were added: Tutbury to Burton-upon-Trent and Stoke to Norton Bridge. The agreement concerning the Derby & Crewe gave the NSR a nominal capital of £3,370,000 but this was reduced to £2,800,000 having regard to that authorised, and also the amount needed for construction.

By supporting these new lines the GJR virtually withdrew any claim to the Potteries and there are historians who feel it 'by no means improbable' that the Midland Railway was safeguarded from absorption.[14]

The Derby & Crewe amalgamation removed some opposition, but the Tean & Dove, Eastern & Western Junction Railway still contested the NSR claim to the Churnet Valley route.

The NSR regarded the company's stand as dangerous enough to warrant buying it out, meeting half the expenses which the Tean & Dove had incurred in promoting its scheme; a total of £13,000. This was offset by one tenth paid by the Midland, and a contribution by the L & B, assessed by George Stephenson at £5,850.

Three NSR Acts of 26 June 1846 gave powers for constructing the NSR backbone which had five outlets; four to the LNWR west of the Potteries and a fifth to the Birmingham & Derby Junction at Burton. Subsequently the Knotty was to get only three more junctions with other companies. The North Staffordshire Railway (Pottery Line) Act sanctioned the line from the Macclesfield branch of the Manchester & Birmingham through Stoke to Colwich and branches to Norton Bridge, Newcastle, Silverdale and Crewe. The NSR (Harecastle & Sandbach) Act was for a branch from Kidsgrove to Sandbach and the NSR (Churnet Valley line) laid down the route from Macclesfield to Burton Junction, with a branch from Uttoxeter to Stoke.

Capital created totalled £2,900,000. Just over half, £1,500,000, was authorised for the Pottery line; £1,200,000 for the Churnet Valley and £200,000 for the Sandbach branch. Borrowing powers provided for one-third of the capital. The Pottery line Act also vested the Trent & Mersey Canal in the NSR.

The Bill went through the Commons and Lords unopposed, apart from some squabbles with road trustees and one or two landowners, including Sir Henry Every of Egginton Hall, who would not allow the Marston—Willington Junction section across his land. The branch was designed to provide access to the Midland at Derby and thence eastern England. The Acts contained clauses that the company was not to enter his property without written consent. More successfully, the NSR came to a financial arrangement to overcome the opposition of another landowner, Lord Bagot.

Each Act laid down a completion time of seven years and detailed safeguards concerning the junctions with other companies. The Pottery line Act laid down that if the Newcastle branch was not opened within twelve months of the main line, it would be illegal for the company to pay any ordinary dividend until it was complete.

ABORTIVE PLANS

With the Knotty in being, we can pause now to look at *some* of the abortive schemes. They fell roughly into three types: through links between Manchester and the south; links between Manchester and Birmingham; and more local lines. There was a scheme by Remington for a Direct Independent Manchester & London; no doubts as to *its* intentions, although its route was a little more obscure: from Manchester to Macclesfield, Leek, Tean, Uttoxeter, Burton; thence Leicester, Kettering, St Albans to King's Cross. Pottery branches were to run from Tean to serve Stoke, Hanley, Tunstall, Alsager and Crewe. There was a concept by Rastrick of a Direct London & Manchester Railway, from Stockport into the high hills of the Derbyshire Peak to pass between Buxton and Macclesfield and run thence via Hartington and Ashbourne to Leicester to duplicate Remington's line to London, although to a different terminus, Farrington Street. The Railway Mania also brought a scheme for a line from Macclesfield, Leek, Cheadle and Rugeley. There was to be a branch through Stoke, Newcastle and Tunstall to Crewe.[15]

Other north—south schemes included the Manchester, Rugby & Southampton Railway, not as grand as the title suggests since only running powers were planned between Rugby and Southampton. The northern section was to run through Macclesfield, Leek, Uttoxeter and Burton to Rugby.

The Manchester & Rugby Direct sought a different route: Leek, Ashbourne, Tutbury and Burton. A variation on this was the Rugby, Derby & Manchester, via Derby, Ashbourne, Leek and the Churnet Valley to Macclesfield.[16] The Manchester & Rugby Direct was to be joined by the Liverpool & Derby, running via Warrington, Knutsford, Congleton, Leek and Ashbourne. A south coast outlet was planned over the Oxford

& Rugby Direct Railway and the Oxford, Southampton, Gosport & Portsmouth.

Liverpool and Manchester were the stated objectives of the Staffordshire Potteries Railway (the second to have the title), engineered by Gandell and Brunton over a 44 mile route from Stafford via Stone, Stoke and Congleton.[17] To avoid joining the M & B at Macclesfield, it was to turn north west at Congleton, cross the M & B main line at Goostrey and join the Manchester South Junction & Altrincham at Hale Moss, Altrincham. From Goostrey the line was to continue to Liverpool, but plans were never completed. They did however, include details of two branches: from Shelton Wharf to the GJR at Crewe (11 miles 6 chains) and Congleton—Macclesfield (7½ miles). The latter was obviously intended as a branch because the approach to Macclesfield was to be on a sharp curve.

Apart from any opposition which there might have been from landowners and rival companies, the plan involved massive engineering works including two long tunnels on the Crewe branch: 2,057yd near Audley and 1,351yd at Weston. On the main line there was to be a boring of 2,332yd at Goldenhill and four others in the Potteries were to be of between 600yd and 1,000yd. A 244yd viaduct was projected across the Dane valley near Congleton.

The M & B strongly pressed the NSR to build a joint line between Manchester and Lichfield through the Blythe Valley. It got a cool reception from the NSR which told a deputation from the M & B on 10 October 1845 that the scheme would not justify the large capital involved having regard to 'the much superior scheme by this company'.

A further scheme involving Lichfield was the Birmingham, Lichfield & Uttoxeter. The latter town figured in several other schemes: the Tean & Dove Valley & Staffordshire & North Midland, passing south of the Potteries from Stafford via Uttoxeter and Ashbourne to join the North Midland at Ambergate. This scheme had stronger backing than most, but only for a short time for on 15 July 1845 Ricardo stated that Robert Stephenson had said that far from promoting the line, he would give it every discouragement and had promised to induce his father to withdraw as engineer. Yet the scheme lingered for on 15 February 1846 the promoters sent a deputation to the NSR to discuss plans, since their trains would need to run over about 4 miles of the NSR between Rocester and Uttoxeter. The Tean & Dove & Eastern & Western Junction (similar in concept to Remington's direct line) was to run from Macclesfield via Leek, Uttoxeter, and Burton to Atherstone, with a branch from Tean to Stoke, Newcastle, Crewe and Nantwich.[18]

Uttoxeter and Stafford were to have a branch of the West Midland Railway: Crewe—Hanley—Cheadle—Ashbourne, to the North Midland at Belper.

The Derby, Uttoxeter & Stafford Railway[19] was planned as part of a through route from Eastern England to Holyhead. It was abandoned on 10 March 1846 and is dealt with later in the context of a line that did materialise, the Stafford & Uttoxeter.

North of the Potteries there was talk of a Buxton, Macclesfield & Congleton Railway; a Buxton, Congleton & Crewe[20] (which the NSR decided to oppose on 27 April 1846) and even more grandly, a Sheffield, Buxton, Leek, Potteries & Crewe Railway.[21]

Among these schemes, many failed to comply with Standing Orders: the Manchester & Lichfield; Buxton, Macclesfield & Congleton—and also that to Crewe; the Staffordshire Potteries; the London & Manchester direct railways; the Rugby, Derby & Manchester. The rest of the Mania-promoted schemes were, in the NSR view, 'swamped by their own faulty construction', or else they failed to deposit plans.

How valuable might these lines have been? The Staffordshire historian, Dr J. R. Hollick, once drew attention to vague details about Rastrick's route over the high section of Axe Edge.[22] He favoured the Staffordshire & North Midland as giving the best access to the north east and the east Midlands coalfield since it would have avoided the long haul for coal via Derby and Uttoxeter. He liked, too, the West Midland scheme, pointing out that engineering works would have been easier between Ashbourne and Belper, rather than via Ambergate. A useful link would have been the Liverpool—Knutsford—Leek section of the Liverpool & Derby, modified to join the NSR.

If most schemes seem wild in retrospect, they were con-

Page 33 (above) *Class 'M' 0-4-4T No 11 at Stoke on 6 October 1922 with flared top to bunker;* (below) *class 'K' 4-4-2T No 8 on Derby—Birmingham train of Midland clerestory coaches at Tamworth 1923* *(see page 262)*

Page 34 (above) *Class 'F' 0–6–4T No 117 crosses the river Blythe with a D'Oyly Carte theatrical special from Hanley to Nottingham one Sunday in 1922;* (below) *class 'C' 0–6–4T No 30 on a goods near Derby in 1923*

sidered serious threats at the time. Ricardo said in 1846 that the company had not come into being without considerable expense and some sacrifices which were necessary because of the existence of 'powerful interests' with which the undertaking had come into collision. Another fact was the 'remarkable and deplorable' spirit of speculation which arose in 1845 subsequent to the formation of the company. Ricardo regarded embryo companies and the four which originally opposed the creation of the NSR—the L & B, GJR, Churnet Valley and the T & M Canal—as 'nineteen more or less formidable opponents'. The expenses to which Ricardo referred included £140,000 spent before a rail was laid, equal to about 16s 9d a share. Meeting opposition from the L & B, including the Churnet interests, cost £30,133 7s 0d. The cost of meeting opposition of the GJR, including the Derby & Crewe was £18,637 14s 8d and Parliamentary expenses totalled £2,000. Engineering expenses were £66,475 10s 0d. Expenses concerning smaller schemes made up the total bill.

Unexpected expense arose when NSR engineers examined the plans and sections of the Churnet Valley promoters after that scheme had been thrown out of Parliament. It was found they could not be used 'safely' and a new survey was necessary.

As the dust of the Railway Mania settled, one further abortive scheme was authorised on 22 July 1847: the Manchester, Birmingham & North Staffordshire Junction Railway,[23] which was to have a main line of 3½ miles from Poynton on the Macclesfield branch of the M & B via Cheadle Hulme to join the main line of the M & B on the outskirts of Stockport, just south of the spot where the Buxton—Altrincham line now crosses the main line. Despite its title, the line had nothing to do with the NSR.

Among companies which never even got to the Prospectus stage was the provisionally registered Sheffield, Shrewsbury & South Wales Direct Railway. It was to run via Bakewell and Leek and use part of the Tamworth—Macclesfield line to reach Newcastle. It was to have crossed the GJR at Whitmore and ran thence to Market Drayton.

Notes are on page 294

CHAPTER TWO

Construction

THE MAIN LINES

Authorisation of such a large system as the NSR in one stage caused many problems for the consulting engineer, George Parker Bidder (1806-78). Yet in the first two years during which he was in charge, he proved more than equal to the task. Born at Moretonhampstead in Devon, Bidder graduated at Edinburgh University and became a railway engineer only after meeting the Stephensons, although he could have turned to many things as he was renowned for quick mental calculation.

The promoters were confident of their project from the start for as the original prospectus of the North Staffordshire, or Churnet, Potteries and Trent Valley Railway stated:

> No difficulties present themselves in an engineering point of view and there is every reason to believe that the land-owners will be favourable to the undertaking.

Control of the T & M canal gave the NSR a number of advantages in construction. Bidder estimated that it would reduce the cost of the Churnet line from £25,000 a mile to £13,000 and give a total saving of £192,000. The cost of Harecastle tunnel would be cut by £55,000, and another £25,000 would be saved by the company being able to take the railway over the canal where it liked. About £10,000 would be saved in the carriage of materials, the calculation being 2s a ton on 100,000 tons.

Preparation of Parliamentary levels and plans was well advanced by autumn 1845 and on 10 October Bidder stated that besides those for the Liverpool extension, the survey of the Norton Bridge branch was complete, although the plans would not be ready before the end of the week. Those of the Churnet Valley and termini at Willington & Burton were completed. Half the Stoke—Uttoxeter line had been surveyed and plans of the remaining half would be ready by 25 October.

Sometimes plans were altered to meet local objections or needs. When the Burslem authorities petitioned against the first plans, Bidder was told to give them 'every practical help'.

Strong influence to try and dictate the pattern of construction was exerted by shareholders worried in case they were unable to get a quick return on their money. At their first meeting at Stoke on 23 September 1846 they asked the board not to erect hotels 'or other buildings not absolutely required for the immediate purposes of the railway' before a special meeting had been held; and also not to take further action on three branches then under consideration, those to Ashbourne, Apedale and a short loop through Burslem. The shareholders wanted all available money and effort concentrated on completing the main lines.

The first shareholders' meeting was followed by an elaborate ceremony to cut the first sod. It was an occasion for a public holiday in the Potteries—and of gate-crashing by local people. The site, in a field near Etruria had an enclosure roped off for the directors, while the rest was reserved for their guests. But on the arrival of the mile-long procession, headed by Ricardo and his colleagues on horseback, crowds broke through into the field. Ricardo, badly jostled, had difficulty in putting the silver spade into the ground. When he did it buckled, and he had trouble lifting the turf. Later he lost his hat.

By now the Potteries were growing fast for, as Osborne[1] had observed a few years earlier

> They contain a larger population, a greater proportion of good houses, more manufacturies and wealth, more intelligent and ingenious people, more churches and chapels and schools, and probably more civilised and religious persons, than any other similar extent district. There is certainly a great deal of drunkenness and immorality, but by no means so much as in a cotton or woollen or coal and iron district.

What Osborne did not mention was that for all the wealth

Opening ceremony at the Dane viaduct, Congleton, as depicted in the *Illustrated London News* of 23 June 1849

and the opulence there was also terrible poverty and it was perhaps understandable if on that September day men got drunk at the prospect of work, which the advent of the railway was likely to provide.

Construction then started quickly on the first contracts totalling 77 miles. They included the sections Stoke—Uttoxeter, 16½ miles; the Sandbach branch of 6½ miles, and, by far the most important, the route of almost 47 miles between Macclesfield, Colwich and Norton Bridge. This last contract went to Thomas Brassey and it included several major works. There were the three tunnels at Harecastle; north, middle and south of 130yd, 180yd and 1,750yd, They were to be separated by deep cuttings—of 350yd between the north and middle tunnels and of 333yd between the middle and south. Two lofty viaducts were needed to bridge two valleys near Congleton. Both were built of brick spans and the longest of 1,255ft had 20 spans and a maximum height of 106ft. The smaller viaduct, which was a foot higher at one point, was 697ft long and had 10 spans.

The contractors had to meet strict requirements: Brassey had to avoid obstructing the Macclesfield canal because the company were bound to pay a penalty of £5 an hour if traffic was delayed. This penalty doubled after 72 hours.

The northern boundary with the LNWR at Macclesfield was at Hibel Road Station 17¼ miles from Manchester London Road. Although the NSR built an engine shed and goods yard north of the station, they were reached only by the exercise of running powers.

Viaducts and tunnels were the biggest constructional projects, yet the most complex and troublesome obstacle lay not in the country, but in a town, Macclesfield, where houses already covered most of the level ground which formed the floor of the narrow valley under a craggy hillside on which the town centre stood. So congested was the valley that with its original plans the NSR deposited an alternative for a line 2½ miles long that would have taken it west of the town, from a junction with the Manchester & Birmingham Stockport branch between Macclesfield and the village of Prestbury to the north. This would have reduced the demolition of property by 75 per cent of the amount which was carried out after the adoption of the original plan.

Once the Act was passed, no time was lost in buying houses for demolition and diverting roads and Bidder stated in February 1847 that they had possession of a large number of houses 'to allow the contractor to build forthwith'.

There were legal objections to overcome when the owners of large cotton mills and a brewery sought an injunction after the NSR pulled down an old bridge leading to the brewery and diverted a turnpike road leading to the Sutton Bridge district. The brewery contended that this added 14 yards to the distance into Macclesfield and so caused inconvenience and injury to the premises. A court refused the injunction, ruling that it was a question for compensation.[2]

The route surveyed by Stephenson was magnificent and despite the hilly country the ruling gradient between Colwich and Macclesfield was no stiffer than 1 in 330. But there were steeper banks and it was necessary to build the line at 1 in 102 for 2 miles to lift it from Macclesfield to the level of the Moss which lay to the south.

Besides land needed for the line, the company also bought some adjoining to provide earth for the 40,000,000 bricks needed for the viaducts and Harecastle tunnels. One of the first jobs tackled by the navvies was the excavation of seven main-line cuttings. Several months of work were saved on one planned at Great Haywood by Lord Lichfield agreeing to a deviation of just over 2 miles through Shugborough Park. This reduced the length of what was to have been the longest of the cuttings. The deviation was planned by Stephenson and Bidder.[3]

By February 1847, 1,318 men and 60 horses were working between Macclesfield and Colwich and by then they had removed 80,000 cubic yd of earth, sunk six of Harecastle's nine shafts to their lowest level and driven 843yd of tunnel heading. They had also erected 12,000yd of fencing.

Bad weather during the winter delayed survey work in the Churnet Valley and the contract was not let to Messrs John and Solomon Tredwell until 12 July 1847. By then tunnelling was under way in eight shafts at Harecastle and 60yd had been bricked. The number of men at work between Macclesfield and Colwich had risen to 4,000 and the number of horses to 240. Seven million bricks were ready for use; six million more were in a green state. Clay had been cast for another 40,000,000 bricks and some bridges were finished. Colwich junction was almost complete. Six miles of the Uttoxeter section were ready for ballasting and bricking was in progress in Meir Tunnel (847yd).

BRANCH PROGRESS

On the Crewe and Sandbach branches, Merritt had 540 men at work with 30 horses and 115 wagons. One and a quarter miles of the Crewe line had been laid and ballasted. In the second half of 1847 work was speeded up and the number of Harecastle shafts doubled. By the beginning of 1848 the clearance of buildings had been completed at Macclesfield, where agreement had been reached with the LNWR in 1847 over a joint station, and good progress made in arching over the river Bollin and building retaining walls which were completed later in the year.

The Stoke—Uttoxeter contractors, Price & Leishman, employed 600 men who used 100 horses, 470 barrows and 400 wagons. Three steam engines had to be erected to overcome flooding in the Meir Tunnel (spelt 'Meer' in some reports), but it remained troublesome and costly for several months. Five shafts were driven. Waterworks of a different kind involved the simultaneous construction of a reservoir to safeguard the Duke of Sutherland's supply to Normacot, Longton & Lane End. One million bricks were delivered to works on the stretch and another 2,000,000 had been made on the site.

Station designs had been commissioned and that at Stoke was completed later in the year, and work started on those at Lane End and Blythe Bridge.

In the Churnet Valley, Tredwell was converting part of the canal between Froghall & Uttoxeter, abandoned under the NSR Act, into a track bed. The conversion, one of the earliest in Britain of canal into railway, resulted in the line having many sharp curves. Tunnels were built at Leek and Oakamoor and excavations, including cuttings, involved removing 150,000 cubic yards of earth.

For the lines as a whole, over 16,000 tons of rails and chairs had been delivered by 1848, together with turntables, points, crossings and water cranes.

Another bad winter and a general shortage of money led at the end of 1847 to a change in the original plan not to open the Macclesfield—Colwich section until it was completed throughout. Some people found themselves unable to take up shares and as those who had began pressing for a quick return on their capital, work was concentrated on completing the easier sections at the expense of the more difficult. The directors were worried that if what was called 'the panic' continued they might not have any money to continue construction. If one section was opened they would at least have something of value.

Difficulties with landowners were described as 'unusually numerous and vexatious' and their claims delayed work on Longton viaduct and station. G. P. Bidder described their demands as 'of a character rarely paralleled, even in railway experience'. These works were originally in charge of the resident engineer, Samuel Parker Bidder, another member of the civil engineering family. He had been appointed by the NSR on 23 September 1846, having been engineer of the Preston & Wyre Railway. In 1848 Samuel Bidder was made the first manager of the Knotty and James Curphey Forsyth became resident engineer, George Bidder continuing as consulting engineer for the construction work. Samuel Bidder left the NSR in 1853 and went to Canada, later becoming a director of the Welland Railway, although in the 1860s he returned to England and settled at Mitcham, Surrey.

Meanwhile, in 1848, trouble in getting land was delaying work on the Crewe and Sandbach branches, although no trouble was anticipated in completing them by the time the main line was ready.

The promoters ran into so many legal difficulties with Lord Crewe over the Crewe branch that they found it necessary to go to Parliament to get sanction for an alteration. This was received in the Act of 2 July 1847, which authorised several branches. The deviation,[4] which stretched just over 3 miles, branched away from the main line at the first bridge south of Crewe station and re-joined the original route at Radway

Green. The Act also formally authorised a deviation of the Colwich section through the Shugborough Hall Estate; and, more significantly, of the 4½ miles from Marston Junction to the Midland about ½ mile east of Willington, a route modified to keep away from Sir Henry Every's lands. There was also authorisation for the Apedale branch; one of just over ½ mile to the Earl of Granville's ironworks at Etruria, routed past Etruria Hall on a maximum gradient of 1 in 50; and for an extension of the Newcastle branch to join a private system built by Ralph Sneyd, owner of ironworks at Silverdale.

The Act also consolidated all the company's earlier ones and laid down that no ordinary dividends above 5 per cent were to be paid until the Churnet Valley and Willington lines had been opened. This was to be a spur to prevent the neglect of routes with obviously less potential than the Pottery and Sandbach lines.

The Burslem Loop authorised by the Act was never built. It was to have served a part of Burslem different from that served in later years by 'The Loop'. Projected for just over 2 miles, it was to have stemmed from and run east of the main line, branching away a little north of Bradwell Wood and rejoining it near Etruria, just north of the Newcastle—Hanley road. This was later to be the site of the loop junction being the last point where it could rejoin the main line to allow trains to serve Etruria. The loop scheme was planned to have a branch of about ¼ mile starting near St Paul's Church and running to Burslem Mill. The work was to involve the stopping up of the Burslem Branch canal off the T & M.[5]

At the same time as it passed the Act for these lines, Parliament rejected a scheme first suggested by the Churnet & Blythe company a year earlier and subsequently revived by the NSR. It provided for a link between the Churnet, at or near Marchington, and the Trent line at Hademore. Not only would it have provided the shortest route of all between London and Manchester, but it would also have succeeded in its promoters' intentions of frustrating two companies planning to thrust into the Potteries from South Staffordshire. The corner-stone of the schemes was an Act obtained by the South Staffordshire Railway for a branch into the Cannock Chase coalfield, where it was to have been joined by the Derbyshire, Staffordshire &

Worcestershire Railway, authorised (also on 2 July 1847) to continue the Cannock line east to Uttoxeter. There were to be fresh and decisive battles with this company when it was revitalised as the Cannock Mineral Railway in 1855.

The compulsory purchase of land was sometimes followed by landowners' claims for compensation. After one court action, compensation was paid to a prominent Longton brewer called Glover because of level crossings constructed on two private roads from Longton and Fenton to his mansion and 60 acre estate on the opposite bank of the canal. The brewer contended that his property had depreciated because the crossings had to be kept locked as people could not see approaching trains until only a few seconds before they reached them, and the crossings were not guarded by signals. The keys had to be collected from a railway keeper living 130 yards away.[6]

Many roads were built in the Potteries before railways and providing crossings was one of the heaviest expenses, not only in construction, but in operation because of the need for keepers.

OPENING PLANS

In January 1848 shareholders were given a timetable for the completion of lines later that year.

Stoke—Norton Bridge	1 March
Stone—Colwich	1 May

The Stoke—Harecastle—Crewe and Uttoxeter—Burton sections were to be ready by 1 August so that the NSR could capture through traffic from Liverpool to Derby and the East Midlands.

Bad spring weather prevented the first goods train running between Stoke and Norton Bridge until 3 April. The 'official opening' to passengers followed on 17 April. Nothing more of the main line could be opened because earthworks were incomplete between Etruria and Harecastle, where 80 yards of the tunnel were also unfinished. Completion of Stoke—Norton Bridge gave the Potteries a link with Birmingham and

London. It was an immediate success, profits of the first two months of £1,668 being said to 'exceed expectations'.

This was quite an achievement when it is remembered that there was no junction at Norton Bridge, NSR trains running into their own station. While the NSR built a footbridge across the LNWR main line (then only double-tracked) to its station, it did not succeed in negotiating a junction. That was not to come until about 1850 when NSR through trains started using the up platform and locals ran into a dead-end bay alongside. The station was—and still is—deep in the country, yet in those early days it was busy enough to have a refreshment room for a period.

While the branch was such a success it did little to speed up construction of the rest of the system for the prevailing mood continued to be one of economy and this was echoed in a progress report on 15 July in which Ricardo claimed that no line of the same length (128 miles), with works of the same magnitude, had been completed at less cost.

> I am satisfied that it admits of being as economically worked as it has been economically constructed.

His words may have high sounding echoes since so little of the NSR had been opened and the next section was not to be ready for three weeks.

The Stoke-Uttoxeter section was opened on 7 August, followed by the rest of the main line to Burton on 11 September. There had been talk of opening the Stone—Colwich line the previous May but in his report of 15 July, G. P. Bidder described it as being 'retarded according to the instructions of the directors'.

The Crewe branch and the main route between Harecastle and Congleton were opened on 9 October when the permanent station at Stoke was brought into use to replace the temporary one used for the opening of the Norton Bridge line.

Not all stations were completed in time for the opening of lines and, in January 1849, those at Congleton, Harecastle, Longport and Trentham were still under construction. Although the opening between Stone—Colwich was only a few months ahead (1 May), the section was then still without stations, turntables or sidings. This was in contrast to construction on several lines where sidings were laid before there was any likelihood of traffic.

Another major section, Congleton—Macclesfield, followed on 18 June after delays caused by subsidence affecting several piers of the Congleton viaducts, which had to be re-built on rock foundations.

The joint station at Macclesfield was still not completed by the time the NSR reached the town. Although four years had passed since the opening of the Manchester & Birmingham line in 1845, the NSR got the biggest welcome. The reason, says a Macclesfield historian, was that perhaps the fears of high speeds by trains had been overcome.[7]

Next to open was the Churnet Valley from North Rode to Uttoxeter on 13 July, together with the 4½ mile branch from Marston to Willington Junction. There were few better examples of the impact which railways made on small towns than at Uttoxeter, where three stations were immediately built. Before the link between the north and west junctions was completed Churnet trains used Dove Bank station, situated beside the level crossing on the Derby Road, and then ran to the Junction station opposite the racecourse to connect with Derby—Crewe trains. The latter trains made a second call in Uttoxeter at Bridge Street, opposite Bamford's works. All three closed in 1881 when a new station was built and the north and west junctions connected.

With so much mileage open £7,000 a year was allowed for track depreciation, but that may not have been enough in 1849 for it was a year of 'unusual floods'. The track stood up well and damage to it was recorded as 'not worth mentioning' —which poses the question—why was it?

The Churnet Valley opening took the mileage total to 113 by July 1849 and the NSR, proud of its flourishing system, published an elaborate table of distances and a map of lines which also marked the 'North Staffordshire Canal' as it was annotated. The distance table was an impressive array of figures with its longest columns having 43 entries. It was supplemented by a table headed: Junction Distances to Principal Places. They ranged from Derby (6 miles from Willington) to Plymouth (255 miles from Norton Bridge). It

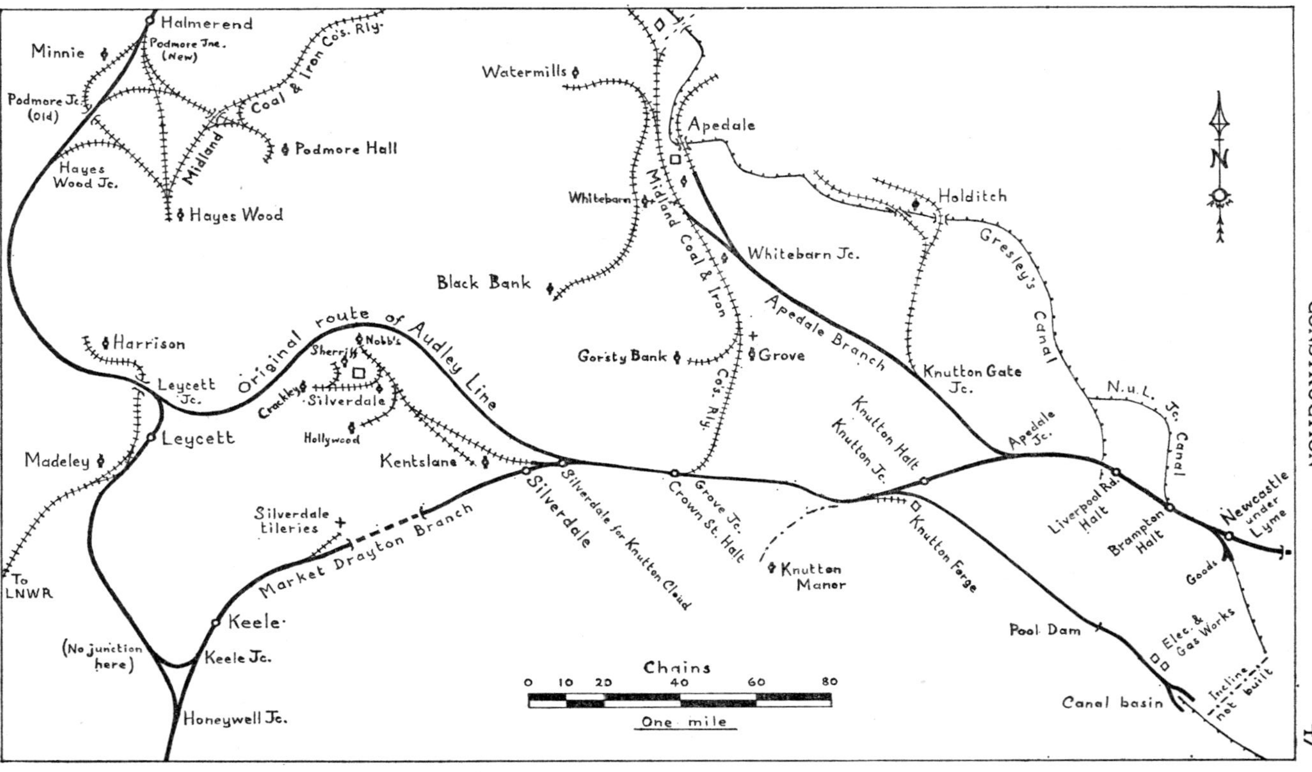

Silverdale and Newcastle

stretched the total mileage to 124 by adding the Sandbach and Newcastle branches although they were not yet open.

PRIVATE LINES

Sandwiched between the completion of the first major wave of construction in 1849 and the next (and more modest) work in 1852, was the completion of the branch to Lord Granville's ironworks at Shelton, between Etruria and Hanley. There was some difficulty in getting land but the line was opened some time in 1850. More important was the opening of a link to join the Silverdale ironworks system, west of Newcastle, owned by Sneyd. He took construction into his own hands when he became convinced (rightly, as it turned out) that the NSR would not build for some time the authorised branch through Newcastle to his ironworks. He started work in 1849 on a line of 2 miles 28 chains from his works to Pool Dam, Newcastle. Known as the Silverdale & Newcastle-under-Lyme Railway it was finished in 1850. Another of Sneyd's suspicions was that the NSR would not build the branch beyond Newcastle, being content to have a terminus beside Robert Heathcote's canal from Apedale.

The Apedale pit, then the deepest in Britain having been sunk to over 2,100 feet, was owned by Heathcote and on 30 March 1846 the NSR signed an agreement with him to apply for a Bill to make a branch from the Newcastle line to the furnaces at Apedale. A marginal note in the Board minutes, signed by Ricardo, stated: 'This clause to be made as stringent as possible'. The NSR was to carry his traffic at its own expense if the canal was obstructed during construction, and in return Heathcote was to hand over the canal section east of Apedale to Newcastle wharf within seven days of the railway's completion. Construction was estimated at £9,000 and the NSR was to have a traffic guarantee of 4 per cent a year. Plans, signed by Stephenson,[8] showed the branch running for 1½ miles from Apedale Junction, ¾ mile west of Newcastle on the line to Silverdale.

Geography was against the builders of the Newcastle branch almost as much as money, for although Newcastle station was to be only 1¼ miles from the main line junction, it was necessary to drive tunnels of 96yd and 605yd at Hartshill, where a ridge rose to over 500ft. Construction of the branch started in 1849, but it was halted the following January because of injunctions by landowners and the company had to get extra powers. It received them under an Act of 15 July which also provided for a time extension for the line through to Silverdale and the Apedale branch.

When work re-started early in 1850 it was quickly dogged by cost. 'A considerable difference of opinion' developed between the engineer and contractor and costs increased when extra brickwork was needed in Hartshill Tunnel. When Sneyd asked the NSR to extend the branch to meet his still isolated line at Knutton, it agreed in return for a traffic guarantee and took over part of Heathcote's Canal, which was now obsolete, and adapted it as the track bed for ¼ mile between Newcastle and Brampton. The line from Newcastle Junction to Knutton Junction was opened on 6 September 1852. The short stretch was estimated to have cost £27,000.

Another part of the canal was filled in to provide a goods yard at Newcastle, where reasonable level land was scarce. The goods station was opened over a year later on 7 November 1853 at the same time as the official opening of the branch to 'Apedale Goods'. However this line was used earlier by regular ironstone trains which began from the Whiteburn Ironworks, served by a siding just south of those at Apedale, to Broomfield, near Tipton, on 11 July 1853. The branch was later to serve the Holditch Colliery and the large works of the Midland Coal & Iron Company. Stanier and Broad, who were working the Apedale Ironworks in 1853, agreed to pay the NSR £500 a year for thirty years to use the branch as a connection to another of their ironworks at Knutton Junction.

Parallel with branch building ran smaller projects and a good picture of their nature and size is provided by seventeen discussed by the board on 20 February 1853. Totalling £11,000, they included one of £1,000 for a carriage shed at Stoke, ordered but delayed because a site could not be found. Stoke goods shed was to be enlarged at a cost of £1,700, £100 spent on two ticket collectors' boxes and £80 on a shed for a fire engine. A goods shed and approaches at Newcastle were to cost £4,000. Work was then under way on a goods shed and siding at Harecastle, and money was set aside for sidings at Lane End; a goods shed and approaches at either Alton or Oakamoor. Sidings at Marchington were to cost £400. Another £600 was to be spent on sidings on the Crewe branch, for which rails and sleepers were already available, and there were to be stables for seven horses at Longton (£75) and one for shunting horses at Stoke (£30). Enlarging Mow Cop and Barlaston stations was to cost £200. At the end of the month it was reported that a site had now been found for the Stoke carriage shed, which was to be on the up side north of the station.

Early in 1854 the Chief Bailiff of Burslem complained bitterly about facilities and a committee was appointed to meet him. When £600 was needed to improve the road between Burslem station and Longport, the local Board of Health asked for financial help and the NSR agreed to pay one third.

Other schemes considered in 1853 and dealt with about this time were for a siding wanted by a firm at Harecastle and a siding and carriage landing at North Rode, which Forsyth advised that they were bound to build under an agreement with a local man named Daintree. The board stipulated that work should be done 'at the least possible cost'. More urgent, said Forsyth, was a goods and cattle landing at Stoke. This was approved on 6 October together with a siding at Crewe Junction, extra ones at Stone and the provision of a crane at Trentham. In May 1853 the Newcastle-under-Lyme Canal Company got power to extend the Silverdale & Newcastle Railway for half a mile from Pool Dam to the Newcastle-under-Lyme Canal, which branched from the T & M near Stoke station. This was labelled, rather magnificently, as the Newcastle-under-Lyme Canal Extension Railway and built by the canal company to improve supplies of coal, iron and limestone to the area. The Act stipulated the use of 'horse haulage only' on the Extension.

THE ASHBOURNE BRANCH

Meanwhile the Ashbourne branch had been opened although there had been a two year delay between authorisation in 1848 and the start of construction. The market town of

Page 51 (above) *Trentham station in 1957, designed by Sir Charles Barry to serve the Duke of Sutherland's Trentham Hall;* (right) *Church Lane crossing keeper's house at Stone*

Page 52 (above) *Rushton station frontage in 1953;* (below) *the exterior of Stoke in 1967 after renovation*

Ashbourne had long been a strategic stop on coaching routes between London and the North West (and Bonnie Prince Charlie had marched through it on his way to London). But in the view of NSR shareholders it was little more than an out-of-the-way town. They wanted instead links with the larger companies which would give a two-way flow of traffic.

Shareholders disagreed with Ricardo when he told them on 19 January 1848:

> The inhabitants of Ashbourne have expressed a strong desire for this extension and the directors feel confident that a fair return may be expected for the moderate outlay required, and for which the present capital of the NSR will suffice.

The following month the shareholders began trying to delay branch construction and held a special meeting at the London Tavern in Bishopsgate on 29 February to consider getting the branch deferred until 'times of well secured prosperity'. It turned out they were divided, for the opposition motion was defeated and the bill went ahead.

Five months later shareholders were assured that it was not proposed to start construction until the main line was completed, despite the prospect of carrying large quantities of limestone from the Ashbourne district to Apedale and Silverdale ironworks. In the opposite direction coal was expected to flow to Ashbourne from the pits around Newcastle.

In July 1851 work started, the first sod being cut at Clifton. The contractor was Brassey, who was allowed £48,500 plus the cost of land. He worked the line from opening on 31 May 1852 guaranteeing 4 per cent for five years in return for all branch receipts and one third of any increase in main line traffic originating from the branch.

The Act of 22 July 1848 stated that the railway should not come within 60 yards of Ashbourne's magnificent parish church but it got pretty near. The clause was designed to protect what was—and is—regarded as one of Britain's outstanding parish churches with a spire of just over 200 feet. The NSR Official Guide for 1908 reminded tourists of Boswell's description

> One of the largest and most luminous churches I have seen in any town of the same size.

The arrival of the railway not only threatened the church, but badly affected the coaching trade of the town. It ended a coach service which had run from Ashbourne twice daily to connect with Churnet Valley trains at Rocester from the opening of the line in 1849.

Two other lines were opened in 1852: the Newcastle branch on 6 September and, nine months earlier, the Sandbach branch between Lawton Junction and a goods depot at Ettiley Heath in the country short of the town. It was used from 21 January. By now the branch had long lost the value it had for the NSR during the early struggles and it was not completed through to the LNWR Crewe—Manchester line at Sandbach for another six years.

Even then it was a goods only branch. There was no potential for passenger traffic and many years were to elapse before such trains were proposed. When they started running on 3 July 1893 it was 35 years since the completion of the line and 47 years since it was sanctioned, possibly a record for any line in Britain. A more certain, though more local distinction of the branch, was that it was the only one that the NSR built *entirely* in Cheshire.

PRESSURE FROM COAL OWNERS

In the following year plans were deposited for another route which had one terminal in Cheshire: the Potteries, Biddulph & Congleton Railway, which was projected to leave the main line 300 yards south of Stoke and run to a terminal at Congleton, ½ mile west of its eventual one at Brunswick Wharf. This was not the only section never built. Only one of two spurs projected to the Stoke—Macclesfield line at Congleton was ever constructed. This ran for 38 chains on a gradient of 1 in 38 to give a north facing junction, which meant that Biddulph Valley passenger trains had to reverse into Congleton station. Yet, because of the lie of the land, they would have had to reverse even if the other spur had been built. This was to have left the Biddulph Valley in the opposite direction and curved and climbed sharply to just north of Congleton station.

Two other branches were planned, one of just over 2 miles from Botteslow to Adderley Green colliery, over a route virtually identical with that taken as far as Anchor Road some years later, by the Longton, Adderley Green & Bucknall Railway, and a ¾ mile hook-shaped branch which was to have left the Biddulph Valley a little south of what became Milton Junction, and climbed to Birches Head at Burslem. The plans were designed to meet agitation from pit owners in the coal-rich valley, who told the Knotty that they would build their own line if the company did not. The NSR board called for an engineer's report on the owners' scheme on 5 November 1853 and three months later, on 27 February 1854, met the coal owners who said that they would abandon planning a line from Congleton to Biddulph, the main village, if the NSR pledged to do so instead and paid their expenses.

A week later the board agreed to go ahead with the Potteries, Biddulph and Congleton Railway and the line was authorised on 24 July by an Act which included protection for the Macclesfield Canal, owned by the MS & L. Construction costs of up to £200,000 were to be met out of existing capital and five years were allowed for completion, under danger of suspending dividends. It was to be a near thing, for construction was initially delayed because of the failure of the NSR—LNWR amalgamation Bill and it was not until 10 December 1857 that tenders were invited. They were considered on 30 March 1858 when Forsyth was allowed £250 for laying out the line and other expenses. Among eight tenders discussed on 30 March was one from Brassey of £103,000. This was £50,000 below the highest yet well above the lowest, £77,800 by A. W. Ritson. Soon after this had been accepted, Ritson confessed he had made an 'important omission' and proposed to add £7,000. The board declined, complained of the difficulties he had caused by not taking proper precautions and said they did not want a fresh tender from him.

Instead it accepted that of £87,500 originally submitted by William and Solomon Tredwell. The first sod was soon cut—on 27 April. Construction was reported well under way by September but haste was needed to open the line within the deadline of 3 August 1859. The Traffic Committee inspected the line on 21 June, and on 3 August it was declared open to meet the requirements of the Act. But the line was far from complete and Tredwell was still at work late in the year.

The coal of the valley also supported ironworks which wanted rail access and the first trains were those carrying minerals, although it was about a year before they started running, on 29 August 1860. Prolonged arguments surrounded the introduction of passenger trains. Following a Board of Trade Inspector's report of 29 September 1863, opening to passengers was postponed and a further report of 7 October brought passenger trains no nearer. The NSR protested on 23 October that the inspector's requirements were unnecessary and asked for leave to open the line. This was refused and it was not until the following spring in a report of 26 May that the line was pronounced satisfactory.

It finally opened on 1 June 1864 when the *Macclesfield Courier* reported:

> On Wednesday the first ordinary passenger train left Stoke at 8.45, the engine driver having decorated his 'iron horse' with oak and laburnum, interspersed with a few flags emblazoned with the Staffordshire Knot.

Before coal was discovered, the Biddulph valley was a pleasant spot, flanked by moors. Much of that rural character had been changed before the arrival of the railway, for as the same reporter noted:

> Within the last decade roaring furnaces have opened their ponderous jaws and are belching forth volumes of smoke and liquid fire—the bowels of the earth are being dug out and converted to the requirements of the age.

The initiative of the Biddulph coalowners in planning a line of their own was not an isolated example: in June 1855 a firm of solicitors—Challinor & Company of Leek—deposited a Bill for a mineral branch of 6 furlongs 4 chains from Ipstones to the Churnet Valley at Froghall. It was probably intended to serve shallow pits near Ipstones. The NSR does not seem to have been worried—indeed it might have favoured it—for it noted the facts without comment. Maybe it thought the ruling gradient would decide its fate. It was planned as 1 in 21.

Notes are on page 295

NORTH STAFFORDSHIRE RAILWAY.

COAL RATES.

On and after the 2nd April, the following will be the Charges for the Carriage of Coal, viz.:—

Three Farthings per Ton per Mile in Owner's Waggons, and One Penny per Ton per Mile in the Company's Waggons, with One Shilling per Ton added for the use of Sidings and other Terminal Expenses.

All Waggons not unloaded within *three days* after arrival at their destination, will be subject to a charge for Demurrage, at the Rate of Two Shillings per Day per Waggon.

All Carriage to be paid by the Senders.

By Order,

S. P. BIDDER, *Manager*.

STOKE, 26*th March*, 1849.

TABLE OF DISTANCES.

FROM. / TO.	Crewe.	Congleton.	Harecastle.	Burslem.	Stoke.	Trentham.	Stone.	N. Bridge.	Longton	Blyth B.	Cresswell	Leigh.	Uttoxeter.	Sudbury.	Tutbury.	Burton.
Crewe....		15	9	12	15	18	23	26	18	21	23	26	32	36	40	45
Mow Cop..	11	4	2	5	8	11	16	19	11	14	16	19	25	29	33	38
Harecastle.	9	6		3	6	9	14	17	9	12	14	17	23	27	31	36
Stoke	15	12	6	3		3	8	11	3	6	8	11	17	21	25	30
Longton..	18	15	9	6	3	6	10	13		3	5	8	14	18	22	27
Burton ..	45	42	36	33	30	33	37	40	27	24	22	19	13	9	5	

CHAPTER THREE

The Small Octopus

SQUABBLES WITH THE LNWR

The NSR was once tagged as a 'small octopus' by its chairman and it took its final shape from a group of secondary lines authorised, though not constructed, in a five year period from 1861. Their development was influenced to some extent by the LNWR, for although the NSR had been formed without Parliamentary opposition, it quickly came into conflict with that giant which came into being only three weeks later.

Unlike the NSR which had little but financial resources, the LNWR inherited wealth and strength from member companies, and being in a virtually unchallengable position financially and geographically, it was immediately powerful enough to challenge anything it disliked which its neighbours were planning. Such was its power that there was soon talk of it taking over the NSR. Rumours got so strong that Ricardo felt it necessary to comment even before the NSR was formed. At the September 1846 meeting of shareholders he dismissed the idea contemptuously saying: 'I do not see why we should not buy up the L & NW Railway instead of selling our own'.

Just how rash such a statement proved to be was demonstrated three years later when the NSR had to negotiate an agreement under which the LNWR was to give it 'every reasonable facility' over its lines, and a share of through traffic. It laid down that the LNWR was to use the Potteries line for direct Manchester traffic.

Ricardo was confident it would work, 'I cannot see by what pretext, either in law or in reason, the agreement can be rendered void'. But the LNWR did and the companies were soon locked in legal battle. For its part, the NSR re-inforced its tactics along lines set out in a policy statement of 30 January 1850, in which Ricardo contended that by firmly asserting its rights, the company would ultimately obtain the traffic it expected.

He warned the LNWR that they had been forced to survey another outlet: a line to the MS & L at Marple, which led not only to the Manchester area, but to the populous districts of Yorkshire. The NSR was also interested in the Midland Railway branch from Leicester to the GNR at Hitchin since it would provide an independent route to London.

The NSR embarrassed the LNWR by planning a link to a branch which the MS & L was building to Whaley Bridge.[1] The LNWR was angry because it was seeking the help of the Midland and Lancashire & Yorkshire railways to keep through traffic off the MS & L, then friendly with the GNR and thus potentially able to start a rival London—Manchester service through Retford. The LNWR was forced to reverse its attitude and to start wooing the MS & L and managed to persuade it to become party, with the MR and L & Y, to a seven-year agreement to divide goods traffic. After this came into force on 1 February 1850, the track of the partly completed Whaley Bridge branch was lifted.

There was nothing the NSR could do when the agreement with the LNWR was patched up because one of the conditions was that it had to refrain from promoting independent routes. It had also to abandon all litigation.

The board's failure to establish good relations with the LNWR led to a militant group of shareholders forcing an internal investigation into the NSR's affairs. After some weeks of uncertainty, it cleared the directors of taking any wrong decisions. They claimed however that it had placed them in a weak position while negotiating a new agreement with the LNWR which took effect from 13 April 1850.

It led to further friction and there was also trouble with the Midland Railway, but relations were patched up after the NSR threatened to build its own stations at Burton and Derby. While relations were strained with the LNWR, the NSR surveyed a route from Colwich across Cannock Chase to the Oxford, Worcester & Wolverhampton Railway, and also an extension from Sandbach to Liverpool.[2]

The best solution seemed to lie in amalgamation between the LNWR and the NSR but a Bill to effect it was withdrawn after a Select Committee reported against amalgamation generally. During a second attempt, the LNWR took over maintenance of the NSR permanent way from Wright, the contractor, who was working the system. This second attempt at amalgamation was barred by the Cardwell Act which followed the Select Committee report.

A third attempt failed because of opposition by the GWR, MS & L and MR, which did not want to see so lucrative a system as the NSR fall into LNWR hands. Ricardo resigned on 19 February 1855 when the Staffordshire Potteries Chamber of Commerce said it would only agree to amalgamation if the NSR reduced tolls. The reduction was to apply to all staple commodities and Ricardo felt it would badly damage the company. Thomas Broderick took over as chairman until the board and the shareholders persuaded Ricardo to return as chairman from 31 July.

Soon afterwards a link was planned to the OWW at Wolverhampton and a third attempt made to reach Liverpool. The company also planned to take over the Cannock Mineral Railway at the suggestion of that company. This had been formed originally as the Derbyshire, Staffordshire & Worcestershire Junction Railway, authorised on 2 July 1847 from the South Staffordshire Railway at Cannock to the Trent Valley at Rugeley. It lay dormant through lack of funds until the company became the Cannock Mineral Railway on 14 August 1855. It was about to join the NSR when the LNWR offered the CMR shareholders 5 per cent, slightly better terms than those offered by the NSR.

The NSR had to accept defeat and this may have helped to improve relations with the LNWR, which were consolidated on a friendly basis by an Act of 13 August 1859.

THE FIGHT FOR TRAFFIC

From the running of the first train, Knotty passenger services were dominated by a single factor: the need to provide connections which met trains run by neighbouring companies.

An early effect which was to linger and worry the Knotty

for years was a wide discrepancy between the growth of local traffic, which was flourishing, and through traffic, which was not. In 1849, the company carried nearly half a million passengers (443,362), but through bookings were only a small fraction (11,609). In the closing half of the year, 82,775 tons of goods were carried, but 79,186 tons constituted local traffic.

Late in 1849, closed third class carriages were introduced on all trains. They were termed 'intermediates' and passengers were charged 1¼d a mile, although those who used the same coaches on Parliamentary trains paid only 1d. The immediate popularity of the closed thirds was reflected in passenger returns for September 1850 which reached 80,437—over 22,000 more than in the corresponding period of 1849. Receipts were up by £1,200. Steady increases were also maintained during winter months.

In 1851 goods carried reached 96,231 tons; minerals, 76,092; while through goods traffic totalled only 4,522 tons. Even so the infant Knotty was profitable, making in the period a net profit of £28,244 15s 3d.

By this time mineral traffic was stated to be flowing 'almost beyond the means at the disposal of the company for its accommodation', while through traffic was reported tersely as 'altogether undeveloped'—although there were hopes of a considerable increase as a result of steps (unspecified) which were being taken. Yet if they were, they had little effect for six months later the board was again complaining of a 'remarkable disparity' between the totals.

Passenger returns passed the half million mark (508,928) in the closing half of 1850 and the increasing intensity of traffic was reflected in more through bookings though only by a few thousand (17,244). Individual events were sufficient to make a temporary impression on traffic returns. A rise in passengers during a single week in January 1851 was attributed to the sitting of Stafford Assizes.

Later in the year the Great Exhibition in London was blamed for *reducing* passenger traffic. The NSR claimed it suffered in two ways: through low rates at which passengers had been carried to this 'attractive spectacle', and because of the short distance over which the NSR was able to handle a few of the trains. Overall passenger revenue in the period increased by

7½ per cent over the corresponding period in 1850.

By January 1852 the accumulated passenger total reached nearly three million, a good achievement since it was reached without any benefit from through services which the LNWR did not start until the following year.

Strained relations were manifest in the development of mail traffic. For several years the NSR felt it was being starved of it for in the early fifties the Potteries mail was still being delivered to Whitmore and taken 7 miles by road to Newcastle. The Knotty was not alone in complaining about the speed and inadequacies of the postal services. People in the Potteries constantly sent memorials to the Postmaster General. Ricardo lamented that the authorities had not thought fit to take any further notice of their representations than to abruptly refuse to meet their requirements.

Although it had the united support of towns between Macclesfield and Longton, the NSR was still not carrying mail by the start of 1852, but the directors felt that it was only a question of time before the mails were on the railway 'instead of being carried through the thinly-populated country between Colwich and Cheadle in Cheshire and distributed to towns of nearly 200,000 souls, by gig posts in the dead of night'.

Ricardo wrote from London in 1853 to Bidder who was then managing the line, saying he was prepared to arrange the carriage of mails on NSR trains from either Crewe or Stafford. The charge on ordinary trains would be 2d a mile: on specials, 2s a mile. Twelve days later the Postmaster General accepted the ordinary charges, although they could not state which trains they would use. The letter added that 'His Lordship does not at present entertain the suggestion that the Post Office at Stoke be at the station'.

Night mails were discussed by the board later in the year and on 16 January 1854 the NSR offered carriage between Macclesfield and Stafford at £1,000 for five years, providing amalgamation with the LNWR took place. The offer was rejected by the Post Office on 30 March, yet on 17 April it asked the company to carry mail between Stoke and Uttoxeter, seeking the same terms as those between Stoke and Stafford. The board refused saying that the Stoke—Stafford mails were carried at a rate which was unremunerative to help the people of the Potteries, and they did not feel they could extend the concession. The following month the NSR stated its price for the Stoke—Uttoxeter mails: 6d a mile.

A 'privilege' renewed at this time was that to W. H. Smith to sell books and newspapers. There was no increase in the terms.

The militant attitude of the NSR was evident again in January 1855 when the company had a fight with the Inland Revenue over duty payable on passenger receipts of the Parliamentary trains, which, it contended, were exempt from duty by law. The NSR got a prompt reply in which a compromise was agreed, and an allowance given to trains which were allowed to deviate from the approved times of starting. In return the company had to pay duty of £274 15s on receipts of £5,495 to the collector at Stafford.

FRONTIER BATTLES

The main characteristic of the NSR's original development was the creation of over 100 miles of mainly through lines. The second period, stemming from the lines authorised between 1861-6, was of a different nature for it included a number of small branches. The Loop became the most famous of them, but the most significant strategically was a line to Market Drayton. The latter was built as the outcome of a battle which developed when the LNWR tried to penetrate the Potteries with its own line. The attack began with a road invasion in which Whitmore was used as a base for a fleet of horse-drawn vans serving Newcastle and Stoke. This service was supported by a move to promote a line from Madeley to Silverdale. (Whitmore was not a suitable junction being separated from the Potteries by a ridge of high ground.) From Silverdale, the LNWR was to have running powers to Stoke.

At this period the Knotty's western frontier was at Knutton Junction: the line west to Silverdale belonging to Sneyd, who also owned the railway to Pool Dam. The LNWR threat came through its support of a private venture by the Shrewsbury & Potteries Junction Railway,[3] which planned a line between Wellington and Crewe through Madeley, with a branch to join Sneyd's system at Silverdale.

The danger from the NSR point of view was averted through its friendly relations with Sneyd, who met the threat by promoting a Bill to turn both his private lines into public railways. The NSR naturally supported him and he got an Act on 13 August 1859 while the S & PJ Bill was rejected.

The NSR lost no time in consolidating the frontier and on 31 August 1860 it leased both Sneyd's lines for £1,250 a year, paying another £600 annual rental for the canal.[4] The S & PJ revived its scheme in 1860 but its position was hopeless because the LNWR was now on the NSR side because of the 1859 agreement. The following year plans were deposited for extending the Apedale branch to Audley and this proposal was later modified by the Wellington, Drayton & Newcastle Railway, which proposed a line of that route with north-facing spurs on both sides of the LNWR main line at Madeley.

A fresh threat came in 1862 when the GWR made a determined bid for an independent route to Manchester. It sought to exploit a scheme promoted by the Wellington and Cheshire Junction Railway for a line from Wellington to Market Drayton, Nantwich and Northwich. This met the united opposition of the NSR and LNWR and the NSR solicitor, William Burchell, of London, reported on 1 August that they had succeeded in rendering the Bill entirely innocuous by inducing a Commons committee to throw out the section between Market Drayton and Silverdale, thus destroying its main object. This left only the section between Wellington and Market Drayton, which would not interfere with NSR traffic.

A month later the NSR was surprised to find that the LNWR was about to survey a line into the Potteries from Madeley, and Broderick wrote to Richard Moon, the LNWR chairman, on 29 September saying he understood survey instructions had been given to the southern division engineer, William Baker.

'I mentioned in my last interview with you,' wrote Broderick, 'that such a line was expected from us and that we are prepared to make the necessary survey. I cannot help thinking that it will seem absurd that two companies in friendly alliance should be preparing to make lines between the same common points.'

Broderick asked for the survey to be halted until they had held a meeting. Moon replied on 1 October that he understood any such line was to be made jointly. Baker had stopped the survey on the understanding that whatever was decided would be by mutual consent. When the meeting took place at Euston Square on 15 October, the LNWR suggested it should make the line. This annoyed Broderick and afterwards he followed Moon to the chairman's room and asked him if he would object to the point being referred to Buller.[5] Moon refused.

The NSR strengthened its 'defences' in 1862 by doubling the section between Knutton Junction and Silverdale, although the second track laid on the north side of the original one was used only by passenger trains which ran to Silverdale.[6]

While the impasse remained over the Market Drayton branch the GWR actively promoted its scheme and in 1863 it got a Bill as far as the Lords. The NSR countered with a scheme for a line from Silverdale as far west as Madeley. If the line was to be extended from there to Market Drayton it was suggested that the LNWR should complete it, either by itself or jointly with the NSR. The LNWR liked neither idea and left the NSR saddled with the whole project which it advanced as the Silverdale, Madeley and Drayton Railway in 1864.

This went before Parliament as a rival to a scheme revived by the S & PJ from Shrewsbury to Hanley, via Halmerend, Tunstall and Burslem. Three branches were included: Kidsgrove—Jamage; Newcastle—Halmerend; and Burslem—Longport basin. The plan was to join a line which Sneyd had built to serve his own pits and ironworks at Talke. This ran for 2 miles 31 chains from alongside the NSR main line at Chatterley. Sneyd had used it from 1860, the year in which he signed an agreement which was to have far-reaching consequences in safeguarding NSR interests. Dated 31 August, it laid down that Sneyd would not carry traffic to or from lines of other companies without the written consent of the NSR.

Sneyd got powers in 1861 for a short extension of his Talke system through a link with the projected Jamage (a corruption of Gem edge) branch at Red Street. It was to serve a pit and chemical works at Jamage. In 1862 Sneyd took things a stage further by seeking a direct connection at Chatterley with the NSR main line. Nothing came of it and up to closure in recent

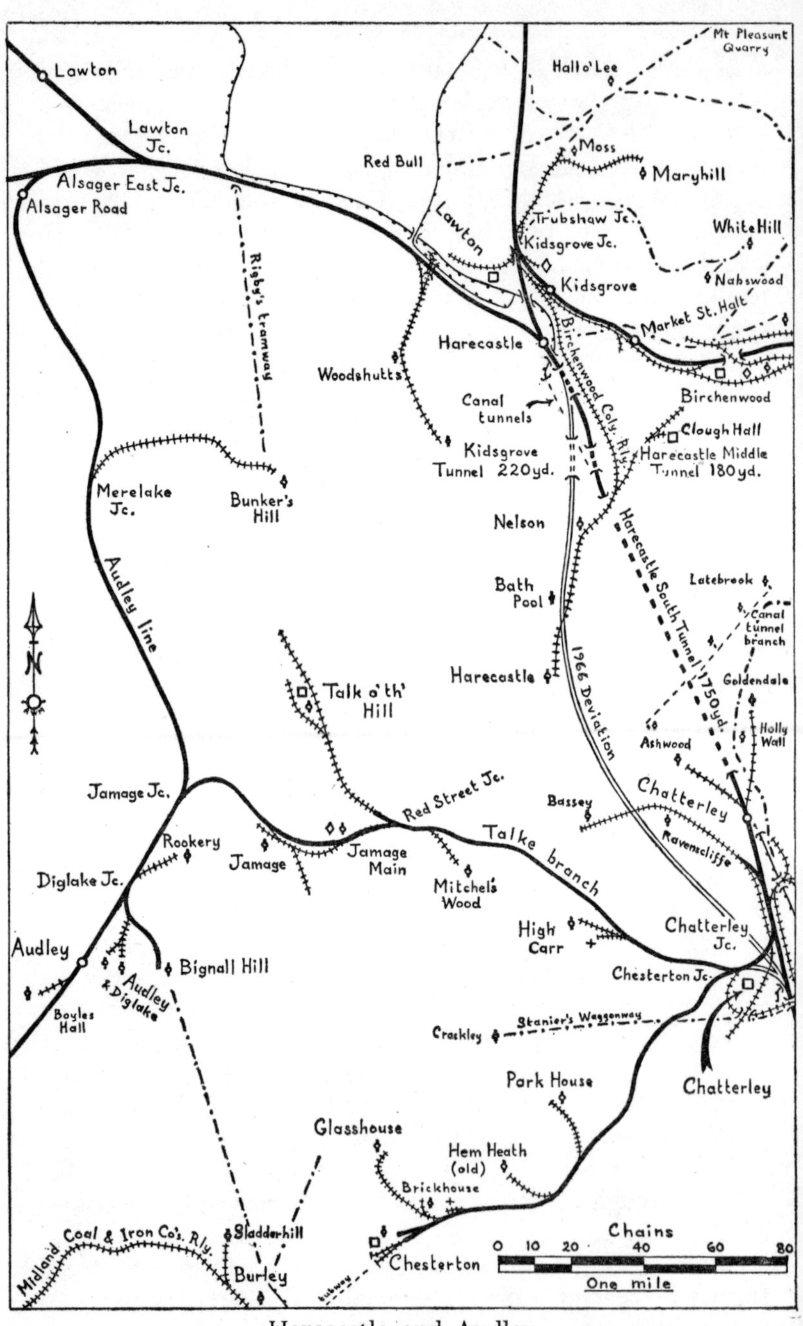

Harecastle and Audley

years, the Talke branch terminated in sidings beside the main line.

The reaction of the Lords on being faced with the choice of Market Drayton schemes was to suggest that the NSR should wait a while before doing anything. It pleased neither company but the position was resolved when the S & PJ's opposition softened and it withdrew, leaving the NSR Bill to pass unopposed by the Lords, who formally rejected the S & PJ's scheme 'with confidence in the NSR.'

THE AUDLEY LINES

The Market Drayton scheme was incorporated by one of two Acts of 29 July 1864 which permanently consolidated the Knotty's western frontier by ensuring its penetration of the ore and mining area around Audley. The Silverdale—Market Drayton scheme was to include a connection to the LNWR at Madeley. Capital authorised was £175,000 with loan powers of £58,000.

The other Act allowed the lease or purchase of Sneyd's Talke branch by the NSR (about which there was already private agreement), and it provided for the construction of the 'Audley' line from Silverdale to Alsager, with branches to pits at Jamage and Bignall Hill and for a short line from Leycett to the Market Drayton branch at Honeywall Junction, giving, in effect, a wide-based triangular junction. The Audley complex was completed by the Chesterton branch stemming from the main line at Chatterley sidings. As a condition of receiving the Act, the NSR agreed to exercise the powers which Sneyd obtained in 1861 for the Talke—Jamage link since it had been in the original S & PJ plans.

This involved no more than 250 yards of line, but its minor length was outmatched by its territorial implications since it would provide the shortest route for minerals sent west from the area, cutting out a long haul. Pits and works around Talke and Jamage were operated in competition and Sneyd, as owner of the former, set out to prevent his own line being exploited by rivals. Behind the scene politics resulted in a compromise by which the NSR agreed to go ahead and build the link, which it did by 1868. But then it was left unused.

The busy Talke line got a further fillip through the opening of another pit in 1873. Six years later the NSR got powers to abandon the Red Street—Jamage line, though not without local protest. Meanwhile the NSR leased most of the Talke branch for £1,250 a year, taking a stretch of 1 mile 55 chains from Chatterley to just beyond the junction proposed at Red Street. Sneyd retained control of the remaining 57 chains to provide a long shunt overlap for trains using his colliery and ironworks at Talke and so avoid paying the NSR for shunting over its lines.

Hopes of a link between the Apedale and Audley lines, in which the NSR was interested, died when Robert Heathcote objected to trains within sight of his house. The prizes for mineral and railway promoters were almost limitless for the Apedale valley was the world's richest in coal with forty-seven seams.

MARKET DRAYTON BRANCH

Returning to the Market Drayton line, this was the third line to reach this little market town. Only the connections offered by the other lines provided an incentive for the NSR to go to Market Drayton. In evidence to a select committee on behalf of the NSR, the North Eastern's engineer, Thomas Harrison, remarked that if there had been no other line to Market Drayton there would be no object in making one to the town.

The first of the other companies was the 10¾ mile Nantwich & Market Drayton Railway, opened on 20 October 1863. It had strong GWR affinities, being worked by the company, although isolated from the rest of the system. It was followed by the Wellington & Drayton Railway, opened 19 October 1867 after having been absorbed by the GWR during construction.

When the NSR ran into a money shortage, the Board of Trade agreed to time extensions for several lines including the Loop beyond Hanley, but there was no concession for the Market Drayton line, which had then to be finished in a hurry. In summer 1868, Forsyth, the NSR engineer, complained of excessive demands for compensation for land. Work costing £87,772 had been completed to the end of June, but the line was not ready for another eighteen months: until 1 February 1870.

There was limited early traffic to Sneyd's race course recently moved from Knutton to Keele Park. The first station built for it, called Madeley, was opened as a temporary block post for race traffic in November 1870. The following May it was renamed Madeley Manor, changed yet again, to Madeley Road, only three months later. In later years race-goers used a station built by the NSR for Sneyd nearly 2 miles closer to Silverdale. That, too, had a short life from October 1896 to 1907.

The railway situation at Market Drayton could have been complicated by the Drayton Junction Railway, incorporated on the same day as the NSR got its Market Drayton Act, to build a line from Prees, through Market Drayton, which it was to enter and leave from the north, to the Shropshire Union Railway near Stafford. The junction was to have been with the Stafford—Wellington line and the line was to have been worked by the Wrexham, Mold & Connah's Quay Railway using an extension which it planned from Wrexham to Whitchurch.

One clause in the DJR Bill provided powers for mutual protection for its route and that of the NSR near Market Drayton because of the likelihood that both companies might want the same land. In the event there was no dispute because the DJR soon passed from the scene, being abandoned by a Board of Trade order of 25 January 1867.

The Chesterton branch was constructed from the Talke branch and opened in January 1866, but traffic soon got too dense for the Talke branch to handle and in 1877 the lines were separated at Chesterton Junction and laid parallel to Chatterley Junction.

At just over 1½ miles in length, the Chesterton branch was longer than that to Bignall Hill, which stretched only 54 chains from the Audley line. This, in itself, was a mere 7 miles 37 chains, yet construction was continually delayed through shortage of money. With four years of time expired, the NSR board met on 25 March 1868 and considered asking for a time extension. No decision was reached, but at its next meeting on 29 April it was agreed that the Audley and Market

Drayton should both be restricted to single tracks. By the end of June, £72,732 had been spent on the Audley line and still it was far from finished. The following October the board decided it was no longer necessary to restrict construction. Yet it was nearly two more years before the line, with the Jamage and Bignall Hill branches, was completed between Alsager East and Honeywall Junctions. The opening on 24 July 1870 was just a week inside the time limit. A picture of the last minute preparations for opening can be gauged from a report by Forsyth on 13 June in which he stated that the line would be 'quite ready' for mineral traffic on 1 July. He added: 'It is important that some trains should run early in the month so as to comply with the Act'. He also reported that Podmore Hall collieries and the Crewe Coal and Iron Company were ready to start sending coal.

The introduction of passenger trains to serve Leycett, Halmerend and Audley was delayed for a considerable time because of trains having to reverse at Honeywall to reach Stoke. Shareholders were told in 1879 that the need for passenger trains was pressing because the area was developing so much, yet the trains did not start until 28 June 1880. The problem of reversal was overcome the following year by the opening of an east facing curve near Honeywall from 1 October. The original section between Leycett and Silverdale was never opened because of subsidence and drainage troubles. The Honeywall West spur was dismantled in 1888. The following year a fourth station was opened on the Audley line, Talke and Alsager Road, brought into use on 1 July. 'Talke' was dropped from the name in May 1902.

There were fresh stirrings on the border in 1888 after the Shropshire Railways was formed and tried to revive the Potteries, Shrewsbury & North Wales aspirations. They had other plans. These included the construction of a line between Shrewsbury and Hodnet, supplemented by running powers over the GWR to Market Drayton and the NSR from there to Stoke. Like the GWR, the NSR objected strongly and only the Hodnet line was approved. Financial difficulties led to the lapsing of this scheme in 1891 and when Col Stephens formed the Shropshire & Montgomery Railway in 1911, he showed no interest in extensions east of Shrewsbury.

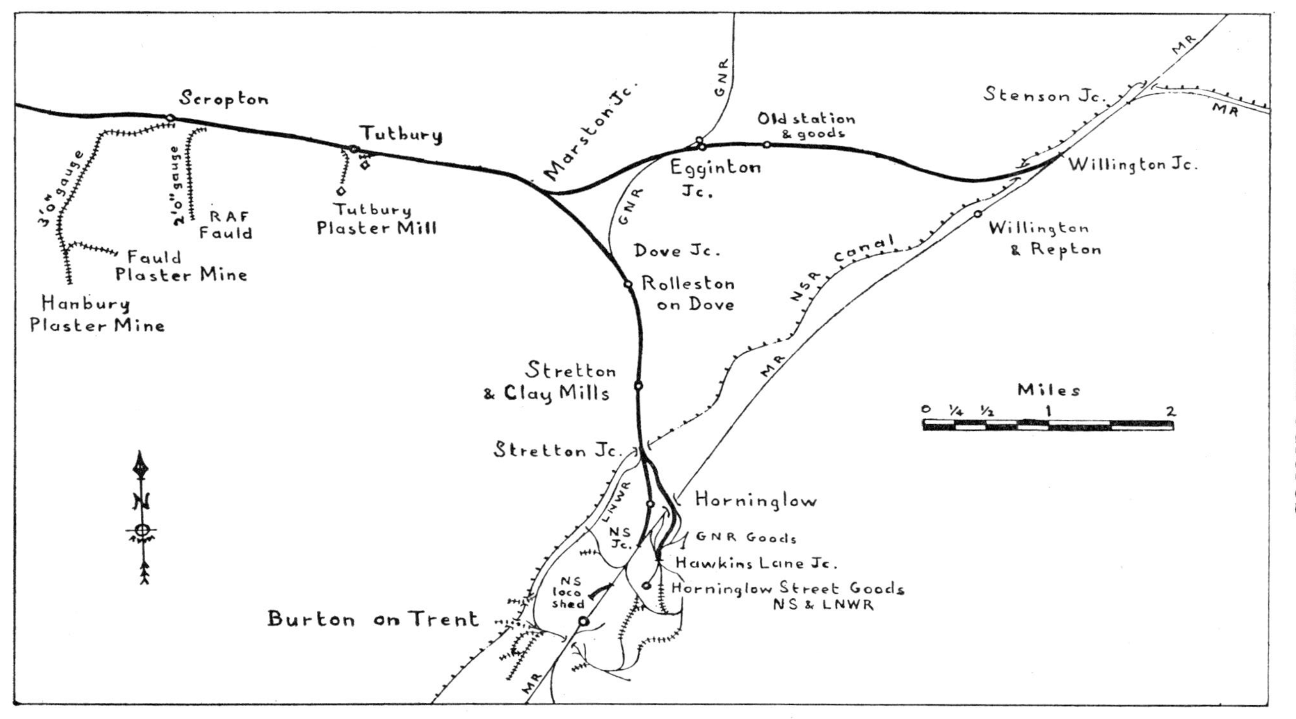

Burton on Trent and Tutbury

Also authorised with the Audley lines on 29 July 1864, though totally unconnected with them, was the Grange branch which stemmed from the main line between Etruria and Longport and ran 1 mile 24 chains to Grange colliery. It was opened on 24 March 1872.

The NSR was always a minor party at Burton-on-Trent but it did manage to get a toe-hold on the Midland's huge traffic through an Act of 13 July 1863 which provided for a line, a fraction over a mile long, from Stretton Junction to Hawkin's Lane Junction, bridging the Midland main line roughly midway. Running powers gave the NSR access to the LNWR goods station at Horninglow Street, ¼ mile beyond Hawkin's Lane Junction. Five years were to elapse before completion on 1 April 1868, only just within the legal limit.

There was also a long delay in completing the Leek branch authorised by the Act to link the Biddulph valley line at Milton Junction, with the Churnet valley at Leek Brook. Forsyth reported on 30 June 1866 that about 40,000 cubic yards of earthwork remained to be dealt with. A small amount of masonry work was also necessary at 'two small roadside stations', although 3½ miles of permanent way had been delivered and points, signals and track linked at the two junctions. Yet it was not until well over a year later, on 1 November 1867, that the line was opened. One difficulty was raising capital: an increase of £100,000 had been provided for in the 1863 Act.

Four days before the Market Drayton Act, the Knotty got powers for two lines in the heart of the Potteries: from Longport to Pinnox, known as the Tunstall Lower branch, and from Pinnox to Newfields (the Tunstall Upper branch). Capital of £66,000 was supported by borrowing powers of £22,000.

Although the Newfields was no more than a branch of 61 chains, there were hopes that it might be extended over Harecastle hill to Jamage, Alsager and Crewe. The original branch was constructed on a timber viaduct between Newfields Wharf and the junction and although conversion to a conventional earth embankment was authorised on 27 July 1892, traces of the timber one were still visible in 1950.

The Tunstall branch was built between Longport and the

Loop at Tunstall Junction, a distance of 1 mile 8 chains. Completion time of four years for this and the Newfields branch was woefully inadequate for that did not open until 1 October 1874. The Tunstall spur, equally well known as the Pinnox branch, did not open until 1 June 1875 and while first a mineral line, it was sanctioned as an 'emergency' passenger line on 27 July 1892.

The Pinnox branch provided the best outlet for a group of pits owned by the Chatterley—Whitfield company which in 1872 began developing its own system, the Whitfield Colliery Railway, to move coal from pits around Whitfield to Chatterley ironworks. The original connection was to the Biddulph valley line near Black Bull, but as the Loop was built, a more lightly graded connection was put in just south of Tunstall station. Finally a junction was developed with the Pinnox branch and extensive interchange sidings built.

THE LONGTON, ADDERLEY GREEN & BUCKNALL RAILWAY

Chatterley—Whitfield also had five pits along the route developed in the seventies as the Longton, Adderley Green & Bucknall Railway, a successor to the abortive scheme some years earlier by the Potteries, Biddulph & Congleton for a branch into this rich mining area. The L AG & B was not an NSR initiative, but that of a closely allied company of that name whose plans, approved by NSR shareholders on 10 May 1866, received Parliamentary sanction on 16 July. The Act authorised 4¼ miles of mineral line from the Biddulph Valley line at Bucknall to Park Hall, with two short branches. Capital of £50,000 in 10s shares was supported by borrowing powers of £16,000. The NSR was to maintain the line and run it at the same expense as the rest of the system, the stipulation being that 'the line so as used and worked by the NSR was to be considered part of the lines of that company'. Despite this the NSR showed little interest in construction and several times powers had to be extended, the first occasion being covered by a Board of Trade Warrant of 13 July 1871. When it expired on 16 July 1872, it was replaced by an Act of 27 July which authorised some deviations, including an extension from Longton (Normacot Junction) to Parkhall to provide a circular route, and the abandonment of part of the route. The line was now legally bound for completion by 27 June 1874.

Even this deadline was not met and the line was not opened until 15 months later: 24 September 1875. It ran from Bottes-low Junction on the Biddulph Valley line, to the Derby line at Millfield Junction: 3 miles 54 chains, and there was a ½ mile branch from Hulme Valley Junction to Hulme Colliery.

A report of the capital account at 30 June 1877 showed it totalled £62,037, including £46,037 taken up in shares. Expenditure to the same date totalled £63,172.

It soon became clear that in one respect the line was too successful for it greatly reduced the distances over which the NSR could haul coal from local pits and in 1883 a move was made to cut the line in two. This was not carried out until the NSR took over from 1 January 1895 under an agreement confirmed by the LAG & B Act of 14 May, which authorised the abandonment of 22 chains between Adderley Green and Weston Coyney, near the junction with the Hulme branch. About five years later this branch was reduced to a stub of 7 chains by the closure of the remaining 33 chains.

THE STAFFORD & UTTOXETER RAILWAY

The Longton, Adderley Green & Bucknall was always a busy line, but the same could never be said of another line with which the NSR had rather looser connections: the Stafford & Uttoxeter. It was the only result of a number of schemes which began in the Mania of 1845. They included the Derby, Uttoxeter & Stafford seen as part of a through route between eastern England and Holyhead. It was soon abandoned.

The NSR and LNWR were friendly enough in the early sixties to unite in opposition to the Stafford & Uttoxeter Railway and against another line planned between Rugeley & Uttoxeter. Burchell, the NSR solicitor, reported on 1 August 1862 that the opposition of the NSR (he made no mention of the LNWR), had prevented the Rugeley promoters getting funds for a Parliamentary deposit and so their Bill had been withdrawn. However, despite opposition, the S & U Bill had been passed. Burchell said the NSR and LNWR had only succeeded in modifying slightly in their favour, powers for regulating the inter-change of traffic between the three systems.

The S & U Act of 29 July 1862 provided for a 13¼ mile link with a branch of 1 mile 77 chains to Weston on the NSR. To reach Uttoxeter, the S & U trains were to run over the NSR main line from Bromshall Junction, 2 miles west of the town. In return, the NSR was given running powers over the S & U.

Doubtless spurred by the Stafford & Uttoxeter's success in getting an Act, the North & South Staffordshire Junction revived plans for a Rugeley—Uttoxeter link. Powers were to be given to either the NSR, LNWR or the Cannock Mineral Railway to work the line. A Commons committee rejected the Bill on 22 April 1863 on the understanding that the S & UR would build a branch to the village of Abbot's Bromley, lying south of its route.

No more successful was the Wolverhampton & North Staffordshire Junction Railway, which aimed to provide a route between the Potteries and the Midlands independent of the LNWR. It was to run from a junction with the NSR ¼ mile north of Colwich, to the Cannock Chase & Wolverhampton Railway at New Hayes. It was to have a ruling gradient of 1 in 70 and cross the Cannock Mineral Railway by a viaduct 92ft high. While the scheme passed two Parliamentary stages, it was withdrawn, mainly because of LNWR opposition.

The S & U took five years to complete and from its opening on 23 December 1867, it was worked by the GNR, then interested in driving west into Wales. The GNR promoted an extension of its lines from Colwick round the north of Nottingham to Derby and the NSR at Egginton, near Burton, where a double junction was developed. The NSR provided the GNR with running powers between Egginton and Bromshall Junctions. The GNR bought the ailing S & U from August 1881 for £100,000.

Just before the Light Railway Act of 1896 there was talk of a link between Uttoxeter and Abbot's Bromley, with an extension to Lichfield, but the LNWR firmly rejected overtures from the promoters.

THE POTTERIES LOOP

Of all the lines built in the Potteries, only one became

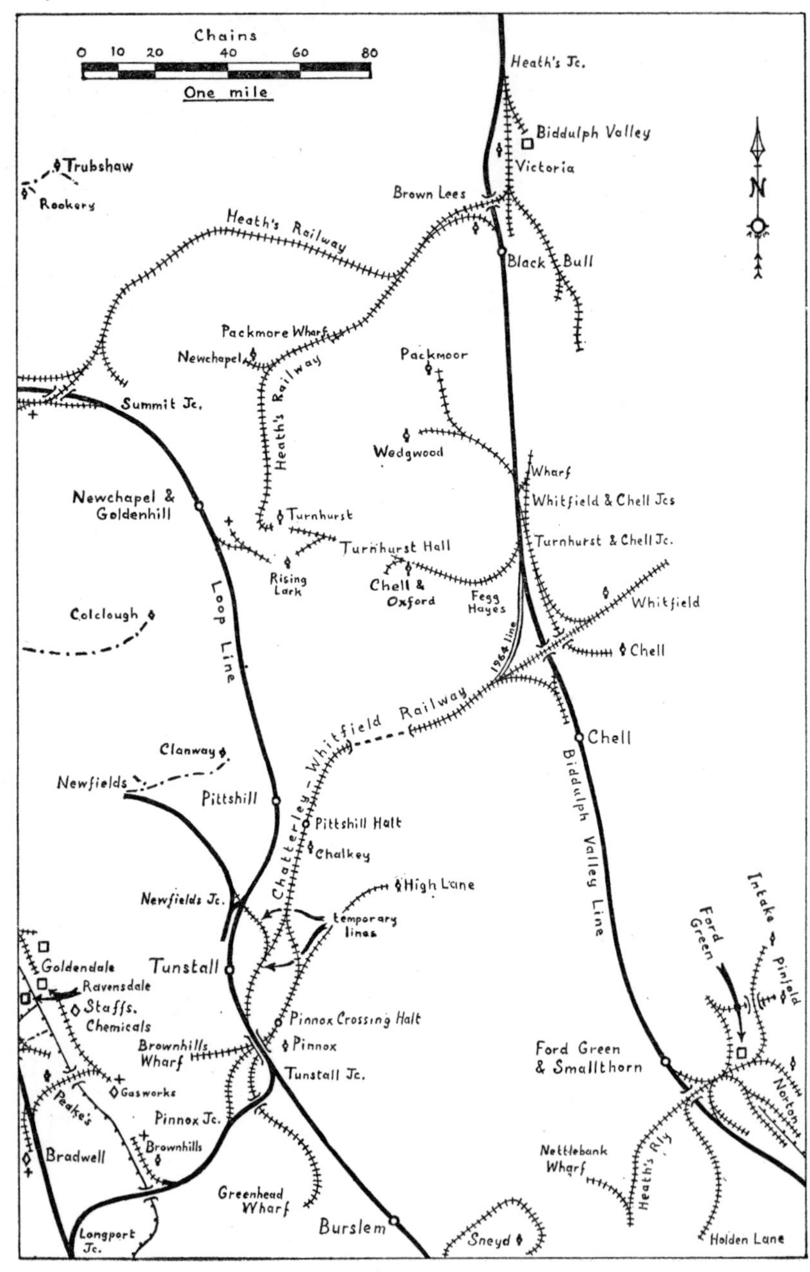

Biddulph Valley and Tunstall

famous: the humble loop, which was to be immortalised in the novels of Arnold Bennett. It was an 'inner circle' for which agitation grew steadily after the completion of the main line, which ran through the Vale of Etruria between Harecastle and Stoke. The Loop was designed to serve the six towns which expanded rapidly on the hilly flank to the east of the Vale and spilled over into the neighbouring valley.

The Loop was first envisaged in 1847 to run from Etruria to Hanley, Burslem, Cobridge, Tunstall and Kidsgrove, a mere 6¼ miles. When the project was revived in 1854 it was estimated to carry annually:

20,000 tons of grain and provisions
40,000 tons of building materials
270,000 tons of coal and iron stone.

On the other hand it was estimated that the railway would reduce the need for 150 men carriers and twice that number of horses.

While the calculations were impressive, it was among projects which the financially-exhausted NSR did not want to know about in the mid-fifties. But something had to be done when there was major agitation in 1858 at Hanley, still without a branch authorised in 1847. The outcome was that in its Act of 13 August 1859 for taking over the Pool Dam line and other projects, the NSR got powers to extend the Earl of Granville's private line to the centre of Hanley. Two years was allowed for the work.

In building the line from Etruria, the NSR faced several problems, including heavy gradients and crossing the T & M Canal which lay on an embankment. A tram road already linked Hanley with the Caldon Canal at Etruria Vale and Lord Granville's line had been working since 1850. The 1859 Act authorised a single goods line to Hanley, following the course of the Granville railway and the tramway. The Granville line survived as an outlet for Shelton Colliery. It never carried passengers because of its private status and after the opening of its main line, the NSR hired horse buses from contractors to provide feeder services.

The Hanley branch of 1 mile 17 chains was opened five

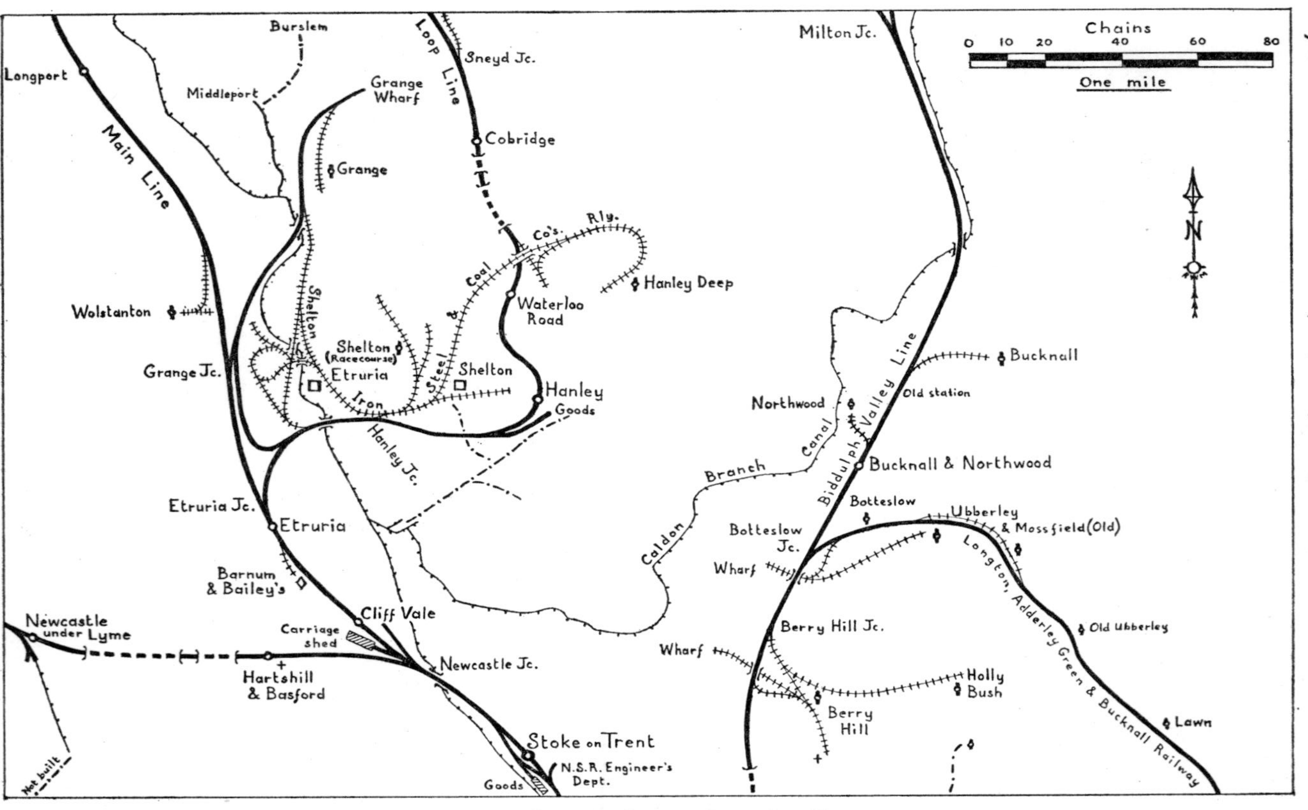

Stoke, Hanley and Bucknall

days before Christmas 1861 and was immediately successful, even though restricted to goods. The Board of Trade refused to let passenger trains run because of a drawbridge over the canal and this was diverted slightly to allow the construction of a conventional bridge, costing £3,000, which also carried an extra line between Etruria and Lord Granville's ironworks.

Passenger services started from 13 July 1864 and they, too, were at once successful. Trains used Etruria's original station which lay between the main line and the branch, but this was soon replaced by a two-platform station a short distance away. The noise from trains and local furnaces led to the removal of the North Staffordshire Infirmary from Hanley, where it was built in the year of Waterloo, to Hartshill, where it remains to this day.

The success of the Hanley branch led to more organised calls for the Loop's extension. Citizens from Hanley joined those of Burslem and Tunstall in a deputation in October 1864 to press for the completion of the Loop. They contended that the Hanley branch was useful, but thousands still had to make long journeys to reach the railway. The outcome was the Potteries Loop Line Act of 5 July 1865 which allowed three years for compulsory purchase of land and another two for the completion of the 7¾ miles. Capital of £300,000 was to be supported by borrowing powers of £100,000.

The onset of a trade depression made progress slow and in summer 1866 Forsyth reported that the preparation of working plans had taken more time than anticipated. Times became so bad that the board decided to abandon the Loop, the Grange and Tunstall branches and in January 1868 a 'memorial' was sent asking for Board of Trade permission. Legal powers were sought under The Abandonment of Railways Act 1850 and shareholders readily consented on 13 February.

Local authorities were angry. The Board of Health at Burslem held a special meeting and decided to offer

> the utmost opposition against the iniquitous attempt to deprive the district of the railway accommodation so long needed, and for want of which its interests have been so largely sacrificed.

At a meeting at Tunstall it was claimed that the abandonment of the Loop could have been suggested only by people having no connections or interest in the advancement of the Potteries.

Shareholders were told on 10 November 1869 about costs: the Loop would be about £200,000, the Tunstall and Grange branches, about £30,000. Horse omnibuses then running between Hanley and Burslem several times a day were stated to be carrying an average of only seventeen passengers. A similar service between Burslem and Tunstall was hardly maintaining itself.

The chairman pointed out that something had to be done because the Loop Act imposed a penalty of £50 a day for non-completion by July 1872, unless there were circumstances beyond the company's control. The need of sufficient funds was not such an instance. The shareholders voted to abandon the scheme, but a Commons Committee had little hesitation in rejecting the application on 23 March 1870. The Board of Trade confirmed the refusal on 6 May amid much local rejoicing. The company at once sought an extension of time, taking as authority a Bill then before Parliament to provide such powers for all companies.

Fresh progress was reported by Forsyth on 13 June. Plans had been sent to most landowners and there was every prospect of tenders being invited before the next board meeting.

The possibility was examined of completing the Loop as a narrow gauge light railway since gradients would be steep and the distance short. The NSR directors examined the latest innovation on the Festiniog Railway: the Fairlie double-ended locomotives. But gauge changes were not in vogue: the GWR were having enough trouble and when construction of the Loop was resumed, it was to standard gauge.

Within three months a tender had been won by John and William Pickering of London and that for the Grange branch had gone to Mackay of Silverdale. Chief bailiff John Watkin cut the first sod of the Loop extension on 21 July on the site of Burslem station, with little ceremony. The NSR directors were not the only people worried about what lay ahead: the contractor remarked that while there were only 6 miles of railway to be built, there would be more excavation and other work than in a projected line of 52 miles which he had just examined. The line was not named.

The summit level of the Loop between Pitts Hill and Newchapel was tackled early, and gradually locomotives replaced horses: the first locomotive, *The Summit*, was put on the rails on 14 November at Turnhurst Hall, once the home of James Brindley.

A second line was laid between Etruria and Hanley and the sharp curves at Etruria were eased. When the Loop reached Burslem on 1 November 1873, a new station was opened at Hanley, and soon afterwards the original one was converted for goods. Just a month later on 1 December, Tunstall was placed on the railway map.

Describing the opening, a local paper reported:

> A large number of spectators assembled on the bank near the station and seemed to regard the arrival and departure of trains with quite as much interest as the dog racing and rabbit coursing in the field close by.

The next section of the Loop—1½ miles between Tunstall and Goldenhill—was opened on 1 October 1874 and Kidsgrove was reached something over a year later: on 15 November 1875. The final cost of the Loop was £493,976, well above the original estimate, but the line was soon to yield a satisfactory return.

The cost of branch construction during the second wave of development up to 1878 averaged £27,212 a mile, calculated on the basis of:

	£
Loop and branches	493,976
Market Drayton	216,926
Macclesfield—Marple	187,079
Audley lines	157,965
Stoke—Leek	50,393
Chesterton	8,413

THE TURNHURST RAILWAY

One project remains to be mentioned in connection with the Loop, for once it was built there was soon talk of a link to the

Biddulph Valley line to give the valley a direct link with Tunstall, its main shopping and market centre. Proposals discussed between 1880-90 favoured the exploitation of the Turnhurst mineral line which local pit owners built from Chell soon after the opening of the Biddulph line. The Turnhurst line was to be extended beyond the pits it served to join the loop north of Pitts Hill. Survey pegs were laid and they remained in position until the early thirties, but the plan never got beyond that stage and the scheme was finally killed by the closure of the Chell pits in 1910.[7]

THE CHEADLE RAILWAY

Some Loop trains ran to Cheadle, the small but busy hub of a hilly coalfield and, more notable, one of the first towns in the Potteries to be selected for a railway—and the last of any size to get one.

The NSR promoters stated in their original prospectus of 30 April 1845 that

> The communication between Manchester and Derby will be maintained by a railway branching from the line a few miles south of Macclesfield and pursuing its course via Leek, Cheadle and Uttoxeter, as already laid down by the Churnet Valley company.

The fact that Cheadle never got a line until years later (and then only a branch), stemmed from a variety of reasons, mainly because, as already related, the original Churnet plans were found faulty. The new survey of routes then made took a line through the Churnet Valley, east of Cheadle and direct to Uttoxeter. Serving Cheadle would have meant great expense in engineering, tunnels and heavy gradients. That would also have been true of any branch from the Stoke—Derby line, which was separated from Cheadle by a high ridge rising to almost 750ft. Among schemes suggested were for lines from Blythe Bridge, via Cheadle to Froghall (1853) and truncated to Cheadle—Froghall the following year; and one to use the Foxfield mineral railway to avoid a tunnel.

The first positive looking scheme, which came in 1874, was

to extend the Longton, Adderley Green & Bucknall Railway from Brookhouse Green, but it was soon discounted because it involved a gradient of 1 in 40. The first Parliamentary powers were obtained by the Cheadle Railway Company, which was authorised on 22 July 1878 to build a branch of 5½ miles from the main line at Blythe Bridge. The company was independent, but it had close links with the NSR, which was to work the line. The NSR was authorised to subscribe £10,000, one fifth of the authorised capital, but there was no other support. As a result the scheme was abandoned by Act of 12 July 1882. Six years later it was revived by the Cheadle Railway Mineral & Land Company Limited, which got powers for a 4 mile line, from Cresswell on 7 August 1888. This time the scheme was successful, but progress was slow and by the time the branch reached Totsmanlow on 7 November 1892, the village had changed its name to Tean. Not that that made much difference to the station which was a mile away. The Act of 1888 gave the NSR powers to subscribe £10,000 and this time it did so. Approval came from Knotty shareholders on 27 December 1894.

The promoters had second thoughts about the authorised route and on 17 August 1896 got powers for a deviation to avoid a long tunnel. Even so a shorter one was necessary and that was to cause trouble for years until the line was taken round the ridge in LMS days. The 1896 Act also simplified the company's title to that of the Cheadle Railway Company and gave the NSR power to appoint two directors. So it was that when the line opened to Cheadle on 1 January 1901, it was leased and worked by the NSR. Its position was further consolidated when the NSR bought the Cheadle Railway from 1 January 1907, confirmed by an Act of 21 August 1907.

One of the NSR's first acts as owners of the line was to refuse running powers to the Midland Railway, although no reason was stated.

THE MACCLESFIELD, BOLLINGTON & MARPLE RAILWAY

While the LNWR refused to co-operate in constructing the Market Drayton branch, the NSR found an ally in the Manchester, Sheffield & Lincolnshire as it sought another outlet:

one of nearly 11 miles from Macclesfield to Marple and a route into Manchester independent of the LNWR. It so consolidated relations with the MS & L that the line was built and maintained as a joint venture. But by the time it was authorised in 1864, the route was a blunted weapon since the NSR—LNWR working agreements had robbed it of the political significance it enjoyed when the NSR threatened to exploit the route as part of an independent one between London and Manchester.

The LNWR was prepared to let the MB & M Bill pass unopposed but only at a price, insisting that the MS & L withdrew support for two independent railways in Cheshire: the Macclesfield & Knutsford and the Knutsford & Warrington.[8]

The MB & M Act of 14 July 1864 empowered both the NSR and MS & L to subscribe £80,000 and to work and maintain the line. Despite the efforts of both companies, and there being only one major engineering work, a low 23 arch viaduct near Bollington, construction was slow. A trade depression was blamed for little progress in 1866-7 and this led the NSR board to state on 26 May 1868 that it would have to consider the best way of raising the remaining £40,000 of unsold share capital. Up to the end of the following month the work had cost £93,165. Eventually the line opened to passengers on 2 August 1869, and to goods on 1 March 1870. It was only single track. Bollington, the only intermediate village of any size, had but a few cotton mills and the only other stations were at Marple (Rose Hill) and High Lane. A more important source of revenue was the Poynton Collieries. These had been acquired by Lord Vernon in 1828 and by 1840 they were connected by horse tramroads. The first railway to be built near them was the Manchester & Birmingham Macclesfield branch. A branch from Poynton to Prince Albert Colliery was opened on 9 June 1845 and by 1857 this had been sold to Lord Vernon and the rail system extended to other pits and the Macclesfield Canal. The line had been abandoned by the time the MB & M was built and a new connection was opened near Higher Poynton station to give the NSR access to the pits. This connection was known to be in operation by 1872, but it was probable that it was in use from the opening of the joint line. The last of the Poynton collieries closed on 1 September 1935.

While the LNWR did not oppose the building of the MB & M,

Page 85 (above) *Double framed 0–6–0 No 87 as rebuilt in 1890 at Burton with the Wellingborough goods. The tender is piled high with hand-stacked coal to avoid recoaling at the Midland shed;* (below) *the 1881 station at Uttoxeter looking towards Derby. The picture was taken about 1890 before the footbridge was enclosed*

Page 86 *Class 'E' 0–6–0 No 75, built at Stoke in 1871, as rebuilt by Longbottom in 1885. Seen at Macclesfield about 1899*

it turned awkward over the construction of a joint station at Macclesfield. The MS & L chairman, Sir Edward Watkin, wanted the LNWR to be third party, but Moon would not hear of it. The situation was further complicated by the town council, which wanted a new station, not on the suggested site, but at Hibel Road, nearer the centre. Once again, as with the building of the NSR, the MB & M arrival at Macclesfield meant considerable demolition of property. Four alternative schemes were considered; the three eventually rejected would have involved junctions with the LNWR north of Hibel Road. Instead the site of Central station was a little to the south and at the foot of a steep cliff, dominated by Macclesfield Parish Church.

At first the MB & M was virtually a branch of the MS & L since the original terminus at Macclesfield was not connected with the NSR. The systems were connected on 13 February 1871 by the completion of a link of just under half a mile. This joined the NSR 6 chains north of Central station, a joint venture between the NSR and MS & L. The new line was not used regularly until 3 April. The next two months brought significant changes. An Act of 25 May 1871 dissolved the MB & M and vested it in the NSR and MS & L (The Macclesfield Committee), eventually destined to become the last surviving part of the NSR. There was equal representation on the eight man Committee. The NSR engineering department was responsible for all engineering work and maintenance, the MS & L (and later Great Central) commitment in this being to supply a steam crane for bridge work.

The second change was the doubling of the line, at a cost of £26,000, which was completed on 26 June. Opening of the Joint station followed on 1 July 1873 when the original one was turned over to goods.

By this time the improved relations between the NSR and LNWR made the MB & M even less useful, for once given the opportunity of through running into Manchester, the NSR chose the shortest, fastest and most convenient route—that via Stockport. Most through trains used only Hibel Road and ran non-stop through Central. Once the MB & M was opened, the need became obvious for a junction with the LNWR Stockport—Buxton line at Middlewood and the companies co-operated over the building of a spur, first mooted in 1878 about a year before the opening of the MB & M Middlewood station, close to that on the Buxton line, although at a higher level. Conflict surrounds the opening date of the station in 1879. Some sources maintained it was 1 April; others, 2 June. The same is true of the $\frac{3}{8}$ mile curve opened seven years later. The only trains to use the curve on Whit Monday, 25 June 1885, were Buxton excursions. Regular goods, and some sources claim, local passenger trains from Macclesfield, began the following day, and through trains from Stoke on 1 June. What is clear is that the curve gave the NSR and LNWR a route between London and Buxton, albeit 19 miles longer than that of the Midland Railway. If the NSR ever envisaged the development of through London traffic via the curve, the LNWR certainly did not for as Neele was to state:[9]

> The through coaches at Macclesfield had to be taken by a reverse journey between the two stations in that town, not a very satisfactory movement in any competitive through route.

OTHER SCHEMES

Macclesfield was for a time the focal point of far more railway schemes than a town of its size could hope to support. Even though the LNWR scotched plans for a Macclesfield—Knutsford—Warrington through route, local businessmen got an Act for a railway under that title on 28 June 1866.[10] It had the support of the NSR shareholders who, in approving it on 10 May of that year, stipulated that the company was not to take any NSR land without consent. The scheme soon collapsed, but had it been completed, the NSR would have had a direct link with the Cheshire Lines Committee (and so Liverpool and Chester). On incorporation of this company, only the MS & L received running powers.

The scheme was revived as the Macclesfield & Knutsford Railway and incorporated on 16 June 1871, only to be dissolved just over three years later (16 July 1874) when its powers were transferred to the NSR.

Two other schemes are worthy of passing mention. The first was an LNWR-backed project of 1866 for a Sheffield, Buxton & Liverpool Railway. This was linked with the other project: the Macclesfield, Buxton & Sheffield Junction Railway,[11] in which the NSR was also interested. It was quickly dropped when the MS & L gave the LNWR running powers to Sheffield.

For some years in the nineties the NSR was faced with the prospect of a connection with the Lancashire, Derbyshire & East Coast Railway, incorporated on 5 August 1891 to run from the Manchester Ship Canal at Warrington, through Knutsford, Macclesfield, Buxton, Chesterfield and Lincoln to Sutton-on-Sea. Its authorised route included a southerly connection with the NSR at Macclesfield. It soon became obvious that while some stretches of the line might be profitable, much bigger portions were not and sections abandoned by Act of 6 July 1895 included those west of Chesterfield.

Notes are on page 295

CHAPTER FOUR

Years of Expansion

PEACE AT LAST

The improved relations with the LNWR, first consolidated by the 1859 agreement, quickly bore a small yet welcome fruit, with an offer from the LNWR to include the NSR in a current Bill covering working arrangements between itself and the GNR and MS & L.[1] The NSR board accepted on 28 February 1860.

This was also a period when closer relations were established with the Post Office and on the same day it was agreed to spend £650 improving and extending PO facilities at Stoke, provided the PO paid 7½ per cent extra rent for the enlarged area. The carriage of mails on all passenger trains was agreed in spring 1864 and a mail special was introduced between Macclesfield and Harecastle. The PO took over the telegraph service from 1 January 1870.

The friendly relations led to the appointment to the LNWR board on 22 February 1861 of one of the NSR's original directors, John Bramley Moore of Liverpool, who was then MP for Maldon. He was destined to remain on the NSR board until 1886 and become the longest serving of the original directors. For the final seven years he was deputy chairman.

The early sixties were a delicate time, not only for relations with other companies, but within the company itself, mainly due to shortage of money. One manifestation of this was in 1860 when it said it had no funds to subscribe to the Longton Stoke & Kidsgrove Soldier Rifle Corps. A fresh attack on the board's handling of affairs was made in 1862, the first public ripples being felt at the summer meeting of shareholders. The Provost of Aberdeen, Alexander Anderson, led a long discussion about allegations of excessive working expenses of locomotives, and in general maintenance and track renewal. The following February Anderson demanded a poll on the directors' report. The meeting adjourned for four days and when it resumed on 17 February, Broderick, acting as chairman, announced plans to end what he called 'further agitation'. The board was willing to accept a large number of proxies supporting Anderson and another man for directorships, and Anderson took the place of Ricardo, who had retired the previous year.

So passed from the NSR scene the greatest of its pioneers, the man who had brought it into being, steered it through the early struggles and made it sound. Ricardo's tremendous influence and powerful direction of the company's affairs meant his departure left something of a void. Broderick, his deputy since 1851, moved into the chair and his place was taken by Lt Col Charles Pearson, destined himself to take the helm only two years later.

Ricardo left behind a company very much of national status. It lay among fourteen which formed a second group behind giants like the LNWR. Grouped with the NSR by an independent advocate of railway reform, William Galt, were such companies as the Bristol & Exeter, Furness, and London, Chatham & Dover. In 1863 the NSR had a mileage of 258, including the T & M Canal. Capital stood at £5,656,849 and receipts were near the half-million mark: £422,673.

Closer relations with the LNWR brought complications. The NSR complained in October 1865 of 'a bad arrangement' which meant that trains did not connect at Crewe and suggested it should be allowed to run trains through from Derby to Liverpool.

Four months later the NSR agreed to act as goods agents for the LNWR in the Potteries, and the LNWR allowed half the mileage between Norton Bridge and Stafford to be set against the NSR working expenses. The LNWR closely watched the NSR activities and on 10 October 1866 the NSR board considered a complaint from Moon that running powers given to the Midland under the NSR branch line Bill contravened an agreement with the LNWR of 1 September 1860. When the Macclesfield, Bollington & Marple wanted to alter its goods station and junction at Macclesfield, the LNWR contended that it would seriously interfere with its own traffic.

The most important step ever taken—or indeed ever to be taken—in relations with the LNWR came through fresh initiative by that company in 1866 and it led to an agreement much wider reaching than the one which had been in force since 1859. It gave the LNWR running powers over the whole of the NSR and in return, the NSR got similar facilities over present 'and future' routes to Wolverhampton, Birmingham, Manchester and Liverpool. Knotty trains were to run direct to Birmingham through Colwich and Norton Bridge; to Liverpool via either Crewe and the direct line, which was to open in 1869, or through Warrington; and also through Warrington to Manchester and, more locally, over the South Staffordshire and Cannock lines—a total mileage of 160, roughly the same as the total mileage which the NSR then had either built or authorised.

The agreement was strongly contested by the Lancashire & Yorkshire Railway, which was concerned about through traffic with the NSR via Macclesfield. To reach Macclesfield, the L & Y exercised running powers obtained by the 1859 amalgamation with the East Lancashire Railway. In return, the NSR and LNWR were said to have running powers to Wakefield, but the NSR denied all knowledge of them.

The agreement was consolidated in an Act of 15 July 1867, which also provided for the LNWR to run on weekdays (except Christmas Day and Good Friday) two fast passenger and two goods trains each way between London and Manchester via either Colwich or Norton Bridge. An LNWR Act of the same day vested the South Staffordshire lines in that company and provided the legal basis for the NSR to use that company's routes.

Years later, the LNWR historian Wilfred L. Steel[2] was to describe the agreement as an excellent one for both parties. Yet if we are to take his following remarks seriously it would seem that the LNWR regarded itself as getting the better bargain. Steel claimed that it meant that if the NSR ever became hostile, or by chance fell into other hands, the LNWR would still have had access to the Potteries with its own trains and be able to use the NSR as an extra link in the chain of communication.

Peace with the LNWR led to the streamlining of the NSR board to a maximum of twelve members from 11 August 1868, including three elected by the Canal preference shareholders. Col Pearson continued as chairman of the new board, which now had three fewer members than ten years earlier.

Other agreements during the year included one with the LNWR for a fixed division of competitive traffic to and from Burton, and with the Post Office, which doubled to £1,000 a year payment for night mails carried between Stoke and Crewe. This agreement ran from 1 January 1869.

A new threat to relations with the LNWR came with the introduction of bank holidays by Parliament in 1871, for while the NSR wanted to run special excursions to encourage people to travel, the LNWR wanted to restrict them. It was an issue on which the LNWR had eventually to yield because of pressure from the NSR and other companies.

Although the NSR owned land on which it built its lines, the question of mineral rights lying underneath were often in dispute and referred to arbitrators. There were double complications at Harecastle, where in 1868, one mining company, Kinnersley, claimed compensation for coal lying both beneath and above the railway tunnels.

The early seventies found the MS & L chairman, Watkin, campaigning for closer relations through a proposed feeder line which would be provided through extending the Winsford branch of the Cheshire Lines Committee, opened 1 June 1870, to the LNWR at Sandbach. Watkin's initiative led to the incorporation of the Sandbach & Winsford Junction railway[3] on 27 June 1872. It was abandoned only three years later, but by then something far more significant had occurred on the NSR. It arose from internal trouble in 1874, when the shareholders demanded yet another inquiry into the whole of the company's affairs. Led by one of the most influential, James Jones Aston, QC, their first move failed after the chairman used his casting vote. Aston then called a special meeting to consider either selling the company or removing the board. Both motions were defeated but on 17 February 1875, three directors resigned and the board was reduced to nine members and joined by Aston. Colin Minton Campbell moved from deputy into the chair.

Directors' fees were at once reduced from £2,250 a year to £1,500.

FRESH TAKE-OVER BIDS

The shareholders' restlessness and changing moods were closely watched by neighbours, ever ready to snatch a bargain. The LNWR obviously remained interested in a direct take-over and the MS & L was considered a second favourite because of its ties through the Macclesfield, Bollington & Marple. There were also the MR and GNR. Battle started in earnest when Watkin found that the LNWR and MR were planning a joint take-over. He sought the aid of the GNR and then all four companies discussed guaranteeing the NSR shareholders 4 per cent in perpetuity. While they were all able to agree that such was its worth, they could not agree terms because the LNWR insisted that if the NSR was reconstituted, it should not retain the running and other agreements it had with the different companies.

The deadlock was broken by a go-it-alone attempt by the MS & L, which proposed amalgamation based on its capital assets being £7,760,000 and those of the NSR, £3,200,000. There was favourable reception by both boards and they issued a five-point plan on 15 November 1875. It provided for ordinary stocks to be at par, and preference stocks to be charged to the amalgamated undertaking. Joint working and management were to start at once with the interchange of two directors and the formation of a joint managing committee of three directors from each company. The fourth point provided for the development of an independent route to the south and was, of course, pinned to the MS & L's burning aspirations to reach London. Joint running powers and other concessions were to be sought from neighbours.

After putting the plan before the NSR board on 24 November, Campbell, on his own initiative, issued a Parliamentary notice for amalgamation between the NSR and neighbours listed in the order: LNWR, MR, GNR and MS & L. A committee of NSR officials examining amalgamation favoured terms with the MS & L and a Bill was approved by shareholders on 12 January 1876. It was suggested amalgamation should be from 1 January

1877 and the LNWR, MR and GNR were to be offered reciprocal arrangements in the interests of the public and any differences were to go to arbitration.

The NSR board was enlarged and negotiations proceeded well until it came to traffic arrangements. The NSR was unable to concede much because of its ties with the LNWR and the MS & L was similarly placed because of its relations with the GNR. The atmosphere at once cooled and when shareholders met three weeks later the chairman did nothing to set aside doubts.

At this stage, the GNR's attitude was one of watching developments, while the Midland was opposed to the link. NSR shareholders had their doubts and one, Porter, pointed out that while NSR working expenses were then 59 per cent of takings, those of the MS & L were only 50 per cent. Dividends were roughly even.

Another shareholder, Lamb, asked whether half-yearly meetings of the amalgamated companies would be held in Stoke or London. Campbell replied that they had not got as far as discussing that, to which Lamb retorted: 'I hope you will bear in mind the interests of those who live in town and who like to hear themselves talk!'

Gradually the NSR board came to realise that MS & L finances were no stronger than their own and this led to negotiations being called off and the amalgamation Bill being withdrawn on 4 May 1876.

An increase in local traffic and a decrease in through traffic in the first half of 1875 were among factors which led the board to press for a reduction in the passenger dues which railway companies had to pay. The NSR thought a reduction would particularly help the poorer classes and it favoured the formation of an association to present the case.

A depression in the iron and coal industries affected through traffic and in February 1876 the directors lamented that when wages were good and people had money to travel, they took long journeys and travelled frequently. The reverse was true in times of depression. Yet the 1876 passenger total of 2,710,612 was only slightly less than the previous year.

Not everybody paid fares willingly and in autumn 1876 local people at Ashbourne retaliated against a rise by starting their own bus service. It was a flop, running for between a week and ten days. Campbell was jubilant: 'The wisdom of increasing the fares has been shown by there being no decrease in traffic.'

Train mileage costs were considered to be favourable with those of other companies, but it was felt that Parliamentary freight rates of 1¾d a ton did not take into account the sort of goods trains it had to run, which stopped at 'everybody's siding' to pick up or leave a wagon.

Trade went through a long depression in the sixties and seventies although the North Staffordshire coalfield enjoyed a boom for a while. In winter 1877 when the iron trade was still depressed and many furnaces were idle, Belgian iron was imported into the Potteries and there was an ever increasing amount of American iron competing with local products. 'America,' commented Campbell, 'seems now not only to be becoming a large manufacturing country, but a very large exporting country.' He felt, however, that the Potteries had plenty of mineral wealth for the ironmasters who with their enterprise and capacity could compete with any nation in the world when trade improved.

That was slow in happening and mineral traffic in 1877 reached only 1,147,000 tons and traffic payments made to the NSR by big iron companies dropped by £25,000. When trade picked up the following year, 1,095,000 tons were carried in the first six months.

Shareholders were often critical of train services and policy and Hugh Sleigh of Leek once complained it had taken him two hours to cover 30 miles from Derby to Ashbourne. He felt development was being concentrated in the Potteries at the expense of outlying places.

Whether or not that was true, the company tapped every source of traffic that it could find and on 23 May 1877 began a pioneering venture by arranging to carry racing pigeons.

The lease of the NSR to the Midland Railway was advocated by a shareholder, Hall, in February 1877, who said it was unlikely the GNR or MS & L would give a better price, while the LNWR wanted the company for 'an old song'. The chairman said the NSR was valued by three great companies and they appeared to have fancied that the undertaking would get down some day to so low an ebb that it could be purchased on low terms. It would not be too difficult to leave the chair and hand over the reins to any one of the great companies that would take them. He did not covet the position, but while he was in it, he would turn it to best account.

When shareholders again discussed take-over a year later, Campbell said it must be remembered that the NSR had a small mileage and had to collect traffic for the large companies which surrounded it. They made profits from good mileages while the NSR had to do a great deal of hard work for comparatively little return. The NSR could never be as good a paying line for shareholders.

> The directors are quite prepared to listen to any suggestions that may be made by any of these companies to join them, but at the present time trade is so depressed that railway receipts, generally speaking, are falling off.

It was now the turn of the MR, MS & L and GNR to consider amalgamating among themselves and the NSR welcomed the move, seeing itself as a vital connecting link between the three systems.

TRAFFIC BUILD UP

For those who had doubts about amalgamation, 1878 was a good year for it brought a narrowing in the gap between the working expenses of the NSR and MS & L. While those of the MS & L dropped slightly to just over 49½ per cent of receipts, the NSR were reduced by a more appreciable amount to 53½ per cent. The NSR dividend in 1878 of 1⅝ per cent was the lowest since 1852, but, more significantly, it was to remain the lowest recorded in almost the next half century to Grouping. After 1878 dividend never fell below 2 per cent and, after 1881, below 3 per cent. During 1878, passenger figures recovered a little to reach 2,676,000.

Concerned at the dismal 1878 dividend, some shareholders wanted to know why wages of drivers, porters and other staff had not been reduced as they had by the Midland and several other companies. The chairman said cuts had not been made because they had to pay wages not less than those of neighbouring companies. There was also concern over the activities of the Railway Commissioners. The chairman said in August 1879 that they had no intention of building more hotels or opening more refreshments rooms until it became necessary, or until they were compelled to do so by the Commissioners. 'At present,' remarked Campbell, 'the Commissioners seem to take upon themselves a power to compel railway companies to do anything they like.'

Campbell claimed that they were suffering from a large amount of capital which had been expended on the line, but the present directors were not responsible for it. They were trying to lay out as many lines as possible so that if the company were handed over to another, they might get a much higher price than if the line existed in a 'tumble-down' state.

The transition from the eighteen seventies into the next decade was important for the NSR, for, as the chairman remarked on 13 February, 1880: 'We now seem to have turned the corner and there are much more encouraging prospects.' Trade was improving, particularly iron and coal, although pottery was not doing too well.

Economies were made wherever possible: in 1880, for

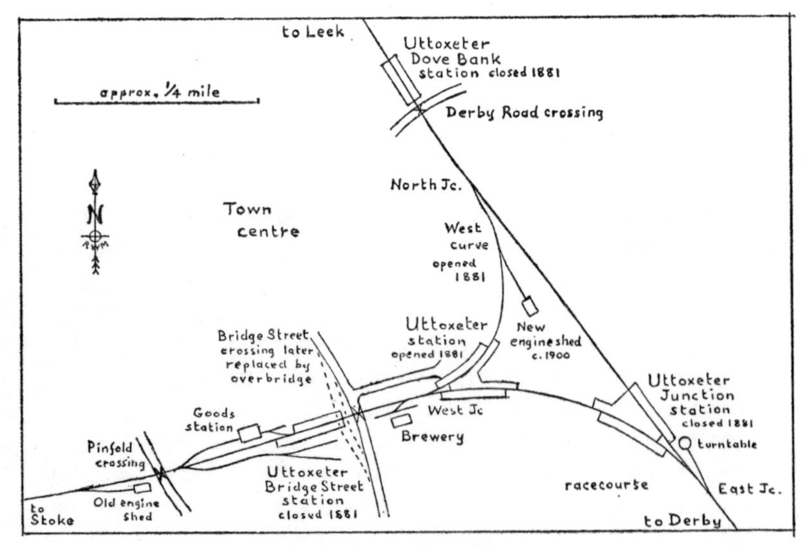

Changes at Uttoxeter, 1881

instance, NSR services to Nottingham were withdrawn to save £700 which was paid to the Midland Railway for the use of its station. On the other hand, money was spent where improvements could help efficiency and during 1880 authorisation was received for the construction of a 28 chain curve at Uttoxeter. When it was opened in October 1881, the old stations were closed and a new one (which still survives) was opened near Bridge Street, just to the south, at the junction of the Derby and Leek lines.

Gradually, operating practices were modernised as improved equipment became available and proved reliable. The first major track improvements were associated with the LNWR decision to speed up expresses through the Potteries in 1876. The Colwich line, little used for some years, was relaid with the LNWR contributing towards the cost. At this time the NSR felt that while steel rails cost a 'trifle' more than those of iron, it was absolutely necessary that the line should be in 'as perfect a condition as possible', to use a phrase popular with company officials. It was one that constantly recurs in references to many aspects of safety. A well-laid main line was necessary for the safety of passengers—and for profit for, in the chairman's view, 'any accident would have been a loss to shareholders'. It was also realised that the better the condition of the permanent way, the more likely they were to attract traffic from other companies.

Taking advantage of the slack steel market, the NSR adopted a policy of laying down as many miles of steel rail as it could. In 1877 it spent £42,900 on track renewal and £12,700 on new sidings and main line station improvements. Two years later, 12 miles of steel rails were laid on the main line, and more sidings were constructed. Another 15 miles of track were relayed with steel rails in 1880 and the two tunnels near Leek were lined with blue bricks—the local product that gave such distinction to stations. This year also saw the building of a subway at Stoke station, and heavy rains said to have been the worst for forty years kept the engineer busy in the Churnet Valley, where £200 was spent repairing part of the line swept into the river. This was a period when many of the wooden bridges which had been in use since the line opened, were replaced by stronger structures of stone or steel. Many of the original crossing gates were also replaced after 30 years of wear, and rails were increased in weight to 82lb—8lb short of the standard which was established in later years.

The mid-eighties brought fresh trade depression and earthenware dispatched to Liverpool in 1884 totalled only 75,000 tons, against 107,000 tons the previous year. In 1885 there was a drop in the quantity of bitter beer sent from Burton and as 1886 brought another decrease in some traffic, the chairman, Salt, drew attention to a basic point concerning all companies. The NSR was suffering particularly from light loads and short trains because long trains carrying heavy loads could be run at about the same cost.

Another factor blamed for delay in the company in reaching its aim of being a 5 per cent line, was the Trent & Mersey Canal. In February 1890 Salt described it as the 'really weak point' and added that if by any ingenious means they could make it a good paying proposition, they would at once achieve their aim.

THE SIXPENNY LINE

In the first half of 1891, the total of third-class passengers reached 92½ per cent of the overall total of 3,273,415. Many were short distance travellers and in this period the Knotty fell from being a 'nine penny line' to that of a 'six penny line'. Salt lamented in 1895: 'We literally pile up the passenger traffic by six pences'. Later he was to cite the takings of an un-named station which in three years between 1893-6 booked 195,710 passengers and took only £2,625. The sparsity of passengers who used the Sandbach branch in four years after the introduction of passenger trains in 1893, is shown by the takings at the Wheelock terminus. They averaged only £300 a year, and those at Lawton only half that amount.

Opening this branch to passengers 47 years after it had been sanctioned surprised many shareholders and the chairman felt it necessary to reassure them that they had not suddenly embarked on a new construction programme. The branch, he pointed out, had been 'in their hands for many years for merchandise'. Introducing passenger trains involved the replacement of wooden bridges by those of wrought iron.

A lot of work for little return included the problem of small change, and a note in public timetables stated: 'In order to prevent inconvenience and delay, Passengers are respectfully requested to provide themselves with suitable Change to pay for their Tickets as the Company's Booking Clerks are not able at all times to give change'.

In the thirty years 1868-98 the combined railway and canal tonnage more than doubled. From 3,000,000 tons in 1868, it rose to 4,000,000 tons in 1878, to 5,000,000 tons in 1888 and reached 6,250,000 in 1898. It was to increase by a further million in the following five years.

The Light Railway Act of 1896 was seen as a source of possible revenue and it was exploited in two ways: by a limited amount of new construction, which will be dealt with in the next chapter, and by the acquisition of powers to operate some short branches as light railways so as to introduce passenger services without great expense. The company sought permission to convert twelve lines and got approval for nine, being refused light railway status for the Pool Dam, Tunstall and Newfields branches. Orders were granted covering both halves of the Adderley Green branch, the Apedale, Talke, Chesterton, and Grange branches; the Burton branch between Stretton Junction and Hawkins Lane Junction; the freight-only tip of the Biddulph Valley line from Congleton Lower Junction to Brunswick Wharf, and the northern tip of the Sandbach line between Wheelock and Sandbach. All were later to return to their original status as mineral lines, following an inquiry by the Railway Commissioners on 19 July 1905 into the use of mineral lines as light railways. The increasing traffic generated by the NSR towards the end of the century contributed to the build-up of traffic at Crewe and led to many improvements by the LNWR including doubling the size of the station.

A spur was also built to carry trains from the NSR Crewe branch under the main line into Basford Hall sidings. The spur, sharply-curved and graded, ran under the main line just south of the LNWR carriage sheds on the up side.

Just before the turn of the century, an electric railway was built in the Potteries—but not by the NSR. It was a private line from the Churnet Valley at Cheddleton to the North Staffordshire Mental Hospital then being built on a hill about half a mile away. From 1895 the line was used by the contractor, Lovatt, for carrying materials and worked by small steam locomotives but on completion of the hospital four years later, the steeply-graded line was electrified with an overhead system and besides carrying coal and stores, trains were run for hospital visitors until about 1920.

The line never came within the Light Railway Act of 1896, but that did provide the incentive for another private scheme: the Derby & Ashbourne Light Railway, first mooted in that year as a 4ft 0in gauge road tramway and modified, after a public inquiry in October, 1897, to standard gauge. Although there were plans to extend it to Leek, it quickly disappeared even from paper.[4]

A more lasting impression was made by a second line which did reach Ashbourne—that opened by the LNWR from Parsley Hay on 4 August 1899. On its completion, a new joint station was built at Ashbourne and that of the NSR closed. The NSR retained its small engine and goods sheds and stables. To match an expected increase in traffic, the NSR applied to the Board of Trade to widen the Ashbourne branch and this was agreed, provided that it did not interfere with any plans of Staffordshire County Council.

For years there were outcries against Ashbourne station, the last in August 1898 when Col Jelf complained that it was a disgrace. There had not been waiting rooms for 35 years; only a small booking hall in which local children congregated to warm themselves. The chairman admitted the station had caused them 'much anxiety' for some years, but it had not been improved because of preparations to share one with the LNWR. From 1899 the station layout at Ashbourne was generous with lines forming a passing loop and serving two platforms and bays. This was in contrast to another branch station, Rocester, where there was only an up platform because the crossover from double to single line lay short of it.

STATIONS: DEVELOPMENT AND STYLES

When Stoke became the focal point of the railway system, it was not the most important of the Pottery towns, yet no effort was spared to give it the atmosphere befitting of the head-

Page 103 *The Caldon Low Tramway in 1904;* (above) *the Hughes' 1877 0–4–0ST 'Toad' with quarrymen and wagons on the 3ft 6in gauge lines at Caldon quarry;* (below) *general view of the terminal basin at Froghall taken from the foot of the incline, with 3ft 6in and standard gauge wagons. The canal is on the right*

Page 104 *Two accidents;* (above) *a class E 0–6–0 which tried to demolish a junction distant signal, being rescued by a Cowan & Sheldon 1899 steam crane;* (below) *class C 2–4–0 No 14 which has come to grief at Uttoxeter*

quarters of a company. Not only was the station magnificent, but around it was built a square of equal elegance. It was the work of an unknown architect, R. A. Stent. He took a Jacobean motif and gave the whole scheme Dutch gables, mullion windows and round arches. He used local brick, dark red, offset by patterns of darker brick and stone dressings. The centre of three gables of the station façade lay above the boardroom window on the first floor. For the North Stafford Hotel on the opposite side of the square, Stent took his inspiration from a Jacobean manor house, again using gables to great effect. The concept was completed by two matching two-storey houses.

Stent's was not the first station at Stoke. A temporary one built by the contractor, Jay, at Whieldon Grove was used until the permanent one was ready. Costing £31,438, the new one also became the headquarters of the Canal company. The square and stables cost £8,843; officers' houses, £6,272 and 20 cottages, £3,000.

In designing the station, Stent may have had the help of a fellow architect called Hunt for a similar station at Stone is attributed to him. Stoke is among sixty British stations which the Victorian Society consider especially worthy of preservation.[5]

In its present form it is not entirely original for the roof was first destroyed by fire on 30 October 1868. As the walls remained sound, the new roof was able to be supported on iron girders costing £800. Another £200 was needed to replace workmen's tools destroyed in the blaze. Although several parts of the railway were then covered by fire insurance, Stoke station was not and this loophole was closed soon afterwards by the creation of a fire insurance fund covering the entire railway.

The second roof was replaced by a third in 1893-4 when the station was virtually reconstructed. The new roof, of 7,910 sq yd, cost £4,000 and provided more height and light by a single span of 85ft, which replaced the three earlier ones. The station was now lit by a new wonder: electricity. The company built its own underground power station adjacent to the south side of the southern subway. Electrical workshops were established next to the engineer's works.

The civil engineer responsible for many improvements was G. J. Crosbie-Dawson, appointed in 1886 after having been a resident district engineer on the LNWR and chief assistant engineer of the L & Y. The electrical engineer was Andrew F. Rock, who was to remain in office to Grouping. He took a major part in the conversion of Stoke yard to electric lighting, another early project which, like others, was delayed by lack of money and resources. Rock's predecessor had been John Neale, who died in 1901 at the age of 68. He had been appointed inspector in charge of NSR telegraphs, and those of the LNWR in the Midlands, in 1854 and had become telegraphic superintendent of the NSR when the government took over public telegraphs in 1870. Three years later he patented an acoustic single needle dial and the single wire block instrument used by the NSR. He also invented a block instrument for permissive block use, showing the number of trains in section, and also a rail treadle for trains to signal their approach to level crossings.

When electric lighting was experimentally fitted to coaches it was run off batteries, which were installed in the carriage service road next to the Newcastle bay platform. They were recharged in the old refilling room for foot warmers at the north end of platform 1. In winter, clouds of water vapour escaped every time the door was opened, recalls Doctor E. G. Ashton of Rotherham. He added in a letter: 'Presumably a two to one mixture of oxygen and hydrogen escaped at a later date, but nobody saw this!'

The most important trains handled at Stoke were the London expresses and while local trains were crammed two or three along the platforms, the Londons spread themselves over the whole length. For years, wrote Manifold,[6] 'a preliminary ceremonial hush settled over Stoke station when they were due and the top-hatted stationmaster turned out for the noon to London'.

The 'Eustons' did not run every few minutes like the locals which won the praise of several writers. J. W. Walker[7] wrote:

> Station times are fair, though nothing resembling hustling is in vogue. The destination boards resembling the arms of a roadside finger post, which are affixed at right angles to the brake

vans, are simple enough for anything, but most passengers would like the information before trains arrive. As two or three trains at one platform is common, a conspicuous indicator pointing out their position and destination would be useful.

Walker found something unusual to praise at Stoke:

Railway tea is usually an abomination, but the cup that cheers provided here is really excellent. There are also good toilet and other conveniences. The "official atmosphere" is not excessive and on the whole, Stoke is quite a well appointed station.

Travellers could use the railway telegraph system at normal rates to order luncheon or tea baskets from the refreshment room at Stoke, or from those of any other company.

Stoke was among forty postal agency 'stations' at which the public could send and receive messages. Stoke telegraph offices on the up and down platforms were always open to handle messages to all Britain's major towns and telegrams were delivered within three miles radius when the local Post Office was closed at night. The service was also maintained up to 8 pm on Sundays. Fourteen smaller stations at places like Black Bull, Norbury and Waterhouses delivered telegrams to local people at usual postal rates.

The Knotty was proud of its Stoke facilities and mentioned it in timetables:

For the convenience of Passengers, Lavatory and Dressing Room accommodation, with various toilet and travel conveniences, are provided at Stoke Station, under the management of Mr Faulkner of London. A lavatory &c. is also provided at Uttoxeter.

The last major improvement carried out by the NSR at Stoke was to open out the entrance into a spacious booking hall with the way to the platforms through an arch erected in memory of Knotty men killed in the first world war. Costing about £1,000, it was unveiled on 18 August 1922.

Such features as blue-black grooved platform-edge tiling, and diapers of blue bricks to offset the more extensive use of red bricks gave distinction to many NSR stations. Thick cream slabs surrounded station houses—structures often more imposing than the stations themselves. A fine example at Keele survives, showing the Staffordshire Knot framed by bricks.

At Trentham the company provided the platforms and the Duke of Sutherland constructed the buildings to his own specifications to conform with the design of Trentham Hall. Both were the work of his architect, Sir Charles Barry, designer of the Houses of Parliament.

The Knotty built some pleasing country stations like Madeley, which was tucked into a hillside at the entrance to a deep cutting, lying within sight of the LNWR main line.

The company had its share of joint stations like Colwich, where in May 1865, the NSR and LNWR joint committee called for accommodation on the up side, the LNWR having provided it on the opposite platform. In return, the LNWR agreed to help the NSR in difficulties it had encountered over the siting of a level crossing.

Station arrangements were even more complex at Norton Bridge, where the NSR had shared the cost of the passenger station and met the whole of that of the passenger sheds and goods station, built partly on LNWR land. The LNWR used NSR land to avoid shunting wagons across the main line.

Improvements were carried out whenever money became available and in June 1867, a block of buildings was demolished in the market place in the heart of Longton to make way for a better approach to the down platform. The work cost £1,300 and twenty-two years later £4,000 was spent on placing a lattice girder bridge across the market place. The bridge, with low clearance, is there today, adorned and half-hidden by advertisements.

Tutbury station was re-modelled in 1880, 'not so much because the traffic demanded it,' said the chairman, 'but because we are under agreement with the owner of the property in that neighbourhood to expend a certain sum of money on it'. This was the bargain made in return for the company being given the land on 'reasonable terms'.

Leek was a particularly fine station with a colonnade in front of the main buildings, but its architecture did not prevent critics complaining for years about its shortcomings. They failed to budge management and it seems fairly obvious that this was because of a dislike which Phillipps had both for the station and its staff.

Walker pin-pointed the troubles when he wrote: Leek on market days makes an interesting study in confusion and delay. How to accommodate a thousand passengers with their numerous baskets on a platform 12ft wide and by no means long, is a problem that would puzzle any institution but the NSR. Talk of a new station of generous dimensions with island platforms etc has been in the air for a time, but Leek still remains about the worst place on the line. He did not state which was the worst, but he did remark that any up train at Leek with less than eight to ten minutes station time to its credit, was lucky.

Several other fine stations in the Churnet Valley were designed by A. W. Pugin, a noted Victorian architect. At Alton he partly-designed Alton Towers, seat of the Earl of Shrewsbury, as well as the station.

Station improvements often took time. A new one planned at Rocester in 1885 was eventually completed ten years later.

Longton got a practically-rebuilt station in 1898-9 and a new roof was put on that at Burslem in the same period.

Generally, Walker felt most stations were 'equal to present requirements', although some of the older ones retained scanty waiting and seating accommodation. Platforms varied in height and many were far too narrow.

Notes are on page 296

CHAPTER FIVE

Blaze of Glory

TRAM COMPETITION

The turn of the century broadly marked the start of the ebb in the railway's passenger fortunes for while it did much to develop electricity, this was exploited far more successfully by its chief rival—the tramways.

Six towns, tightly-packed, hillside-built, industry-coal-steel-potteries-houses, all jammed together, were hardly the ideal area for a railway to exploit in every way, but it was rich ground for trams as a more flexible form of transport, and few railways faced competition earlier than those in the Potteries. Horse trams were running in the area only two years after they were introduced into Britain at Birkenhead in 1860. A Burslem—Hanley service started on 13 January 1862, was operated by a company formed by the American pioneer of the Birkenhead tramways, George Francis Train. These original horse-trams of the Staffordshire Potteries Street Railway Company Limited, ran on step rails, which, like Birkenhead's, were raised above the road surface. It was a short lived innovation for by the end of 1864 the trams were running on grooved lines flush with the road surface.

This was the Potteries' only tramway for twenty years but by 1880 the NSR was worried about their potential and in February of that year, when the Loop line was only five years old, the chairman felt it necessary to answer fears that the trams might diminish the Loop traffic. He said he had never found such competition very dangerous and did not for one moment fear that Loop traffic would not continue to increase. One shareholder, Freeman, said that if Parliament had sanctioned trams, the NSR must do the best it could for itself. 'After all,' he added, 'many such schemes have died an early death.'

But it was such pious hopes—not the tramways—that died and in 1882 the North Staffordshire Tramways bought the Burslem—Hanley service, converted it to a steam tramway of 4ft 0in gauge and extended it to Stoke and a district to the south west; and also from Stoke to Fenton, Longton and Normacot. The route mileage was not great: 6 miles 64 chains, but it went past people's homes. Traffic grew quickly and between 1896-8 the steam trams carried a yearly average of almost 4,000,000 passengers: 3,913,746. They ran 360,156 car miles and were profitable: receipts of 14.15 pence a car mile being well ahead of expenses of 9.31 pence.

Electric trams started running in 1899, operated by the Potteries Electric Traction Company, formed a year earlier. The last steam trams ran only a year later and by 1905 the company was running 115 electric trams (all single deckers because of low railway bridges), on 31 miles 73 chains of lines, including those of the North Staffordshire Tramways, which it had leased.

The routes covered six towns and Newcastle and besides being in direct competition with the Loop trains at all stations between Goldenhill and Meir, they linked places not served by trains direct, including Chesterton, Sneyd Green, Adderley Green and Hanford Bridge. They also provided direct links between Tunstall, Burslem, Hanley and Newcastle.

During the first two years of tram competition, the NSR reduced its passenger mileage by 18,000 to a total in 1901 of 600,000. As passenger receipts remained the same at £125,000 it meant earnings had improved slightly.

The Knotty was, of course primarily a mineral line and in that field it was not doing so well. In 1900-1 it was among only four of Britain's eighteen major companies that failed to increase goods mileage earnings. In 1901 it increased goods mileage by 5,000 to well over half a million (583,000), but earnings dropped by £6,000.

It is unlikely the fluctuating position worried Phillipps as general manager, but he might not have been too keen about statistics surrounding competition and indeed railway operation. He was no lover of them, as he demonstrated when *The Statist* magazine discussed the national railway position around the turn of the century. He wrote refuting the value of ton-mile statistics, favoured by the North Eastern general manager, George S. Gibb.

Phillipps contended that trading conditions had been changing and merchants no longer ordered goods in large and heavy consignments as they had done in the age of canals. Instead, they did so in 'endless small lots of goods, all requiring the promptest despatch in through trucks direct to destination'.

> The 12 and 15 ton 'broad' gauge waggons were never replaced when the Great Western Railway converted their line into 'narrow' gauge—probably their experience showed that they were not economical.

His letter was dated 17 December 1901.[1]

Returning to tram competition, Salt had spoken earlier in that year of his hope that in time trams might provide the railway with traffic by serving their important stations. It was a sentiment quashed six months later by his deputy, Tonman Mosley, when he addressed shareholders on 7 August.

He confessed: 'It is almost impossible to compete with the electric tramway for several reasons'. He pointed out that their lines were laid on roads which meant that they did not have to buy land, unlike the railway companies; they did not have the same encumbrances placed upon them by the Board of Trade; they crossed all roads on the level, but there were not the same requirements for trams as they were for trains.

His statement came at a time when NSR dividends were at a low ebb. In the first half of 1901 they reached only $1\frac{5}{8}$ per cent, but the situation improved sufficiently for the annual dividend to reach $3\frac{3}{4}$ per cent. While this was the lowest since 1886, it was to be, with the exception of 1908, the lowest of all the remaining years.

A decline in rail passengers between Stoke and Newcastle was reported in February 1905 when a countermeasure was announced. Mosley revealed that they were considering 'motor coaches on rails', to run through populous districts, stopping between stations to pick up passengers at road crossings and take them where they wanted to go.

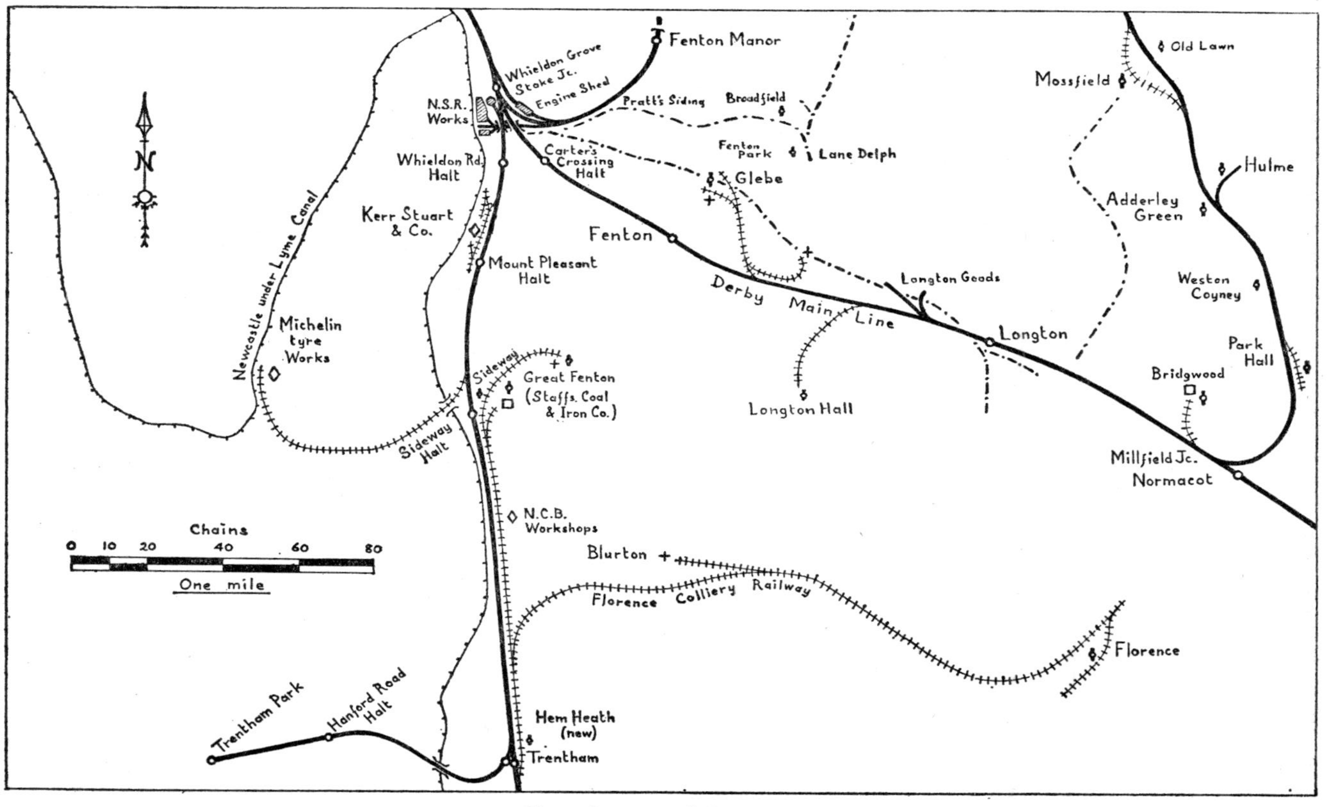

Trentham and Longton

RAIL MOTORS

So was heralded the first big innovation of the Edwardian years. The 'Rail Motor Cars', third-class, hand-baggage only, which were introduced in June, picked up passengers at stations and eight halts opened from 1 May: Crown Street, Knutton, Liverpool Road, Brampton, Hartshill and Basford (two areas where there had been agitation for a station since 1892); Whieldon Road (platform on upside only); Sideway and Mount Pleasant, built to serve the large railway works of Kerr Stuart. Called California, the works were bought by that company in 1892 and lay between the main line at Stoke and the T & M canal.

The initial service was between either Silverdale, Brampton or Newcastle, and Sideway or Trentham, but because of its success it was soon extended to Leycett and on market days to Barlaston and Colwich. Rail motors ran over the Biddulph and Sandbach branches from January 1906 and by 1908 were maintaining a 15 minute service on the Loop. A Sunday service was re-introduced on 1 June but came off from 1 October through lack of support.

By summer 1910 the NSR board felt confident enough to report that to a very great extent they had made up the leeway caused by tram competition. The success was attributed to careful management and the saving of every penny.

The statement was made soon after the opening of the Trentham Gardens branch, built in an attempt to exploit the rail motors. The last of the Knotty branches, it had been authorised on 21 August 1907 under an Act which also transferred the Cheadle Railway to the NSR. Trentham itself had grown into a suburb and the Hall and its 500 acre deer park were still as great an attraction for local people as when sixty years earlier the Knotty had chosen it as the venue for its first excursions. The Hall had been built a few years ahead of the first railway in the area. In the Edwardian years it had lost some of its status for in 1905 the Duke of Sutherland abandoned it as one of his seats 'owing to the pestilential odour of the neighbouring river Trent, which is made noxious by pollutions in its passage through the Pottery towns'.[2]

The three years between the authorisation and opening of the branch on 1 April 1910, coincided with those of a slight depression in dividends, which fell from $4\frac{3}{8}$ per cent in 1907 to $3\frac{3}{4}$ per cent the following year.

In the sense that the Trentham branch was short, it was characteristic of most other local branches, yet it might have enjoyed better fortunes but for the first world war. This delayed plans to extend it to the Pool Dam branch and provide a western circle line through the heart of a growing residential area. Plans for the Trentham, Newcastle-under-Lyme and Silverdale Light Railway of just over 4 miles got to the construction stage by the erection of a large steel bridge over the main London road outside Trentham Park station. Beyond it lay a steep drop from the embankment to ground level. It was a measure of the line's fortunes.

By the time the Trentham branch opened, it was road, rather than rail, that was carrying local traffic and the only halt, Hanford Road, closed in April 1913. There was one other station called Trentham Junction, which lay just beyond the divergence of the branch from the main line. It was connected to Trentham station by a footpath and used by people travelling south. Despite its seemingly important status, Trentham Junction was never in the time table.

It was originally envisaged that the Trentham extension would carry Audley mineral trains clear of the bottle-neck at Stoke, but by the time the light railway was abandoned in 1921, the traffic flow from the Audley area had changed and ambitious plans for main line improvements at Stoke were being prepared. But for some years the light railway was shown on company maps as a projected route.

Rail motor services lingered until grouping. Dr Ashton, a holder of a contract[3] from Newcastle to Stoke between 1921 and 1923, remembers an occasion when passengers had to abandon a rail motor and walk over the top of Newcastle tunnel after heavy snow. As the telegraph line between signal boxes had been broken the driver could not get a staff to run through.

Besides the Knotty rail motor services, the GCR maintained for a time a shuttle service between Macclesfield and Bollington with a petrol-electric railcar of 1912, which during its career up to withdrawal in 1934, was often known as the 'Bollington Bug'.[4]

If the Knotty rail motor services were never the success the advocates wished, it is worth remembering two points. Firstly, heavy traffic which developed during the first world war was far beyond their capacity and so they had to be replaced by trains. Secondly, the tram promoters never succeeded in carrying their aspirations as far as they had planned. They never built extensions authorised to Blythe Bridge, Bucknall, Kidsgrove, or direct lines from Newcastle to Trent Vale; Goldenhill to Burslem and Tunstall. The reason was, of course, the appearance of the motor bus and the tram company was not slow to test them. The first experiment in 1900 was unsuccessful. but in the following year, two Straker double-deck *steam* buses were bought. Built by Vulcan Ironworks at Fishponds, Bristol, they ran from April 1901, but they were sold eleven months later because they could not master the steep hills of the Potteries. Further bus experiments in 1904-6 were abortive and buses were not introduced successfully until 1913.

By then the motor *car* had achieved success and by 1908 was modestly, but firmly, rooted in the Potteries. One of the NSR's earliest reactions was to consider speeding up trains. The chairman said he had consulted the locomotive engineer several times about accelerations. It was however a little difficult to press him because there might be difficulties arising from his anxiety to hurry trains forward. Very considerable caution was necessary. Mosley went on to express a sentiment which was to prove as hollow as that of the shareholder had been about the advent of trams. He hoped their first class passengers would soon tire of riding about in motors and return to the railway.

During the years that competition was biting into passenger receipts, the NSR was able to take comfort from being 'The six penny line', an image which it was shy to acknowledge. With fares so low, a big drop in passengers meant only a small drop in revenue. While sixpence was the average fare of third class passengers, those travelling second paid an average of twopence more, while the first class average, paid by a minority, was far higher: 1s 9¾d. In one half of 1905, third class bookings earned £90,284 out of a passenger revenue of £110,170.

In the complete year of 1907, passenger revenue was £273,631—only a shade over a quarter of the total revenue of £1,020,437. The balance was made up from goods, mineral and livestock traffic.

Various ideas were put forward for improving traffic. Col Twemlow contended in 1905 that a lot of traffic could be captured on the Market Drayton branch if trains were not so infrequent. This included a great deal of traffic dispatched from Market Drayton by the GWR. He pleaded for branch connections on the London expresses at Stoke so that people could get from Market Drayton to Euston in three and a half hours, instead of five taken by the GWR. He also advocated connections to Stafford and Derby.

To try and break out of the strait-jacket of having to fit in with other companies' trains, a new time table was introduced in 1908 'entirely independent of the LNWR and MR'. It was a disaster. Time margins were found to be too narrow between the departure of NSR trains and the arrival of those of the other companies. The new NSR time table coincided with major train alterations by the big companies and the NSR stated that while it would try and meet retimed trains, it could not run specials for passengers who missed connections.

Despite this set-back, the NSR considered only two years later abolishing second class. For some years it had tried—and failed—to encourage third class passengers to travel second to avoid drawing empty second class carriages. The only public reactions the idea provoked were complaints about third class carriages being bare and draughty. The NSR felt there would be worthwhile economies if the big companies abolished second class but it was then in no mood to take the step by itself.

SUNDAY TRAINS

One source of profitable revenue might have been Sunday excursions but any hopes of developing them were vetoed by the strict Victorian attitude to the observance of the Sabbath, which lingered into Edwardian days. It was exemplified, as we have noted at the beginning of this book, in summer 1908 by the 370 shareholders who pressed strongly for a limitation on

Sunday excursions. But despite the religious hostility to excursions, the NSR allowed wagons to be used as platforms for open air evangelical meetings. Part of the Knotty legend is the story of how children had to be packed into empty coal wagons to weigh them down so that they could scrape under a low bridge and leave Jimmy's Yard at Oakamoor. While there, however, they were close enough to houses to let preachers attract an audience.

THE LEEK & MANIFOLD LIGHT RAILWAY

A line which did help the working classes to get into the country—and on Sundays since there was one train each way—was the Leek & Manifold. The initiative to take a railway into one of the deepest, loveliest—and least populated—valleys of North Staffordshire came from individuals rather than the NSR, which was content to watch as various proposals crystallised. It was careful to give the impression that it did not want to spend any money on such a scheme.

After the passing of the Light Railway Act of 1896, the company thought of building a narrow gauge line from Norton Bridge to Eccleshall and Gnosall. It was considered by the board on 30 October 1894 and later there were statements that a bill was to be presented in the 1900 Parliamentary session, but nothing came of it, probably because of the growing improvement in road transport to rural areas.

The first concerted effort to get a railway into the country and moorland areas around Leek was well timed, for traders at Leek were worried by the LNWR line from Parsley Hay to Ashbourne, then under construction, because they feared it would make it easier for people to go to market in Buxton or Ashbourne, rather than Leek, which could only be reached over rough roads. A meeting at Leek on 27 May 1896 led to the formation of a committee which hoped to secure the help of the NSR.

The plan was for a narrow gauge line through the Manifold valley from Waterhouses, which was to involve the NSR in building several associated standard gauge lines. All were authorised by an Order of the Light Railway Commissioners of 6 March 1899: a line of 4 miles 42 chains from the Churnet

Valley at Cheddleton (later Leek Brook) Junction to Ipstones; an extension of almost equal distance (4 miles 26 chains) to Waterhouses, and a 61 chain branch from Caldon Junction to

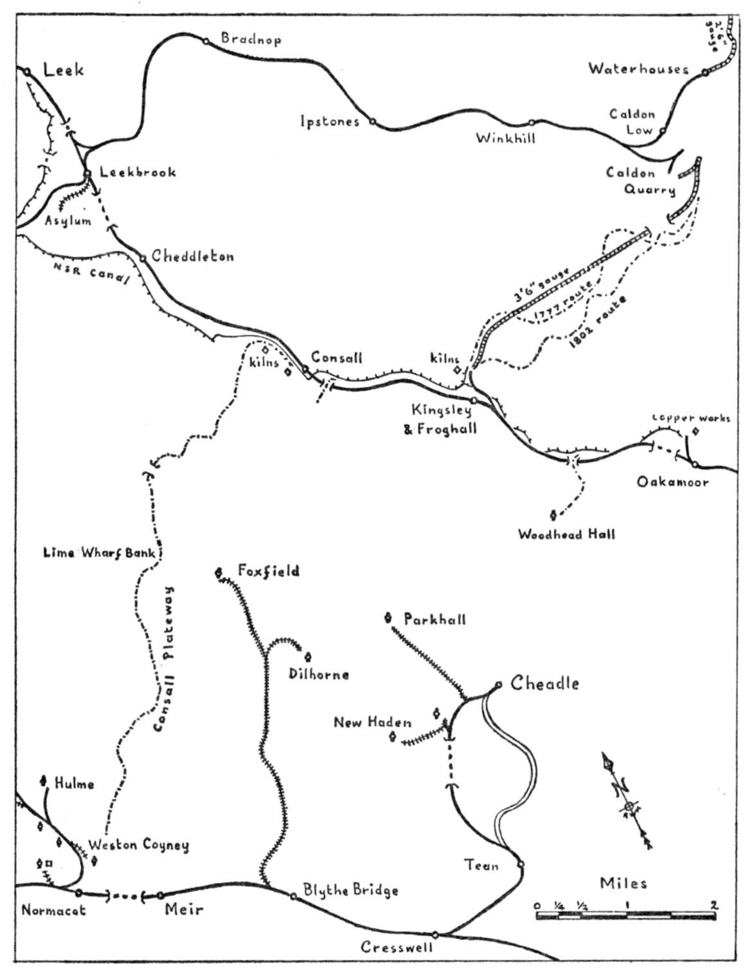

Leek, Caldon Low and Cheadle

the quarries to serve workings about to be started and to provide a better outlet for the stone than over the cable incline to Froghall. The Order allowed for £100,000 in new capital and a loan of £33,000; three years for compulsory purchase of land and five years for completion of the lines.

The L & M share capital of £20,000 was heavily supported by a £10,000 loan at 3½ per cent from Staffordshire County Council, a Treasury loan of £7,500 at 3 per cent, and a Government grant of £17,500. These amount to a little more than the total expenditure on the line which reached £52,600. The agreement provided for the NSR to work and maintain the L & M for ninety-nine years at 55 per cent of gross receipts.

The official NSR party used the Caldon tramway to reach the spot where the Duke of Devonshire cut the first sod on 3 October 1899 and in view of the financial position it is perhaps worth speculating what might have been in their minds on that journey. Doubt? Doubt about both the line's value and potential. If the chairman's recent remarks were to be taken seriously this was definite. Doubt had been first expressed publicly at the summer shareholders' meeting a year earlier when Salt referred, guardedly, to 'long dealings and a good deal of trouble' with Government departments. His hope on 8 August 1899 was that the L & M would be a 'successful experiment'.

What was the line's potential? It was to run from Waterhouses (which, after all, was not Leek) and market travellers would have to change trains to Hulme End, which was envisaged as a useful railhead for the upper valley and the only two villages in the area: Longnor, quite some distance away, and Hartington, which in any case, was to have a station on the Buxton—Ashbourne route. It was estimated there were enough people in the area—3,366 in 1891—to sustain 35,000 single journeys a year.

Difficulties were quickly encountered and NSR shareholders were told on 11 August 1900 that it had been hoped to make a start on construction but it had been delayed, partly by the company's hesitation to embark upon more railway construction at a time when prices were high, and by difficulties in obtaining land. This difficulty was again referred to six years later when Mosley remarked: 'When the line was first considered, great representations were made to the NSR regarding the cheapness of land which it would have to pay for'. The cheapness of land, he added caustically, had been unknown to them.

To return to 1900, nothing was done either in that year or

the next—a year during which the chairman remarked sceptically that the line *might* be the means of bringing in agricultural produce.

Construction began in March 1902 and the line was opened on 27 June 1904. E. R. Calthrop, the engineer, took over construction fresh from building lines in India and he pleased country lovers with the way he did the job. Charles Masefield[5] recorded:

> On the whole, there is little to regret in the advent of the railway. From the utilitarian standpoint it has placed a once very remote pastoral district within reach of a market for its milk, and even the most conservative lover of nature undefiled, is bound to admit that the making of the line has done wonderfully little to desecrate the scenery.

Calthrop stamped the L & M with an oriental touch in massive-cabbed locomotives and deep-windowed coaches with verandas: glorious flamboyant creations.

While the railway may not have damaged the scenery, the NSR was accused of damaging local roads. The complaint was made after the company started running two steam buses, built by Strakers, which were needed to provide connections to the L & M until the completion of the Waterhouses branch. The NSR got Parliamentary sanction to run the buses on 24 June 1904 (three days before the L & M opening), and they at once proved popular, conveying 1,838 passengers in the first month and earning £45 in fares. The second month they did even better, carrying 2,225 passengers and taking £60 in fares. Although they weighed under three tons, the County Council complained they were breaking up the road surface. In 1905 the company gave the Council 20,000 tons of stone quarried in making a new cliff face near Waterhouses—but denied the buses had done any road damage.

Storms and bad weather delayed the completion of the Waterhouses branch for almost a year. There were numerous small land slips and one embankment was flattened out before the line was completed in two stages: from Cheddleton to Ipstones on 15 June 1905 and through to Waterhouses on 1 July. The original plan had been for a curve at Leek Brook to allow through running to Stoke, but Leek traders were

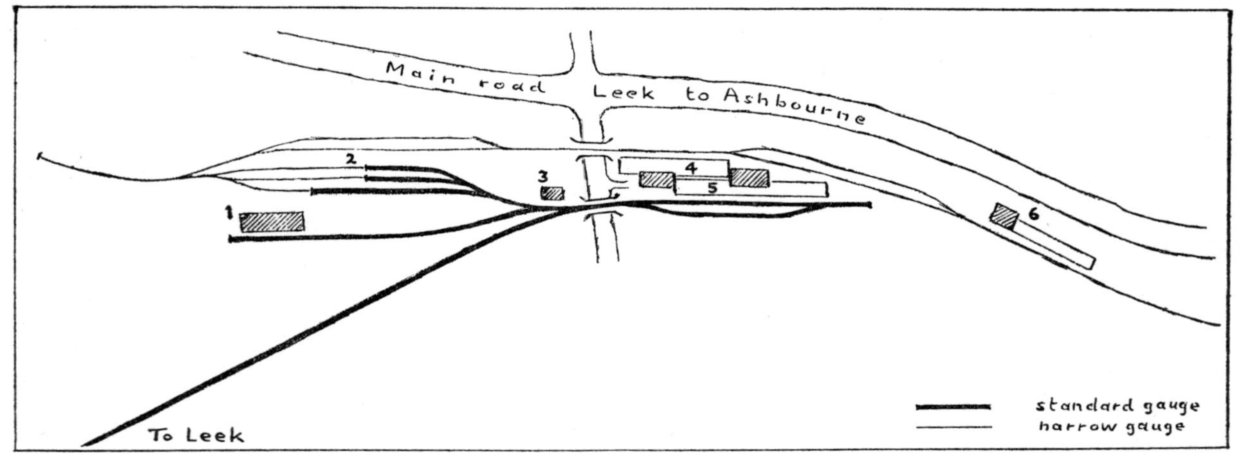

The mixed gauge layout at Waterhouses station: I goods shed, 2 interchange sidings for loading and unloading the transporter cars, 3 signal box, 4 narrow gauge station, 5 standard gauge station, 6 original temporary narrow gauge station

inflamed by the idea of local trains running straight to Stoke while any to their town would have to reverse. The NSR had to get Parliamentary powers to meet the protests by building a ¼ mile north-facing curve. Authorised in 1899, it was opened at the same time as the line to Ipstones.

The NSR purpose in buying two buses was not purely as a temporary feeder to Waterhouses, but also to run others. One route envisaged was between Hulme End and Hartington.

Leek traders cannot have been happy when shareholders supported a plan put forward in 1904 for extending the L & M through Longnor to Buxton. It was never seriously presented further otherwise it would have been opposed by the LNWR.

The NSR made its influence on the L & M felt in several ways. It insisted on steel, rather than wooden bridges, and never conceded to the pressure of L & M directors who wanted more connections.

From 1 January 1912, the NSR paid the L & M a fixed annual payment of £675. This later rose to £750. The passing of time reinforced fears that the railway could never pay and by the end of 1921 the debit against net revenue was £14,403. The slimmest hopes of profitability were removed as road transport gained an ever increasing hold on market traffic.

OTHER IMPROVEMENTS

Growing road competition was reflected in some NSR improvements elsewhere early in the century. The Loop got a new station on 1 April 1900: Waterloo Road. Improvements were made in 1901-2 to stations at Uttoxeter, Consall, Leek Brook, Aston-by-Stone and Stretton-on-Dove. A new cattle station was opened at Brunswick Wharf, Congleton, and up and down goods lines were laid between Stoke and Grange Junction, and Etruria's two platforms were replaced by an island. Fenton got a new station in 1905 and another was opened at Hassell Green on the Sandbach branch on 17 April. The extension of electrical power continued. Parliament had underlined the company's original enterprise by the Railways (Electrical Power) Act of 14 August 1903, which gave all railways authority to use it. Longton goods yard was electrically lit from 1906 and that at Hanley two years later. Work there, which cost £600, included power capstans. Power was used as a tourist attraction at the Caldon quarries after the opening of the Waterhouses branch. A cave was opened in 1906 and electricity used to illuminate its stalactites and stalagmites. The words 'Alight for Froghall Quarry'—the official name of that at Caldon Low—was added to the name-board at Waterhouses.

Early in the century more wooden and cast iron bridges were replaced by heavier structures of wrought iron and steel. Oakamoor and Harecastle tunnels remained troublesome and needed constant maintenance. In 1904, 1¾ miles of new sidings were laid at Longport, Harecastle, Stoke, Tutbury and Uttoxeter and 7½ miles of main line was relaid with 90lb steel rail, replacing the 72lb iron rails. In 1905 a relaying programme of seventeen miles a year was forecast and the standard permanent way became bull-head sections of 90lbs a yard with sleepers 8ft 11in by 10in by 5in. They were spaced 2ft 10in centre to centre. Chairs weighed 47½ pounds.

The cinder bed made the track bed—and the surrounding areas it seems—fertile. Walker noted that platelayers were said to be doing almost as much haymaking as farmers. Another ballast used was that of limestone from Caldon, liked for its hard quality.

In 1909 the two mile section of the Loop between Newchapel and Kidsgrove was singled and a new halt, Market Street, opened at Kidsgrove on 1 July. At first it was used by locals in both directions, but later it was only a stop in the down direction because of the stiff gradient.

The opening of a new Post Office at Stoke on 2 April 1909 brought an end to a period of difficulties and delays for which the NSR was sometimes blamed. It vigorously refuted its critics and the chairman said he fancied that if the shelves of the Post Office where the papers and correspondence of the NSR lay could be examined, they would be found inches deep in dust—no one having looked at them for a long time!

Leek remained a target of the critics and when it was suggested in autumn 1905 that Staffordshire County Council should loan £5,000 for the L & M, the *Leek Post* commented: 'Leek has never been considered anything but a gold mine to be cruelly and selfishly worked'. Five years later its traffic potential was recognised by the doubling of the section from Leek Brook to Endon on 25 March 1910—an improvement which was followed in February 1914 by the widening of the entrance to the goods yard. Associated improvements at the stations included the widening of platforms.

IMPROVING THE IMAGE

The Knotty featured the L & M in guides which it issued from 1890. At first they were called *Official Illustrated Holiday Guides* but by 1908 'holiday' had been dropped from the title. Typical was the edition of that year which went on sale at booking offices and the accountant's department at Stoke, as well as at stationers in local towns.

The guides' main object was stated to be that of dispelling, by facts and photographs, the notion held by many that the Potteries were a 'bleak and stony county'. The text was supplemented by maps 'obtained at considerable expense from the Board of Agriculture'.

There was plenty of evidence that outsiders thought ill of the area, which found another defender in Walker[6]

> No description of the Potteries is necessary here, but give even the devil his due; there are many manufacturing centres quite as bad—and worse. Leaving Stoke the line continues flanked by innumerable short branches and sidings, through the same industrial scenery. Gradually the prospect brightens, the sky resumes its natural tint, and after passing Harecastle with its dirty tunnel and five converging sets of rails, pleasant country accommodates the line to the L & NW Junction at Crewe.

Walker mentioned something which the guides ignored: a free and unofficial medical service provided for local people. It came about that parents believed that the atmosphere in local tunnels had medical properties and they started taking children with whooping cough into tunnels after trains had passed. 'Whether the treatment is effective or not, the writer cannot say, but if sulphur has curative properties, it ought to be,' was Walker's comment.

The guides sang the praises of such things as the company golf course at Rudyard, doubled in 1910 to eighteen holes.

NORTH STAFFORDSHIRE RAILWAY.

THE

"North Stafford" Route

IS THE

SHORTEST, QUICKEST, and BEST for both

GOODS AND PASSENGERS

BETWEEN

Leicester, Newark, Nottingham, Lincoln, Grantham, Boston, Cambridge, Bedford, Northampton, Market Harborough, Sheffield, Chesterfield, Derby, and Burton,

AND

Chester, Birkenhead, Liverpool, North, South, and Mid Wales, Ireland, Isle of Man, Buxton, Lancashire, and the North.

TOURIST TICKETS by this Route are issued from the former to the latter districts each Season; also EXCURSION TICKETS (Day and Week-end) in most instances between the same points and by the same Route.

The Company's TOURIST AND EXCURSION PROGRAMME, giving full particulars, will be forwarded free upon application.

TOURIST and WEEK-END EXCURSION TICKETS are also issued from most principal places to ALTON, RUDYARD LAKE (the "Name-place" of Rudyard Kipling), ASHBOURNE (for DOVEDALE), and BUXTON, each Season.

These and other places of great interest, such as—

RUDYARD LAKE—The Windermere of the Midlands—Fishing, Boating, Bathing, Golf. Arrangements can be made for Camping-out in delightfully wooded, sheltered nooks on the borders of the Lake. Apply to Station-master at Rudyard, or to the undersigned.

Hotel Rudyard—Recently Enlarged—Very Comfortable.

WATERHOUSES, for the Caldon Low Limestone Quarries—the happy hunting ground of the geologist.

MANIFOLD VALLEY TOY RAILWAY—2 ft. 6 in. gauge—runs along the Valley of the Manifold to the point where it sinks into the earth to reappear at Ilam, four miles away—the most beautiful scenery in Staffordshire.

LEEK, for Rock Hall, the Roaches and Morridge Hills, and for the Manifold Valley Toy Railway.

TUTBURY, with its Ancient and Historical Castle, Beautiful Church, and Glass Works.

DENSTONE, for Croxden Abbey Ruins, Denstone College, and the Weaver Hills.

CONGLETON, for the Splendid Old Church at Astbury, Moreton Old Hall, Biddulph Grange, The Cloud, The Dane Viaducts, &c.

And also the magnificent Wood, Hill, and River Scenery of the Churnet and Dove Valleys, are easy of access by the "NORTH STAFFORD" Route.

The Public are particularly requested to ask for Tickets by the "NORTH STAFFORD" Route, and to see that such Tickets are supplied to them.

Applications for information as to Traffic for this Route should be made to—

W. D. PHILLIPPS, *General Manager,*

Railway Offices, STOKE-ON-TRENT; or any of the Company's Agents in the various Towns.

Advertisement of 1809. No doubt the Knotty was a good line!

There was a eulogy about the lake. 'It is a splendid sheet of water and the number of pleasure boats which visitors can obtain at moderate charges, has been very considerably increased of late; there are also two motor launches. The lake has also been stocked with over 30,000 fish'. Rudyard traffic doubled between 1904 and 1906 and the company's hotel was improved to deal with the tourists and day trippers.

There were however more important matters which had to be dealt with in 1907 when there was talk of amalgamation between the GCR and the GWR. It was a move which the NSR felt might prejudice its interests and so while it was friendly with both companies, it felt obliged to take measures to protect itself. There was also a move in 1907 to consolidate relations with the GCR and under an Act obtained by that company, the name of their joint undertaking, the Macclesfield Committee, was changed to the Great Central & North Staffordshire Railway Committee. Membership remained at eight, but at Grouping the NSR was represented by only three members.

When nationalisation of railways was talked about in 1908, A. Emil Davies,[7] in presenting the case for state take-over, examined seventeen companies in England and Wales with over 100 miles of line. At the end of 1906, the NSR lay thirteenth, with paid-up capital including loans and debenture stock of 10.6 million pounds. Working expenses were 59 per cent, a good average since those of the GCR were then 66 per cent and of the LNWR, 63 per cent.

Taxation began to get heavier and the NSR was often critical. In 1901 it complained about high rates of 7s 1d in the pound at Stoke, 8s 0d at Hanley and 8s 10d at Longton. In the year up to June 1907, rates and taxes totalled £35,117—about £170 for each mile of railway, on which gross earnings were £4,401. In summer 1909 the company complained against the taxation of licensed property which meant heavier costs for running the Stoke hotel, Rudyard Lake Hotel, the Churnet Hotel at Leek and a small licensed property at Hanley.

In 1910, the company started giving £500 a year to the North Staffordshire Infirmary which treated nine out of every ten people hurt on the railway and also many of the men and their relatives.

PEAK YEAR

So to 1913. For the NSR, as for many other companies, it was to be the year of its high-water mark. The company had £190,574 available for dividend and for the first time since 1891 it became a 'five per cent' line. Not only was income a record, but the stock, track and all other parts of the system were in excellent shape. 'They have never been in such an efficient condition,' the chairman proclaimed.

It was also a year of minor expansion, new sidings being laid at Longton, Cobridge, Leek, Etruria, Uttoxeter.

There were plans for improvements but because of the changing international situation, they were destined to remain so for ever. They included the change to light railways of a number of mineral lines, among them the Adderley Green and Biddulph lines and the projected extension between Trentham and Pod Dam.

Notes are on page 296

CHAPTER SIX

Management and Men

STATUS AND DIGNITY

Locomotive and train operation may be the stuff that most interests those who study the railways of the past. To satisfy this desire historians use thousands of words to gild an already glamorous lily. But railways were conceived by men, built by men and run by men. Society in Victorian and Edwardian England recognised the railwayman for what he was: a man following a secure, worth-while and honourable calling. It accorded him a status which placed him above that of many workers in other industries; a status that added dignity to his labour.

Within his ranks there were distinctions: in early days station masters wore uniforms with gold buttons. Knotty inspectors of 1850 had imposing frock coats with silver embroidered collars and silver buttons—a uniform completed by blue cloth trousers, hat and greatcoat of blue pilot cloth. Men of the passenger department had white Staffordshire Knots on their uniform; those of the goods department, red.

By 1849, apart from enginemen, well over 300 men were working for the company, being classified as station masters, clerks, ticket collectors, porters, police, watchmen, guards, gatemen, pointmen, breaksmen. There were also eleven boys being paid upwards of 4s a week. Clerks in the offices of the company secretary, engineer and the audit office were classed separately.

If history has paid more attention to the navvies who built the railways, it is because they were characters, while the strictly disciplined railwaymen of Victorian days, were not. Their virtues of reliability and stolidness did not lend themselves to colour. Little attention was paid to the views of railwaymen until they began to unite into trade unions like the Amalgamated Society of Railway Servants, a general, rather than a graded union, formed in 1871. Then they began to oppose with growing effectiveness the powerful influence of the companies who, nationally, were represented in Parliament by over eighty directors.

DIRECTORS IN PARLIAMENT

No less than four of the Knotty's fourteen directors were MPs in 1858: the chairman, Ricardo; Lord Alfred Paget, John Bramley Moore and Smith Child. Lord Paget was also a director of the Norfolk Railway (of which G. P. Bidder was then chairman), and of the South Staffordshire Railway, of which Richard Moon was also a director. Ricardo was also chairman of the English board of the Norwegian Trunk Railway, being built from Christiania to lakes forty miles away, and one of the trustees of another Scandinavian project: the Royal Danish Railway.

The importance which the NSR attached to Parliamentary connections was shown by its decision in April 1856 to give £15 to funds for the protection of railway interests in Parliament. It represented £3 for each £1,000,000 of the company's paid-up capital.

The board was careful not to antagonise men at election times and before a general election in 1868 it instructed the general manager to tell 'officers and servants' that they must not do anything to interfere with the independence of those employed under them.

Wages always dominated relations between management and men and there was a wide gap in the early days between those of the directors and senior management. In 1849 directors received £2,500 (an amount equal to that which they had received for their services up to the passing of the Acts of incorporation). This was just over three times the salary of the secretary, Samuda. (He was, incidentally, to get an annual allowance of £300 when he retired in 1876.)

There were the usual fluctuations in directors' pay. In 1851 they voted themselves half-pay because of general difficulties and backdated it six months. In the more prosperous year of 1884 they gave themselves a £500 rise to £2,000.

Chief officers' salaries were increased on 1 July 1853, Forsyth, as general manager, getting a rise of £200 to £850. He was among the highest paid officials. Men like Charles Lockhart, the coaching superintendent, were then receiving only £200 a year.

In 1882 a new manager was appointed to succeed Martin Smith, who had held the post for six years after moving from a similar one on the Vale of Clwyd Railway. He was W. D. Phillipps who was still to be connected with the company, as a director, when the twentieth century was over twenty years old and the NSR was about to become part of the LMS. There was more to distinguish William Douglas Phillipps than the unusual spelling of his surname: his shrill way of speaking, his caustic tongue, used to great effect on occasions; his stance with his head on one side. Born in 1839, he was apprenticed to Scott Russell, builder of Brunel's *Great Eastern* steam ship, and before he was twenty-one, he was manager of the Llanelly Railway. (He was a nephew of the chairman, Biddulph.) When this company was bought by the GWR, Phillipps joined the LNWR as district goods manager, Swansea. He became in 1874 district superintendent, Manchester. (This post had been held from 1852 to 1862 by Charles Cooper, a former NSR passenger superintendent.) Phillipps did well on the LNWR and later Sir Richard Moon was to compliment him after his negotiating on behalf of the NSR by remarking: 'We taught him too much!' Phillipps lived to be the longest serving member of the Goods Manager's Conference of the Railway Clearing House, which he joined in January 1866. By 1916 he could claim to have been with the Knotty for thirty-four years, rather more than half of the company's lifetime.

Life colleagues of many companies, all directors enjoyed high local esteem and often national prestige and their private addresses were given in time tables. The board of 1921 was led by Lord Anslow, CB, of Bangor's Park, Iver, Bucks, who had been in the chair since 1904, sitting until 1916 as Tonman Mosley. His deputy since 1909 had been Captain Sir Beville Stanier, Bart, of 'The Citadel', Preston Brockhurst, Shrewsbury, who had joined the board in 1903. Listed next was Rodolph

Fane de Salis of Portnall Park, Virginia Water, Surrey. At Grouping, he was the longest serving director, having joined in 1899. Other directors who lived away from the Potteries were Lt Col Sir Thomas Anderton Salt, DSO, another Baronet, who was chairman of Lloyds Banking Company. Sir Thomas, who lived at Hooke Court, Beaminster, Dorset, joined the Knotty in 1910. Col A. H. Heath lived at Street Ashton Lodge, near Rugby. He was a 'newcomer' who took his seat in 1918. Another director was the Earl of Harrowby of Sandon Hall, whose address was given as 10 Upper Belgrave Square, London. Like the chairman he was a Privy Councillor.

Besides Phillipps, who lived at Cresswell Manor, Stafford, and who received a seat in 1917 in recognition of his services to the railway, there were two other directors: W. Morton Philips of Heybridge, Tean (1909-23) and Major Francis Hamilton Wedgwood of Barlaston Lea, Stoke, a member since 1911. Except for the deputy chairman, all were to serve to Grouping.

Traditions of long and faithful service were not confined to some directors, they belonged as well to men like R. E. Pearce who spent his working life with the railway. He succeeded his father as registrar and assistant secretary in 1891 and took over the secretaryship three years later on the death of Percy Morris, who had shrewdly handled affairs since the reorganisation of 1876. Pearce was to remain as secretary until Grouping. He was a man conscious of his position and he had a bell fitted to his home at Stone so that the signalman could give him enough warning so he could arrive at the station with the dignity befitting the secretary of the line.[1]

DISCIPLINE

Just as the gap between their pay was wide, so too was the type of lives lived by management and men. For the men, discipline was strict. Forsyth laid down in March 1848 that all workers, except engine drivers, had to remove beards and moustaches or be dismissed. In the mid-sixties this became one of the few rules to be relaxed, even though it remained an offence for a man to have a beard on the LNWR, whose rules the Knotty closely copied.

[N]ORTH STAFFORDSHIRE RAILWAY
LOCOMOTIVE DEPARTMENT.

[R]egulations for Engine Drivers, Firemen
ETC.

[S]ubject to the General Rules and Regulations of the Company, the following conditions apply to the classes of men named below.

TIME.—All Engine Drivers and Firemen to be paid at the rate of 10 hours per day. Time to be taken when the men sign on and off duty by order. Allowance before train time—30 to 60 minutes according to circumstances.

OVERTIME.—Overtime will be paid at the rate of 10 hours per day.

SUNDAY DUTY.—All time worked between 12 o'clock midnight on Saturdays and 12 o'clock midnight on Sundays, will be paid for at the rate of 8 hours per day.

TIME OFF DUTY.—So far as the necessities of the service permit, at least 8 consecutive hours off duty will be arranged for.

WORKING ARRANGEMENTS.—The Company will endeavour to find a full week's work for as many of the men as possible. Men will not, however, be entitled to a full week's pay unless it is actually earned. Men coming on duty, by order, will have a day's work found for them.

WAGES.—Engine Drivers will be paid at the following rates:—On Shunting Engines, 1st year, 5/- per day; 2nd year, 5/3 per day; afterwards, 5/6 per day. Extra Drivers when working trains, assisting, or piloting, 6/- per day. When permanently appointed on regular trains: 1st year, 6/3 per day; afterwards, 6/6 per day, until appointed in Nos. 1, 2, or 3 Goods Links, at Stoke, or on ordinary passenger trains, which are paid 7/- per day. Passenger Train Drivers, 5 years after appointment to a regular passenger train: 7/6 per day. Regular Drivers, when working as Pilotmen, or assisting trains, will be paid at their standard rates. Extra Drivers working as Shedmen or Engine Turners: 5/- per day of 10 hours, exclusive of meal times.

FIREMEN.—1st year, 3/- per day; 2nd year, 3/3 per day; afterwards, 3/6 per day, until permanently appointed on train engines, when they will be paid: 1st Half-year, 3/6 per day; next Two years, 3/9 per day; next Three years, 4/- per day; afterwards 4/3; Passed Firemen 4/6 per day.

Drivers and Firemen at out-stations will only be advanced in rate of pay, or otherwise promoted, according to seniority as compared with Stoke men.

Passenger men at Stafford, Manchester, and Crewe, also men working the Sunday Derby Passenger train, will be paid for one hour after the actual arrival of the train, to stable their engines.

RELIEF.—Time occupied in getting to or from Shed, when going to relieve, or after being relieved, when not exceeding 30 minutes, to be paid for at standard rates, if over that time at 5/- and 3/- rates respectively

When through slackness of traffic a reduction of staff becomes necessary, Engine Drivers and Firemen will be put back to lower grades, and their rates of pay accordingly reduced, at the discretion of the Locomotive Superintendent.

TURNERS.—Paid at the rate of 5/- and 5/6 per day of 12 hours.

CLEANERS.—At the age of 16 years 1/8 per day, and advanced 2d. per day per year, until a maximum of 3/- per day is reached.

LODGING ALLOWANCE.—When men are required to lodge away from home for the convenience of the Company, they will be paid as follows:—Drivers and Firemen 2/- (except at Liverpool, Manchester, Wellinbro' and Colwick where it will be 2/6); and Cleaners 1/- per night.

LEAVING THE SERVICE.—One month's notice to be given by either party.

PREMIUMS.—£520 will be given annually by the Company amongst those drivers and firemen who have kept the most correct time, whose consumption of fuel and general stores is lowest, and whose conduct has been good.

CLOTHING.—One Jacket yearly, or, One Overcoat every two years, to Drivers, Firemen, and Passed Cleaners.

By order of the Directors,

[Stoke]-on-Trent,
[A]pril, 1901.

L. LONGBOTTOM, Locomotive Superintendent.

McCorquodale & Co., Limited, Newton—Printers to the Company. 1715

Thos Salt. Chairman
April 7th 1901

Knotty workers had to live where they were told and could not, like the directors, take part in the affairs of other concerns, the stipulation being that they were not to keep shops or trade without permission. The penalty was dismissal, as it was for men who did nothing more than swop shifts. The general manager and resident engineer could, however, substitute a 'heavy fine'. There were fines for 'slight cases of idleness, inattention or neglect'. Not less than half a crown was to be deducted from the wages of footplatemen late for duty.

Men leaving the company had to give a fortnight's notice or forfeit pay due to them, and they were warned that the company reserved the right to prosecute such cases before a magistrate.

Fighting, swearing and immoral and indecorous language were strictly prohibited, as were violent altercations and threats. Any man could report another for misconduct, but he was not to enter into 'any discussion or give rude answers to any one'. The public was encouraged to report men if they did. A small-print notice in time tables stated: 'The Directors request that any instance of incivility or misconduct on the part of persons in the service of the company may be directly reported to the General Manager'. The men were not allowed to take gratuities.

The Knotty's reputation as a reasonable and (as many thought) good employer, was based on acts which often displayed foresight and sympathy in decades when they were not always common between employer and employee. One of the earliest was the formation of a Friendly Society in 1849. The board helped the development of education when it agreed in 1857 to a request from the chief inspector of schools to accept certificates of school attendance from the age of nine, as proof of education by youths seeking jobs.

After the death in 1850 of the goods manager, Henry Samuel Miller, it was found that there was no provision for his wife and family. That situation was met by his widow being given £250—half his annual salary. This was in line with early policy of treating individual cases of hardship on their merits. There was another example in 1868 when the widows of two other men were given pensions of £10. There was help, too, for men who were injured in accidents on the line; men like

'Bob' Johnson of Ipstones, who lost both legs in an accident in Stoke yard. He had to find another job for there was no question of compensation and he was given work by the company as a signalman. He went to Bolton's Sidings box at Oakamoor and spent many years on the levers, quickly mastering even the 'distant' which lay 1,100 yards to the west.

WORKING HOURS

Working hours of railwaymen were notoriously long in Victorian days and while the companies were also notorious for making sure they remained that way, the NSR made occasional concessions. One of the first was a reduction in the working week of drivers, cut to 72 hours under an agreement of 6 February 1866. It included an hour and a half on shed daily.

Generally, progress towards shorter hours was slow and it was not until thirty years later—on 22 December 1896—that an eight hour day was introduced for foremen and yardmen at Stoke.

There were, however, one or two concessions in the interim years. From 1880 men were allowed to keep old uniforms and from 1894 free coffins were provided for those killed on duty—without distinction as to whether or not it was their own fault. But there was one qualification: they had to have at least five years' service.

Agitation for the introduction of shift work was much in vogue at the time of a collision at Stoke station on 21 February 1872, and apart from the widely reported statement by the inspecting officer, Col Rich, on the signal boxes being too comfortable, he had some other interesting comments. He suggested that if shifts were to be reduced to eight or ten hours, they should be worked in two parts so that men working a ten hour shift would not be free for fourteen hours a day. If they were, he felt they would either get other work and arrive tired for railway duty, or spend their time in 'frivolous pursuits'. The labouring classes did not know what to do with free time.

There were occasions when, through no fault of their own, men did have more time on their hands than they wanted.

This happened when the company workshops were put on short time. The board's policy about this was outlined by the chairman, Salt, who said in August 1885 that they were then working in this manner 'without any serious injury to the men'. He added: 'We have considered the necessity of lowering wages, but we do not wish to if it can be avoided, but the moment may come when it will be necessary. We shall have to act in that case in concert with the larger companies who are our neighbours'. They would be pleased if they could continue short time and maintain wages until things improved, but if they had to cut them, they would meet the 'convenience' of the men as much as possible. 'Our present rule is to keep all the good men we can, and where we have to reduce staff, to get rid of those people who are worthless'.

A detailed picture of how the NSR directors saw their role towards workers over thirty years from the mid-eighties until the first world war, emerged from the statements of successive chairmen. When redundancy occurred in summer 1886 following the decision to merge the two main workshops to save time and money, Salt commented: 'The only painful part is that we shall probably reduce the number of men very considerably—at least forty to fifty'. They hoped to deal as generously as possible, either in time or money, with any workman 'who has served us well'. One shareholder, Hicks, pleaded with the board to exercise great caution in discharging workmen so as not to injure the railway's efficiency.

The company subscribed £500 to the North Staffordshire Friendly Society and in announcing the news in February 1887, the chairman was at pains to point out that this sum was 'much below what is given by other railways to similar societies'.

By August of that year the workshops were again on short time, which meant a five day week. It was estimated that this pattern would last for three-four months out of six. It was a plan adopted to avoid dismissals.

The board's next reference to labour relations, made two years later on 7 February 1889, was laced with a warning. Salt said that while they desired to make the men as comfortable and happy in their employment as possible, they were determined that they would not keep men 'but such as are good men

Pages 137 (above) *The 12 15pm Manchester—Euston restaurant car express passing Macclesfield Central in 1910 hauled by class 'H' 0–6–0 No 84;* (below) *local train from Congleton via the loop line arriving at Blythe Bridge about 1900. Note the typical pork pie hats of the station staff*

Page 138 *In the beautiful Churnet Valley in 1910. Class 'B' 2–4–0T No 28 with four and six-wheeled coaches*

and worth keeping'. He added: 'I believe that that is our duty both to the men themselves and the company', a statement well received by shareholders.

When he returned to labour relations eighteen months later, Salt reported that they were on excellent terms with the men. They had instructed heads of departments that whenever there was a grievance among the men, it was to be remedied at once, provided it was found to be real and substantial. They were also doing a great many little things for the men's comfort. 'We have raised their wages where they ought to be raised and I believe every one is happy and content'.

GROWING UNREST

Such pronouncements and others that were to follow, were no doubt prompted to assure shareholders that all was well on the NSR at a time when there was growing unrest among Britain's railwaymen generally over wages, hours and conditions. The tide was flowing against management and the management did not like it. The situation was highlighted by the Hood case on the Cambrian Railways, which was followed by the Railway Regulation Act of 1893, which reduced the men's working hours.

There was again short time in the workshops from autumn, 1893 until 1 March 1894, curiously at a time when the system was busier than usual due to a national coal strike which lasted from 14 August 1893 until 11 September and lingered in South Wales until 20 November. Once the pits went back there was a tremendous rush for coal and the NSR found its engines and wagons over-taxed in handling coal pouring from local pits. Heavy trains were dispatched to many parts of the country as the coal boom continued into the spring. The rush meant a good deal of overtime for the Knotty men and they also got a bonus not, as the chairman stated, 'so much as a matter of payment, but as an outcome of their goodwill and loyalty for the extra work'.

Five years later the position was reversed when traffic in the Potteries declined because of a coal strike in South Wales.

If the Regulation Act of 1893 favoured the men, the Truck

Act which followed in 1896, favoured management and the company lost no time in applying it by introducing in January 1897 fines for minor offences. Men who were late for work, or cheeky to superior officers or passengers, faced fines of up to five shillings; twice that sum if their negligence delayed trains or damaged goods in transit. If their negligence put lives in danger, the men could be fined one pound. In the context of weekly pay at that period, five shillings represented about one-third of that of a porter; one-fifth of that of a senior clerk.

General unrest by railwaymen throughout Britain was referred to by the chairman on 15 February 1898, when he stated that of all workmen, almost the best in position were those connected with the railway service. They had the advantage, with the exception of a few men who were taken on for summer work, of regular and good employment and good wages. In many cases they were given clothes and other advantages. Privilege tickets and holidays were given to a reasonable extent. The company had a Friendly Society and they had been discussing for a good many months the possibility of establishing a pension scheme.

He pointed out that such things could not be carried out so easily in a small company as in a large one which had greater resources, but on the other hand, men in small companies had other advantages. They did not go far from home and they were more easily looked after. The directors were most anxious to meet the needs of the men in every possible way. A man coming to the NSR should feel that he could look to remaining with them for the rest of his life.

Salt then referred to a recent claim by the men for more pay, shorter hours and changes in conditions. It had been referred to departmental managers, but he felt it right to tell shareholders that as far as they had examined the claim, the cost would be at least £40,000, equal to a dividend of 1½ per cent. This would entirely alter the character of the undertaking and could be achieved only at very great cost.

If, however, the increases were quite clearly for the benefit of the men and if it was their duty to accede to them, they would do so, but there were two great difficulties in the way. There was no knowing that if they did give the men £40,000 tomorrow, they would not come back in twelve months and ask for the same thing. They had experience of this since it was only a year ago that, through their 'able managers', they met the men and gave them a substantial addition to their pay and the latter had said they were perfectly satisfied.

Salt feared that if the NSR increased wages they would revise the whole wage system for all local factories and do the greatest possible injury, not only to the district, but to the men themselves, because they would create a general rise in wages that would disturb and drive away a great deal of trade. Therefore, while they were perfectly willing to meet the men and were anxious to do the most they could for them, glad that they should get high wages as long as they were industrious and honest and doing well, there were larger considerations. What was the position of the men? They got good clothes, regular work and many other advantages. It was open to a railwayman to go away if he did not like the conditions. No one wanted or would compel him to stay, so there was no hardship in that matter.

Referring to hints of a national rail strike, the chairman said the workpeople of Britain, who were extremely able and intelligent (many were his personal friends), had their duties and responsibilities as citizens of 'this great country' just as much as shareholders or anybody else.

He felt a moral repugnance that a set of men employed in most responsible work—work necessary for the prosperity of the country—should say that they care for nothing and nobody and would throw everything into confusion on the mere chance of obtaining two shillings more a week, and say that there was nothing wrong in that. He was certain that they acknowledged justice as much as he could himself, but there was something more. Supposing that all the NSR people struck? If that happened, there was a very large number which they could replace at lower wages. The service could not be so bad since the general manager was inundated with applications for jobs. In a very short time and with very little management it was possible that they could replace the greater part of their men. He did not say that it would not be a great loss and inconvenience both to themselves and the public, but they were prepared to do their best for the district and work through for a time with less staff and facilities.

Salt then went on to consider what might happen if the men succeeded in what seemed a most immoral and unwise undertaking. If they did, they would injure the shareholders and those who managed the railway—but they would also damage themselves. 'If they destroy the railway, how will they get their wages?' asked Salt. After a strike some men might return, but the company could afford great loss and inconvenience. Some men would never come back and would suffer for the rest of their lives.

Relations were not quite as bad as they may have seemed for only a few months later—on 10 May—there was a happy and memorable social event at the North Stafford hotel at Stoke: a dinner for twenty-nine men who had joined the company in its earliest years: 1846-8.

The current unrest among the men led to a number of improvements in service, introduced from 1 January 1899. They included 'privileges' in time, wages, clothing, promotion and other fields. 'The majority of the men,' Salt told shareholders, 'are loyal, happy, content and proud of the company. However, among 4,000-5,000 men there will always be some who are difficult and discontent. Our duty is to be just and fair to all, but at the same time, to support the good element and look after the best workers.'

As a step towards that, the company tackled the problem of housing and built cottages at Sudbury and other places to let at moderate rates to workers who could not find cottages near their work, or who had to live in areas where rents were high. By grouping, the company had acquired 371 houses or cottages for the men and also owned what were termed '15 other houses or cottages'.

APPRENTICES

Among the most junior of the staff were the works apprentices. In the eighteen-nineties they served four and a half years as premium pupils getting a thorough grounding in the fitting, turning, erecting, pattern, moulding and copper shops and the smithy. Some spent a year in the drawing office. Afterwards the apprentices went to the running department, working as goods firemen or helping breakdown gangs. They were also involved with the operation of the mechanical tugs on the Trent & Mersey canal.

If their training was long, it was not always rigorous and a diary kept by a man who was apprenticed from September 1894 to February 1899 records that he was able to leave home at Shrewsbury on a Monday morning and he often returned on Friday afternoon. He and his colleagues also enjoyed odd half-day holidays and found plenty of time to enjoy evening dances and music halls at Stoke and other places. But in the final years of an apprenticeship, work was more demanding. Once they had completed it, not all stayed with the company. The diary writer later worked at a London screw factory and on Tyneside before taking over a cycle business.[2]

The board's paternalism towards workers was demonstrated on the outbreak of the Boer War. Twenty-six reservists were drafted for service in South Africa and there were fears that more men might have to go. They were told their jobs would be kept open and the company would meet their payments to the insurance scheme and also give a large donation to the widows' and children's society so that if any of the men died, their widows would be well looked after.

Several years later there was another kind of militancy for another reason: growing unrest over work. The men's attitude hardened first into unrest and finally into strikes. This was in the era of a new chairman, Tonman Mosley, who took over on the death of Sir Thomas Salt on 8 April 1904.

The chairmanship changed at a time of economy and on 12 July 1904 an investigation was ordered to see if locomotive running expenses could be reduced by cutting the working week of goods drivers, firemen and guards to five days. The following February, Mosley made his first statement about labour relations, saying he believed they had a good class of workmen in their shops. They wished to give them a chance of living comfortably and happily in their homes.

Reporting a wage rise two years later, Mosley commented that the directors did not grudge it to the men because they felt it had been well earned, but from a comparison with the previous half-year, it was obvious to the men themselves that shareholders had not been feeding greedily on the increased dividend during the same period. Wage expenses could not go on indefinitely since they were limited to the company's earning capacity. Investors had already been frightened away by the poor chance of getting good interest on railway stock.

Rejecting any moves for workers to share in management, Mosley said the board could not for a single instant allow any divided control in railway administration. The lives and property of the public were at stake, as well as the lives of the men themselves and the railways were expected to provide safeguards as much as possible.

Although their relations with employees had been satisfactory, they had not been without warnings of how easily these necessary provisions might have been prejudiced by the intrusion of other persons activated by motives other than the single one of safeguarding the public. However, they had great faith in the common sense and fairness of their men. Wages, said the chairman, were not everything. Shorter hours were not everything. Privileges, company contributions to the Friendly Society and provision for the sick and orphans and, above all, the permanency and honourable position of their employment, were all factors for careful consideration by the men. Moreover, the men knew that their complaints could be carried to the directors if they failed to get sufficient consideration from the superintendent and officers of departments.

By 1903 membership of the North Staffordshire Friendly Society, founded with only 29 members 16 years earlier, had grown to 2,132 and profits were being used to help elderly railwaymen who were unfit for work. In common with most companies, the NSR belonged to the Railway Clearing System Superannuation Fund Corporation, which got an Act on 20 July 1906 to increase contributions.

The NSR opened a savings bank on 1 March 1908, run by the accountant, J. F. A. Jones. A year later it had 3,448 savers. Two years later the board suggested that men who had put in a 'considerable amount of money' should have the opportunity of taking unissued stock at the normal price of the day, without having to pay brokers' expenses. This would give them the benefit of a price considered to be far below the actual value. He felt that if workmen took shares in the company, they would watch very closely to see their interests were well protected.

A RAILWAY ON STRIKE

For the Coronation of 1911, 'a small amount' was spent on illuminating the station yard at Stoke and the management repeated its gesture of the 1902 Coronation and gave the men a day's holiday with pay.

The action was not greatly appreciated for later in the year the men joined a national rail strike from 17-19 August—much to the surprise of Mosley, who later confessed that he had so much faith in them that he never anticipated their desertion. It occurred when he was away in Scotland and he was unable to get back during the few days the strike lasted, but other directors were on the spot to deal with the situation.

Mosley said he did not want to rake up the past, but that it was sufficient perhaps to leave the matter with the consciences of those who had left without warning in the face of a private contract and a management undertaking. It was better to turn to the brighter side and pay tribute to the loyalty of so many of the staff who in the face of great difficulties, stood by the company like men and did more than their share of work without fear or flinching. The company faced an uncertain future, which would be controlled, not by themselves, but by the larger ones which were forced into leadership by national strikes. Smaller companies, he stressed, must follow in their wake when they got drawn into the 'maelstrom of industrial war'. This happened a few weeks later in 1912 when trade and industry in the Potteries were disorganised by a strike which started on 1 March and continued until 15 April. It led to congestion in the marshalling yards, trapping many wagons belonging to other companies.

Notes are on page 296

CHAPTER SEVEN

War and Peace

MOBILISATION

Although 5 per cent dividend was not to be attained again until 1918, the Knotty remained a profitable line despite the demands made on it during the war years. The outbreak of war in August 1914 quickly evoked a national mood of 'it will all be over by Christmas' and amid this atmosphere, limited development went ahead, notably at Trentham, where the large bridge to carry the Newcastle and Silverdale Light Railway was rolled across the main London Road outside the station on 19 September. When the war did not end quickly, the national mood changed to patriotic fervour.

The first war time shareholders meeting on 27 February 1915 was held as 'The Old Contemptibles' were earning the gratitude of Britain on the Western Front, and the chairman remarked that one thing had been made evident. 'We are not an effete and degenerate race. There were many heroes, as of old time, on land and sea'. On the NSR they had not been backward, as 504 of the staff were serving with the colours.

As in the Boer War, the company showed generosity towards its fighting men guaranteeing them jobs on return at a wage or salary on a scale to which they would have been entitled had they stayed at work. Shareholders endorsed £2,500 a year being spent on 'suitable provision' for the wives, families and dependants of the men during their absence. The chairman reported that two men had been killed and a third badly wounded, although he had now returned to the railway.

On the home front the company had formed a drill and shooting corps and its 290 members were drilling six times a week and preparing to protect the vulnerable points of the

system. The company's .22 miniature rifle range at Stoke provided the volunteers with some of the best facilities that any railwaymen enjoyed.

During the first six months of war, the company carried some 70,000 men and 2,860 horses 'without a scratch' but traffic generally suffered because trade was hit by the 'remarkable' enlistment of men in the Potteries.

As the war lengthened there were other cuts, yet the company continued to advertise the attractions of Rudyard and the Manifold Valley, and these were included in a 1916 guide to a beauty spot much better known nationally, Windermere. (See previous page.)

Attempts were made to find oil in the Apedale Valley, only to be abandoned when volcanic ash was found at a depth of 4,000ft.

War or not, the shareholders wanted more trains and in February 1915, J. R. B. Mansfield complained that there were no Sunday morning trains to Cheadle and buses were giving a service which must be to the railway's detriment. Mosley replied that the company was under constant attack in the newspapers and elsewhere about Sunday trains. They could not start a fresh service unless a strong case was made for it.

BONUS PAY

The war caused a rise in the cost of living and a war bonus was introduced: 3s a week (or 6d a day) for men with basic pay over 30s; 2s for those earning under 30s a week and over the age of 18. The bonus was increased late in 1915 and again in 1917. By 1916 701 men had joined up, 1,876 had attested and 23 had been killed. By 1917 859 men had enlisted, 47 had been killed and 50 wounded.

The NSR operated its share of ambulance trains bringing home the wounded from France. Twenty-one were handled at Stoke in 1916, each carrying up to 200 men and generally the trains were cleared in less than an hour. Between November 1916 and mid-February 1917, 60 ambulance trains, loaded and empty, ran via Stoke to Manchester and Yorkshire. During the whole of 1917 Stoke dealt with 25 trains carrying 3,215 wounded.

NORTH STAFFORDSHIRE RAILWAY.

CHRISTMAS HOLIDAYS.

DISCONTINUANCE OF TRAINS.

On CHRISTMAS DAY Trains will run as on SUNDAYS.

TRAINS and CARS will be DISCONTINUED as under :

5 17 p.m. Stone to Aston	Thursday, December 24th.
6 5 p.m. Aston to Stoke	
9 47 p.m. Keele to Stoke	
7 0 a.m. Stoke to Colwich	Saturday Dec. 26th.
8 24 .am. Colwich to Stoke	
7 15 a.m. Crewe to Derby	
7 20, 8 0 and 10 12 a.m. Leek to Stoke	
7 42 a.m. Burton to Tutbury	
7 55 a.m. Macclesfield to Stoke	
7 53 a.m. Stoke to Newcastle	
8 10 a.m. Newcastle to Stoke	
8 18 a.m. Tutbury to Burton	
8 25 a.m. Rushton to Leek	
9 10 a.m. Stoke to Tunstall	
11 33 a.m. Stoke to Macclesfield	
2 5 p.m. Derby to Crewe	
2 5 p.m. Macclesfield to Stoke	
8 20 p.m. Crewe to Stoke	
7 30 p.m. Stoke to Leek	
5 5 a.m. Tunstall to Blythe Bridge	Saturday, Monday and Tuesday, Dec. 26th, 28th and 29th.
5 15 and 7 5 a.m. Cresswell to Stoke	
5 45 a.m. Stoke to Normacot	
5 50 a.m. Stoke to Tunstall	
5 55 a.m. Blythe Bridge to Tunstall	
6 20 a.m. Normacot to Stoke	
6 22 and 6 45 a.m. Tunstall to Stoke	
6 30 a.m. Stoke to Cresswell	
5 30 and 6 20 a.m. Stoke to Newcastle	
5 40 and 6 50 a.m. Newcastle to Stoke	
8 51 and 9 50 a.m. Stoke to Newcastle	
9 3 and 10 0 a.m. Newcastle to Stoke	
7 23 a.m & 2 45 p.m. Stoke to Trentham Park	
7 50 a.m. Trentham Park to Trentham	
8 10 a.m. Trentham to Trentham Park	
6 0 a.m. Aston to Stoke	
8 29 a.m. & 3 11 p.m. Trentham Park to Stoke	
8 36 a.m. Cheadle to Cresswell	
8 55 a.m. Cresswell to Cheadle	
6 25 a.m. Ashbourne to Uttoxeter	
8 5 a.m. Uttoxeter to Ashbourne	
9 35 a.m. Alsager to Stoke	
2 5 p.m. Blythe Bridge to Normacot	Monday & Tuesday, Dec. 28th & 29th.
4 15 p.m. Blythe Bridge to Cheadle	
5 11 p.m. Cheadle to Cresswell	
5 21 p.m. Harecastle to Alsager	
4 55 a.m. Stoke to Leycett	Saturday, Dec. 26th and Friday, and Saturday, January 1st and 2nd.
5 50 a.m. Leycett to Newcastle	
6 33 a.m. Newcastle to Stoke	
8 0 a.m. Congleton to Manchester	SATURDAY, DEC. 26th & FRIDAY, JAN. 1st

Railway Offices, Stoke Station.
December, 1914.

W. D. PHILLIPPS, General Manager.

SHERWIN & Co. Hanley Ltd, Foundry Street Printing Works, Hanley.

The first Christmas of war, 1914

This was the year in which 54 officers and men of the NSR returned home from France after building railways near Abbeville under the direction of the Royal Engineers' Railway Operating Division.

Besides its donations to the North Staffordshire Infirmary, the board encouraged medical work by supporting the St. John Ambulance Brigade and by 1917 the NSR Ambulance Corps had five divisions of about 300 fully qualified men. In a year they handled 250 cases of minor injury on the line. Spare land at the track-side was turned into allotments and prizes given for the best produce. Guns were carried over the Ashbourne branch for testing on the moors.

From the start of 1917—the year in which the U boats were to bring Britain near to starvation—the national war effort increased and Lord Anslow said in February that they had cleared the lines to handle more traffic. Free running over the railways was required for winning the war and all unnecessary travel had to be abandoned. Since January, 20 per cent of passenger trains had been stopped at the government's request and an increase in fares had reduced passengers considerably. At the same time there was a 'very remarkable increase' in workmen's tickets. The chairman lamented that they could not get back the good LNWR service because they had to yield to war necessity.

Reducing passenger mileage also enabled extra coal trains to be run to the ports and other places and made rolling stock available for common use—earlier the company had loaned 20 carriages for government use.

ENGINEERING WORK

With trains and loads getting heavier, the benefit was being felt of relaying work using 90lb steel rails under a programme aimed at completing 21 miles a year. It was frustrated by delays and shortage of materials and men and in 1915 only 13½ miles was relaid followed by 10 miles in 1916 and 5⅛ miles in 1918. In 1918, 6⅓ miles were re-sleepered, ⅝ mile of sidings relaid and ½ mile of siding moved.

Five track circuit telephone systems were completed in 1916 and in 1917 electric shunting was introduced at Oakamoor copper works with the now-famous battery shunting locomotive. The chairman pointed out that it had released three horses for other work! Sidings at North Rode were extended in 1917 and £1,700 spent on increasing accommodation at Etruria. Improvements were also made at the Caldon quarries and more crushers and cleaners were provided to meet an ever-rising demand for limestone. Two lorries were also bought for quarry work in 1917.

Workshops were kept busy with government work but some locomotive and wagon building continued and by the beginning of 1918 the NSR had repaired 1,343 wagons, irrespective of ownership. All companies were now pooling wagons under a scheme that divided them into 12 groups, each led by a big company. The NSR was grouped into No. 7, headed by the LNWR and also including the Cambrian, Furness and Wirral Railways.

By 1917 147 women were employed as clerks, ticket collectors or on other jobs. Lord Anslow, as Tonman Mosley had become in June 1916, said the women had similar capabilities and talents as the men. Eventually the number of women employed rose to 216, three times the pre-war figure of 71, and the chairman said in 1918 that 'some of the females were even working on munitions and their output was approximately that of the men'.

In 1917 three factors combined to cause a drop of £1,011 in revenue of the company's hotels and refreshment rooms: a big increase in taxation, high prices and a reduction in visitors.

In 1917 dividend remained at the level of the two previous years: 4⅝ per cent, the chairman commenting that it was not exorbitant, and not one that anybody could be jealous of in ordinary commercial practice.

The autumn of 1918 brought the demise of two of the halts built for the rail motor service in 1905: Whieldon Road and Mount Pleasant, both closing on 30 September.

Less than a fortnight before the Armistice there was a serious collapse in Cheadle Tunnel when on 3-4 November 1918, the brick lining gave way because, it was claimed, of imperfect packing during construction. Four hundred feet of roof fell in and left a cavity of between 6ft and 25ft. After emergency repairs coal trains resumed using the tunnel on 9 November, although passenger trains did not run through until 3 December. Reconstruction work, described as very dangerous, involved strengthening the whole tunnel with a concrete ring a foot thick. Heavy wartime traffic caused a great deal of trouble in the tunnels and both Harecastle and Keele had to be relined.

INQUIRY: A SECOND BATTLE

The World War was not the only one in which the Knotty was engaged. In 1917 a sudden volume of agitation grew against everything the company did—or did not do. It was stimulated by an articulate pressure group and it got the Borough of Stoke to complain of inadequate facilities provided by the NSR and its rates. Charges grew so serious that in 1918, even though Europe was still locked in bitter struggle, a public inquiry was ordered and presided over by a King's Counsel, Mr Rowland Whitehead. The evidence he heard for three days —23-25 October—was confined to that of the critics, for the Knotty was legally advised not to take part after being refused advance information about the case against it. The critics' main contention was that traffic rates were too high and connections with trains of other companies were poor. They damned the company sufficiently in the Inquiry's eyes for it to be recommended in its report of 6 December that the NSR should be either nationalised or absorbed by one of its neighbours.

The Company later answered its critics in a considered reply. Rates, it pointed out, were much below the maximum it could charge, and it was doing a lot beyond its statutory obligations, both in its own interest and those of its customers. Other companies—and it cited the LNWR—had powers to charge more for such traffic as minerals. Rates for through-hauled iron traffic were below those of several companies. Pottery and earthenware traffic was fragile and bulky and not economic. Since 1914 every industry in Britain had increased charges by 75-100 per cent except the railways—which were expected to reduce theirs. Connections were often difficult, especially when they might involve the trains of several companies and had to be worked out on the basis of a service compulsorily halved by war conditions.

The NSR directors believed their case was sound. Lord Anslow revealed something of the tactics used by the critics when he spoke to shareholders on 21 February 1919. He said that for about a year before the inquiry there had been agitation which had worked up to something like fever heat.

> The company have for a long time been abused by a few cantankerous individuals whom nothing we did could please, but we could afford to leave them to their grumbles. When, however, advantage was taken by the more influential critics of a Government Committee to make a number of statements prejudicial to the Company behind our backs, we felt that the time had come when we should defend ourselves.

The board felt the railway had served the district well and encouraged the development of industry. The chairman went on to say:

> During the 27 years of my directorship no railway company has opened its mouth to eat us up and naturally we have not jumped down their throats. We are closely connected with the Midland, the LNWR, the GNR, the GWR and GCR railways and I question whether any bill for our absorption would not have been bitterly opposed in Parliament by the others. I venture to question also whether the district would benefit by our disappearance from it, and the headquarters of the NSR were removed to London.

The main recommendation of the inquiry was not implemented mainly because railway amalgamation was in the air nationally and when shareholders met on 18 February 1920 Anslow stressed the importance of what he termed the 'minor' companies getting together to watch that their interests were not swamped or absorbed by those of the larger companies.

DEVELOPMENT PLANS

Whatever the Stoke civic authorities thought of the Knotty, it had no doubts of its own value and almost up to the end, even when amalgamation was becoming a certainty, it remained progressive and in 1920 started the construction of a new power plant and lighting at Stoke.

More important were moves taken to remove the traffic bottleneck at Stoke by an ambitious scheme for which it got Parliamentary powers on 19 August 1921. The aim was to ease congestion in the 2 mile core of the system around Hanley, Etruria and Newcastle Junction, through which most trains, including those of the Loop, had to pass.

Mineral trains from the Pinnox and Grange branches and the Loop line, which all lay east of the main line, were to cross it to reach the goods lines west of Stoke station. The goods loop was to leave the loop line near Shelton, cross the main line and continue in a tunnel (not more than 25ft deep), under a ridge to the west passing under the Newcastle branch and joining the main line a little south of the T & M Canal bridge.

The Act provided for the goods lines to be built as two railways (the second being a feeder to the goods loop from Grange Junction) totalling 1¾ miles. It also authorised a ½ mile diversion of the Ashbourne branch starting 3 miles north of Rocester Junction. Consent was given for two economies: abandoning the unconstructed part of the Trentham—Newcastle Light Railway and also dispensing with the Newcastle Canal.

New up and down marshalling yards were planned between Newcastle Junction and Stoke, to replace the Stoke yard and allow the widening of Stoke station to provide four through platforms and bays and a new west entrance and subway giving direct access to the city. A 60ft locomotive turntable, built during the war and stored, was to be installed on a site cleared of houses.

The plan was regarded as long term which would ultimately allow London—Manchester expresses to take the fast line at the junction north of Grange, while Crewe—Derby trains would be diverted on to the slow line. Loop trains would also be kept off the main line. Expresses from London would be able to run into Stoke station without interfering with the Derby—Crewe and the Leek services. Local trains would use the north and south bays.

The Act also gave the NSR authority to meet one need of a

Page 155 *Stoke works in 1895:* (above) *the rail entrance under the main line on which stands a class 9 2–4–0T, a class 'C' 2–4–0 and a row of dumb-buffered loco coal wagons;* (below) *the interior of the locomotive erecting shop with a class 'D' 0–6–0T in the foreground*

Page 156 *Three stages in the building of No 100 at Stoke in 1896 with the newly finished engine posing outside the roundhouse*

world of changing social behaviour, the prevention of crime, by enrolling officers as special constables to protect company property. The company encouraged sport by purchasing the Staffordshire Cricket Ground. near Stoke station in 1920, and forming an Amateur Athletic Association the following year, which was soon to have 576 members.

To try and increase passenger traffic on the Biddulph branch a halt was opened at Mossley in October 1919, but since it was not mentioned in all timetables, it made little impression on passenger figures.

Beside expansion there was contraction here and there, the most notable and, for many, the saddest being the closure on 25 March 1920 of the oldest route of all—the Caldon Low cable inclines. Quarry traffic was switched to the branch through Waterhouses.

As life got slowly back to normal after the war, the Knotty again demonstrated its initiative in attracting passengers, claiming in summer 1920 to be one of the first companies to restore excursions. In a sense it was a worthless gesture for many of the excursions ran at a loss because of the rising cost of living generally, and more specifically, a national rise in rail fares from 6 August.

Industrial unrest continued and traffic was reduced by a national coal strike which affected the Potteries from 18 October to 8 November.

This was still the heyday of coal and in a single week in February 1922, 42,414 tons were sent via other systems—the highest comparable tonnage since August 1917.

The early post-war years brought a decline in passenger traffic, but they began well enough for in 1919 2,500,000 more passengers were carried than the 1913 total of 8,525,419. By 1921 the overall total had slumped, although it remained above ten million (10,142,438). By 1922 it was down to 9,646,579.

The continual growth in road transport was reflected in changed policy and operation. Plans for using buses as feeder services did not develop, but there was a modest expansion in the fleet of motor vans carrying goods and parcels. In 1909 the company had just three, but the final fleet in 1922 totalled 32. There were also 291 carts and road wagons—an increase of over 70 on pre-war days. They were pulled by 181 horses and another six were kept for shunting—six fewer than in 1909.

Another form of rail transport was also used; velocipedes being kept at Endon and Norbury around 1920 for staff to get quickly to the scene of an accident or a breakdown.

Not that accidents were expected, for right up to grouping the company was investigating ways of improving safety and was experimenting with automatic train control, the SYX system being fitted to tank no 39.

GROUPING

The last shareholders' meeting—the 144th—came just after grouping, on 28 February 1923, when the final dividend was 5 per cent for the fifth consecutive year. Lord Anslow felt the deal with the LMS was satisfactory. He pointed out that while the 5 per cent ordinary stock only entitled holders to £71 8s 6d they had obtained £74 and that was likely to increase.

Major Wedgwood joined the LMS board as the NSR became part of its Western Group, while other directors got £14,600 for loss of office and the two auditors, £250.

Many of the younger staff joined the LMS. Some were destined to occupy senior posts, among them George Ivatt, always known as 'the major' in Stoke works. It is likely that at Stoke he would have succeeded Hookham, to whom he was finally chief assistant, but through grouping had to wait some years before becoming a chief mechanical engineer. The chief draughtsman in Knotty days was a Glasgow man, Sinclair, who had moved from the North British works. One of his predecessors had been a Rotherham man, J. W. Hartley, who left to start his own engineering works (later owned by Kerr Stuart) at Etruria. One of Hartley's sidelines was making castings for the NSR which did not have its own foundry.

A trend that was just becoming obvious before grouping, and was to become accentuated afterwards, was in the decline in the number of staff. The total fell from 6,577 on 21 March to 6,360 a year later.

ANALYSIS: THE FINAL YEARS

A broad picture of the company's progress and fortunes in

the twentieth century up to grouping can be gauged by a comparison of statistics for three representative years: 1907; the peak year 1913, and the last year of independence, 1922.

A marked feature was a large growth in passengers from the 1907 figure of just under seven million (6,934,536). By 1913 that total had been exceeded by third class tickets alone (7,069,532), and supplemented by over two million workmen's tickets (2,084,777). First class travellers were comparatively few: 102,709. At grouping the Knotty was among only 24 companies carrying over ten million passengers annually. Of the total of 10,289,013, the vast majority, 9,646,579, originated on the system. The bulk were third class: 6,074,617, followed by workmen, 4,107,560 and, far, far behind, first class—106,836. A wide gap also remained in 1922 between first and third season ticket holders, third class 4,108; first 934.

By grouping, rail motor mileage had fallen sharply and in 1922 the three remaining ones of the NSR (one of the few companies still using them) covered only 32,129 miles—over 20,000 miles less than the fleet had run in 1913: 54,237.

By 1922 passenger train miles had increased to 1,669,479, 105,000 more than in 1907 and 94,000 above those of 1913.

The early years of the century brought decline to both the coal and mineral industries of North Staffordshire and consequently in the tonnage of rail traffic. One reason was the discovery of iron ore in Northamptonshire which was easier and much cheaper to mine than that in North Staffordshire, notably in the Silverdale area. Local mines could not compete in price with this or with cheap varieties imported from Sweden, Spain and West Africa. In 1913 the Knotty carried nearly 4,000,000 tons of coal, coke and patent fuels and just over 2,000,000 tons of other minerals. In 1922 it carried 80,000 tons less coal, and well over 200,000 tons less of other minerals. These reductions were accompanied by sharp drops in goods and mineral mileage—1,066,812 miles against 1,505,557 in 1907 and 1,359,104 in 1913.

In freight ratings the Knotty was one of the 19 British companies handling over 1,000,000 tons a year at grouping. Almost all the coal, coke and patent fuel carried originated on the system, the 1922 total being 3,602,911 tons out of 3,841,194. Yet only about one-third of merchandise traffic did so—573,755 tons out of the total traffic of 1,712,354 tons.

Of other minerals, totalling 1,789,730 tons, 970,490 tons originated locally. Altogether this accounted for 5,147,156 tons out of the year's total of 7,343,278. In addition there was livestock traffic—181,262 head (83,766 of local origin).

ABSTRACT OF STATISTICS

Capital Paid Up	1907	1913	1922
Loans & Debenture	2,893,105	2,845,990	As
Preference Stock	4,252,483	4,487,483	for
Ordinary Stock	3,594,650	3,594,650	1913
Total	10,740,238	10,928,123	
No of shareholders	6,500	7,925	
Capital expenditure during year	53,710	12,719	19,095
Total capital expenditure to date	8,973,909	9,081,696	9,221,629
Receipts			
Passenger, parcels, mail	273,631	292,904	547,296
Goods, minerals, livestock	646,524	723,288	1,340,232
Other receipts	100,282	25,571	54,039
Joint lines	–	17,215	29,257
Total	1,020,437	1,058,978	1,970,824
Expenditure			
Maintenance and renewal of track	110,092	115,330	334,017
Locomotive running expenses	153,371	121,155	317,709
Carriage and wagon repairs	49,675	129,926	246,680
Traffic expenses	150,795	202,694	561,024
General charges	43,338	23,329	85,208
Rates and taxes	35,230	37,614	*65,668
Other charges	82,181	–	–
National Insurance Act	–	3,399	10,669
Running powers (balance)	–	1,181	12,212

* includes Government duty.

	1907	1913	1922
Joint Lines	–	13,132	32,647
Miscellaneous	–	12,946	2,777
Total expenditure	624,682	660,706	1,668,611
Dividend: ordinary	$4\frac{3}{8}$%	5%	5%

Rolling Stock &c totals for 31 December 1922

Locomotives, steam	197
Locomotives, battery electric	1
Rail motor-cars, steam	3
Passenger coaches, bogie	133
Passenger coaches, 4 and 6 wheeled	212
Other coaching stock	193
Goods brake vans	127
Other goods stock	6,128
Service stock	364
Road motors, goods and parcels	32
Horse wagons and carts	291
Horses for road vehicles	181
Horses for shunting	6
Route mileage owned	$203\frac{1}{2}$
Route mileage jointly owned	12
Route mileage leased and worked	$12\frac{1}{4}$
Route mileage of canals owned	119

(Caldon quarry wagons not included)

CHAPTER EIGHT

Working the Line

> The efficiency of the men on the Knotty was proved by the fact . . . I think we can boast, that we never had a major disaster. *Frank Oakes—Traffic*

COSTS: RUNNING AND RISING

The most notable feature of early operation was the working of the line for no less than the first ten years by a contractor: Joseph Wright of Saltney Carriage Works, Birmingham, who was also working other railways during this period. The contract, which ran to 30 June 1859 was subject to a month's notice, and, at first, included the maintenance of the permanent way.

Hire charges were on a sliding scale designed to meet any rises in operating costs. Mileage rates suggested by Wright in 1850 were: engines—1½d (10 shillings on days they did not run); first class coaches: one-sixth of a penny; second class: one-eighth; third: one-tenth. Wagons: one-twelfth.

The company seemed content for Ricardo said on 30 January 1850 that he had investigated similar costs on other lines and felt the NSR was paying as little, if not less, than any other company in the United Kingdom.

By 1853 passenger locomotive mileage was calculated at thirteen pence a mile and other charges were: goods locomotive capable of 18mph, 14½d; capable of 12mph, 13½d. There had been a slight rise too in carriage hire. The company accepted increases philosophically, as when an increase in traffic expenditure was reported in 1855. This was considered 'not unreasonable having regard to development, and the enhanced price of labour and materials'.

Wright was given a fair say in improvements he thought necessary as traffic developed, including the building of a smithy at Stoke. It was sanctioned on 18 May 1853, provided it did not cost over £300 and Wright paid 6 per cent a year interest. He was not so successful in his request for a stationary engine at Stoke, which was rejected by the NSR board.

When Wright's contract expired the company took over operation and the decision was influenced by closer ties being established with the LNWR, which had already taken over maintenance of the NSR permanent way.

Knotty safety regulations were based on LNWR practice from the earliest days. A well run railway was the product of strict discipline in Victorian eyes and there was plenty of that on the Knotty. The management used all the majesty of the language in vogue in those days of pomp to frame safety regulations. The basic ones were grouped under the ambiguous heading of Special General Regulations. There were seventeen of which the first laid down:

> The first and most important duty of all the Company's officers and servants is to PROVIDE FOR THE PUBLIC SAFETY; to prevent any obstruction on the main line which can be avoided, and to remove it instantly should it occur; to take special care at all times, that the signals are properly worked to protect running trains, and trains standing at their stations, and that they are shown for sufficient time to warn all parties of the obstruction *before* any engine, carriage, waggon, truck, horse-box, or other vehicle is placed on, or crossed over the main line.

EARLY SIGNALLING

LNWR signalling practice was closely followed through the use by the NSR of lamp signals, semaphores (with arms, explained the 1865 rulebook); detonating or explosive signals and fusee signals. Red was for danger; green for caution and white for clear. These indications were made by flags in daylight and by lamps at night or during fog.

In addition, stated rule 22:

> A hat, cap or arms or any other object WAVED violently by a person on the line denotes danger and the necessity of stopping immediately.

Caution Go slow,

25. If it be necessary to proceed with Caution from any defect in the Rails, another Train having passed within five minutes, or from any other cause, the Green Flag, will be elevated, thus—

Stop.

26. If required to stop, the RED Flag will be shown, and waved to and fro, the Signalman facing the Engine.

Stop.

27. Engine Drivers must always STOP on seeing the Red Signal.

Withdrawal of signal.

28. As soon as the Engine passes, the Signalman will bring his flag to the shoulder.

Signals to be in good order.

29. Every Servant of the Company will be responsible for having his Signals in good order.

HAND SIGNALS.

Hand Signals.

30. In case of any Servant of the Company being accidentally without flags, the following Signals must be given:—

Hand signal for caution.

31. CAUTION, OR SLOW.—One Arm held up as high as possible, the Man facing the Train, thus—

Hand signal to stop.

32. DANGER, OR STOP!—Both Arms held up as high as possible, the Man facing the Train, thus—

Two pages from the 1865 rule book

SIGNALS.

NIGHT.

33. Every Servant of the Company will be held responsible for having his LAMPS in good order and properly trimmed. The Lamps, both Signal and Hand, must be lighted by Sunset and during Foggy Weather.

Responsibility of servants for good condition of lamps.

34 The Signal ALL RIGHT is shown by a steady WHITE light.

All right signal.

35. The CAUTION Signal, to PROCEED SLOWLY, is shown by a steady GREEN light.

Caution signal.

36. The DANGER Signal, ALWAYS TO STOP, is shown by a RED light, or in cases of emergency, by WAVING ANY LAMP VIOLENTLY.

Danger signal.

LINE AND TRAIN SIGNALS.

37. DESCRIPTION AND PURPOSE OF SIGNALS IN USE, VIZ.:—

LAMPS with RED, GREEN, or WHITE LIGHTS.
POST, or SEMAPHORE SIGNALS, with ARMS.
FLAGS—RED, GREEN, or WHITE.
DETONATING OR EXPLOSIVE SIGNALS.
FUSEE SIGNALS.

SEMAPHORE SIGNALS.

DAY.

38. These Signals are constructed to show either One or Two Arms.

Day Semaphore signals.

A driver got the line clear signal in daylight from a policeman, gateman or signalman standing erect and holding his flags, but not making any signal with them. Another rule bearing the LNWR stamp was the waving of a red flag to and fro to stop a train. While the NSR laid down that the *signalman* was to face the engine, the LNWR held this was the job of the *policeman*.

Detonators were used in conjunction with flags—pretty liberally it would seem judging by the number of people to whom they were issued: guards, under-guards, police, switchmen, engine and gatemen, foremen of works, gangers, platelayers and tunnelmen. Each station master or clerk in charge of a station, was to carry a stock of at least 20 detonators. The detonators were to be kept:

> in an unlocked drawer or shelf in the counter in order that they may at all times be easy of access to all on duty at the station; and every person connected with the Station shall be made acquainted with the place where they are deposited.

Fusee signals, used to signify caution, were lighted and fixed between the rails. Stations and sidings had Auxiliary or Distance signals worked by wires and placed at 'a considerable distance in advance of' station signal posts. A driver finding a distance signal 'on' had to stop at the post and *immediately* draw slowly up to the station or junction ahead so as to get within the protection of the distance signal.

A signalman who saw two trains approaching a junction on different lines had to keep his signals at danger to both and let neither pass until he was satisfied that no collision could possibly occur. There are no recorded instances of how signalmen interpreted this rule but they must have needed a strong faith in early locomotive brakes not to enforce it absolutely.

Under such conditions speed restrictions were naturally severe. Special passenger trains were limited to 25mph, goods and ballast trains and light engines to 20mph 'without distinct orders to the contrary'.

Although the telegraph was in limited use from early days, its extension to all but the busiest lines was slow.

Passenger trains, despite their priority, were often slow,

especially those on lines where a 5min interval system was in operation. Staff and ticket was the first improvement towards branch operating, but here again, its introduction was slow and even on lines which did use it, 5min intervals had to be observed between trains.

SNOW AND FOG HAZARDS

In such smoky industrial areas as the Potteries, fog was often dense in autumn and winter and among many fog regulations were those which prohibited ballast trains from all lines, except in special circumstances. If fog came down unexpectedly, ballast trains had to go to the nearest siding. They had to stay there until it cleared. In fog permissive block working was changed to absolute.

More serious, although more rare, were periods of heavy snow. One of the earliest known instances of trouble was on 4 January 1854 when nine engines were used to charge a drift which trapped a Manchester train at Harecastle. One snow precaution involved guards of trains stopped out of course walking back 1,000yd, instead of the customary 800yd to set detonators. This was because detonators were liable to be swept off the rails by brooms attached to snow-clearing engines.

Dangers caused by rain and sparks often meant extra work for goods guards. They had to refuse to take wagons if a spark or hot cinder was likely to set them on fire unless completely sheeted. If any train was unable to move at more than 6mph, the guard, fireman or other person, had to be sent back 800yd and follow it at that distance.

Goods, mineral, cattle or ballast trains had to shunt at least ten minutes before a passenger train was scheduled to overtake them, and wait until five minutes after its passing before regaining the main line, or until a 'line clear' signal had been telegraphed from the next station. Main lines at stations had to be kept clear for passenger trains, if possible for ten minutes in advance. The general rule that gave passenger trains precedence could be used with discretion on lines with telegraphs, but station masters had to tell passenger drivers how many minutes a goods had left ahead of them.

If an accident or obstruction caused single line working, a

pilot engine was to be used at once and if there was not one handy, an engine was to be taken off a goods or coal train. If that was not possible, a pilotman was to be appointed locally. Pilot working was one of the few instances in which locomotives were allowed to run 'tender foremost'. The only other times when this was to be done was on special orders from the resident engineer or in 'unavoidable circumstances'. Locomotives were not to push trains except on Longton, Biddulph and Macclesfield banks. If an engine broke down it could be pushed to the nearest shunt at not more than 6mph.

No engine was allowed to cross from one line to another without the consent of a signalman during daylight. At night the fireman or guard had to exhibit danger signs if a train was crossing at a place where a night man was not on duty.

Locomotives were not the exclusive motive power: there were horses, too, and it was laid down that:

> No horses shall be used upon the Railway except those which have become accustomed to the sight and noise of Locomotive Engines, and which will allow an Engine and Train to meet and pass them without shying or being frightened . . . No 'Horse Run' shall be at work during the approach of a train.

Guards were forbidden to pass over carriage roofs while trains were in motion 'without urgent necessity'. Equipment for passenger guards consisted of: a timepiece, red and green flags, hand signal lamp, a box of 24 detonating signals, 12 fusee signals, whistle, 'a good supply' of shackles, two or more screw couplings, 2 sprags, box of matches, a box of grease, side lamps and a tail lamp, a working timetable. Goods guards had also to have with them, a tail rope, bucket and 'a good supply' of coupling chains and sprags.

The LNWR influenced time keeping down to the basic rule:

> The Clocks at all Stations are regulated by the time kept on the London & North Western Railway.

The guard of the first stopping train from 'headquarters' had to inform all station masters of the correct time every morning 'on application'. If there were two guards on a train from

Stoke, the man to be consulted was the one in the last van. Guards were told to report all stations whose time was wrong, and they faced a fine of not less than a day's pay if their own watch was wrong, or if they did not give station masters the time when asked. After two days:

> No fault of the Timepiece will be admitted as an excuse for continued irregularity and incorrectness.

Station rules laid down:

> The station master, porter, or other person on duty at a station must, on the arrival of a train, walk the length of the train, and call out in a clear and audible voice the name of that station when *opposite the window of each carriage*, so as to make every passenger in the train aware of the name of the station.

It is not related how efficiently such rules were observed in the case of Parliamentary trains, allowed only 2min at stations like Stoke.

HEAD CODES

Stopping passenger trains, 'ordinary' in the company designation, carried a white light on the front buffer: side not stipulated; except locals for Stafford, which carried two white lights. Goods and cattle head codes were the same: a single green light. Two green lights were carried by LNWR trains working over the NSR. The procedure for specials involved the train ahead carrying a board or flag at the rear of the last carriage and an extra red light at night.

The near side doors of passenger trains running to Stafford had to be locked before they left Stone. This was a variation of the normal rule that off-side carriage doors were always kept locked.

LATER IMPROVEMENTS

Rules changed as signalling improved, although progress was often slow: it was not until 1863 that block working was introduced. In 1880 £12,000 was spent on modernising the

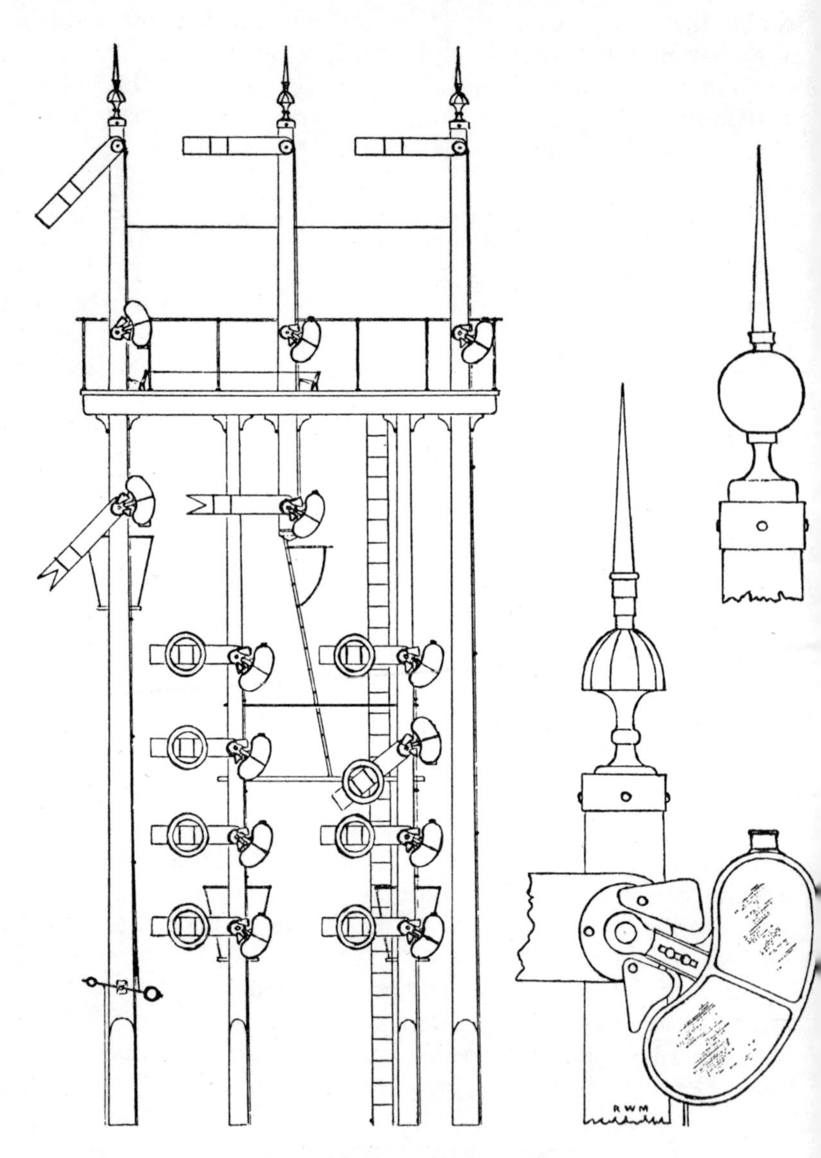

NSR signals: the up gantry at Stoke Junction, with details of the standard spectacle mounting, the older fluted umbrella and spike finial, and the later ball and spike finial

junction of the Audley line, then one of the busiest on the system. Work 'to prevent any accident to main line trains' took six months.

While the Knotty co-operated with the LNWR, it did not join in efforts made by a number of companies in 1884 to introduce standard block telegraph signalling, and neither the NSR or LNWR supported attempts by the GWR to have a standard code of abbreviations for operating telegrams.

One of the most famous Knotty signals was the 'Y' swing over at High Carr on the Talke branch, which has been much illustrated. Yet anyone who regards such a design (common enough on railways in Victorian days) as in any way symbolic of Knotty signalling practice, would be gravely mistaken for the system was signalled efficiently.

Despite its close affinities with the LNWR, the NSR signalling practice was different in several respects. Like the Furness Railway, the NSR used Tyer's one-wire three-position combined block instruments, with bold pointers giving the unusual indications. The commutator was below and the bell plunger in the commutator knob centre, as on Tyer's tablet instruments. The three indications—line clear, train on line, and, in the centre the normal position, line blocked—were obtained by a variation in the strength of the current, hence the single wire. Other railways including the LNWR used three position needles and so needed three wires between boxes, one for the indicator for each direction, and one for the bell.

One observer was critical of Knotty practice. He contended that when the same indication served for line clear and neutral, it provided no check on the signalman's memory and made him dependent on his train book—and it was not difficult to omit an entry. Many of the interlocking frames in boxes survived well into nationalisation.

To reduce delays at crossings, electrical warning bells were set off by an approaching train depressing a rail contact. But there were snags:

> To the cyclist who happens to be on the road after closing time —and gatekeepers generally roost early—this is cold comfort. Either he must turn himself into a travelling crane or risk the wrath of an official in his nightshirt. Cannot some genius invent

a by-pass gate which will allow a cycle to be manoeuvred through without having to hoist it over a couple of 7ft gates?

Walker was not too happy about the strength of signal lamps. Some were almost equalled in brilliance, he observed, by the glow worms on the railway embankments.

Signals were contracted by McKenzie & Holland and many had their characteristic tall, slender posts, completed by finials. Usually they were on a ball raised from the top of the signalpost by a short rod, but some had the finials over an umbrella or mushroom top to the post.

Home and distant arms were 10in wide and extended 4ft 9in from the pivot in the centre-line of the post. They dropped quite steeply to about 60 degrees when pulled off. Distants, although having the usual fish-tail end, had a straight white stripe over the red arm (black over white on the back), as on home signals. Goods and slow line signals had a ring, about 2ft 0in in diameter, around the white stripe. The rings were red (white at back) and midway along 4ft 9in arms, but subsidiary lines were protected by shorter arms of 4ft 0in with the rings 9in nearer the ends. Siding signals had short arms without stripes and only 3ft 0in long, some for shunting having a cut-out 'S' mounted near the end, about 1ft 6in high. Backing signals consisted of a cut-out 'B'. This was 3ft 4in high and 2ft 0in wide. It was mounted on a post with the lamp on top, which revolved through 90 degrees. Ground discs similarly revolved. They consisted of a ring with the lamp in the centre. Calling-on arms were a slim 6in wide and 7ft 6in long, pivoted well to the right of the post.

In early days a second distant with the shorter 4ft 0in arm was used, mounted above the normal distant. The practice of mounting more than one arm on a single post was common and some curious combinations resulted. Also used in early days were point indicators, a few of which survived to grouping. They had a vertical arm inside a slotted frame mounted on top of the post and able to tilt either left or right according to how the facing point was set. Signal posts were painted white, except for the bottom 2ft or 3ft and ornamental tops which were red.

In the years immediately before grouping, signals at Stoke

and Uttoxeter were electrically lit—yet the LMS converted those at Uttoxeter back to oil!

Level crossing gate equipment was fairly standard but some innovations were tried, including a route indicator at Bromshall Junction to show whether trains were bound for NSR or GNR lines. The tallest of NSR signals (there was a notable one at Caldon Junction) had repeater home, but not distant, arms: a practice sometimes used on the LNWR.

Two unusual NSR practices were levers set in frames so as to allow them to be pulled according to the state of tension on the wire, and levers which fell into normal position after locking facing points: the reverse of normal.

Important changes in Victorian days included the adoption of green for the 'all right' signal in 1883, and the alteration of the colour of signal back-lights from green to white, agreed on 7 November 1899. The use of Duplex fog signals was authorised on 12 November 1895 and in later days, Clayton Hand Fogging Machines were used to place detonators on the track at busy junctions.

While the company was content to fall into line with others on matters like signalling, it maintained individualism elsewhere as in distinctive signal boxes with steeply-sloping roofs and heavy overhanging eaves. Box names were on cast metal plates attached to the front of them. The largest box, Stoke, had 51 levers controlling 33 signals and 20 points.

The Knotty was proud of its safety record and in 1887 the chairman boasted that there was no other line in the Kingdom with so many junctions and difficult gradients that was worked so safely. He defended slow speeds by emphasising that trains had to make frequent stops. As they were to be obliged ultimately to use self-acting brakes and new signalling apparatus, they had taken time by the forelock and had already got a system which was nearly complete.

The NSR position as a small company surrounded by big ones was to prove embarrassing when the Government began pressing for the standardisation of brakes. The four companies to which the NSR was connected, the MR, GNR, GWR and LNWR (to quote the chairman's order), all had their own braking systems. No wonder he lamented: 'It is very difficult for a small company like the NSR to know what brake to adopt'.

L

While it could have waited for others to make up their minds, the Knotty chose instead to experiment and on 5 November 1878 it was agreed to fit a train with a communication cord. On 15 June 1880 the order was given for a 'new main line style' train to have Clarke & Webb continuous brakes then much in use on the LNWR. In readiness for more general fitting of continuous brakes, 20 third brakes were sanctioned on 3 May 1881 and on 9 February 1882 it was decided to fit the vacuum brake to cattle trucks.

The broader question was resolved the following year when the LNWR adopted the vacuum brake and on 9 January, the NSR told the LNWR it was fitting this to main line trains. Six years later—on 2 July 1889—continuous brakes were fully adopted at a cost of £7,600.

This was the year of the Regulation of the Railways Act, which annoyed most companies since it forced them not only to fit continuous brakes to passenger trains, but also to adopt the block system and interlocking points and signals on passenger lines within two years. The NSR complied, but echoed an air of self-righteousness when the chairman, Salt, called the fitting of the vacuum 'somewhat tedious and expensive' and stressed that they had given orders for the work without any action by the Board of Trade. He added a personal protest:

> My own opinion is that I very much wish the Board of Trade would leave people alone to manage their own business, which they understand.

Despite opposition, the Act was effective and Board of Trade Returns ten years later showed that NSR trains fitted with continuous brakes were running about 1,500,000 miles a year.

Although goods trains without brake vans were not generally introduced on British Rail until 1968, the practice was followed for many years on a number of NSR lines. For instance, they could be dispensed with on trains between Silverdale Junction and Market Drayton, provided there was a suitable vehicle in which the guard could ride and it was conveniently marshalled for him.[1]

The final fruits of improved track, signalling and brakes were to be maximum speeds of 60mph on main lines and

45mph on secondary routes plus a number of junction restrictions including 25mph at Colwich, Etruria and Marston; 20mph at Stoke and Norton Bridge; 15mph at Leek Brook and through Cheadle Tunnel.

The maximum passenger train loading was 20 coaches; 15 was the maximum allowed on the Loop (reduced still further to 10 between Kidsgrove and Newchapel). Ten was the maximum, too, on the Audley lines. The LNWR would allow only a maximum of 10 coaches on NSR trains between Ashbourne and Buxton. A shortage of brake power was evident even in the twenties when LNWR vacuum fitted banana vans running between Liverpool, Birkenhead and Stoke were marshalled next to engines to give them extra braking power. Electric fitted brake vans were not used for carrying milk after a leak badly damaged an accumulator.

The efficiency of NSR management was reflected in operation by which passenger trains carried a variety of traffic to avoid special goods workings. Private wagons were banned from all trains and on the main line, only one early morning each way (and a local from Macclesfield) were allowed to occasionally convey fish 'trucks' to Stoke. Similar traffic sometimes worked over the Loop and Audley lines.

Mixed trains were run on branches, although the only ones listed in working time tables were two on the Sandbach branch and one to Ashbourne. Cattle trucks were attached to passenger trains on the Churnet Valley, Ashbourne and Leek lines on either Wednesdays or Thursdays. Silk vans were sometimes attached to passenger trains on the Leek and Biddulph lines and the morning train to Market Drayton occasionally carried 'important sheeted goods'. The 10 15 am Uttoxeter—Ashbourne was diagrammed to carry a Tranship Van and a Midland van from St Pancras. Fish trains were always run as express goods and signalmen were instructed to see they had a clear road.

ACCIDENTS

By far the most serious accident on Knotty lines, the Hixon disaster of 1968, occurred on a level crossing, sources of trouble from the earliest days. A system running in so congested an area as the Potteries was bound to have crossings in profusion and even the slow speed of early trains could not prevent fatalities.

After two boys were killed on a crossing near Longport in 1854, it was found that 800 people were using it daily and it was replaced by an underbridge, opened the following May. The level crossing at Stoke station was a cause of constant worry to local people, and trouble to the directors, who resisted moves to replace it with an underbridge. But in 1854 the Commissioner of Police at Stoke intervened, sending a report to the Board of Trade.

But if crossings were not always safe, trains were and by 1852 the company was able to boast that it had carried 3,000,000 passengers 'without loss of life or limb'. Yet there were accidents: early in 1854 a passenger train hit a wagon left on the line near Leek. No one was hurt but the chief porter at Leek was dismissed and the station master severely reprimanded. On 27 June 1854 an LNWR train was thrown off the line in Harecastle Tunnel but only one passenger was slightly hurt.

Records show that the Knotty was prone to Boxing Day accidents—no doubt due to Merry Christmases, although one in 1860 was due to a more serious cause: a burst tyre. It happened as the evening local from Colwich reached Hixon. A 9 year old girl was killed and eight other passengers slightly hurt.

A crash on 21 June 1861 took more serious toll: the driver, fireman and guard being killed as the 7 5 pm from Burton to Stoke was derailed and came to rest in a field. Half of the 16 passengers were also hurt. The sobriety of the driver was questioned, but more likely the crash was due to the instability of the locomotive, which was later rebuilt. (See page 216.)

One of the first accidents involving an NSR train on foreign territory happened at Stockport in December 1868 when a Manchester—Stoke train was in collision and several passengers were slightly hurt. The NSR were later judged to have been 25 per cent responsible.

An unusual accident happened to the noon express from Manchester at Longport on 24 July 1871 when the train—an NSR engine and 10 coaches—was derailed by a rope used for shunting private wagons being left stretched across the line. This crash did not have as wide repercussions as a night collision in Stoke station on 21 February 1872. This was serious not in consequence, but in implication. An LNWR goods from Manchester to London running under clear signals hit the back of an excursion waiting to leave the up platform. The signalman at Stoke North box, who could not see the excursion because of stock stabled on the middle road, thought it had left on time. He had no link with his colleague in the south box and so station movements were always carried out with caution. Four LNWR night goods were the only trains then running through non stop and the NSR refused to waste the stabling space in the middle road, to keep them clear of the platforms. The Inspecting Officer, Lt Col F. H. Rich, criticised signal box comfort in his report:

> When visiting the cabins at the North and South ends of the station (which are large and comfortable cabins), I observed in each cabin a large armchair with high back and sides and cushioned seat. The sides of the armchair have glass windows so that the signalman while enjoying himself may look right and left.
>
> In the South cabin the chair was placed directly opposite the fire with its back to the point and signal apparatus. I was informed that these chairs were provided so that the men may sit down and be protected from the draughts which came up through the holes in the floor through which the levers work.
>
> The signalmen are on duty for twelve hours but I submit it is not desirable that such comfortable means should be provided for the men to go to sleep on duty and I recommend the chairs should be removed at once from the cabins, and if the duty hours are too long, they should be shortened. If the men are too delicate to perform their duty in a well enclosed and roofed cabin where they are provided with a good fire they should be invalided and proper men engaged to do the duty.

Whether Col Rich liked the chairs or not, some survived, and one in Leek Brook Junction box until LMS days is now preserved at Clapham.

Some signalmen may have had plenty of time to sit down—but not all, for at many of the smaller stations, boxes were built on the platform and there a signalman found himself doing other jobs as well: porter, lampman, luggage clerk, and, perhaps, station gardener.

Some accidents influenced changes in signalling, but one in 1873, like that in 1861, led to a major change in locomotive design. It happened on 26 September and involved a goods train of 52 wagons from Crewe to Stoke. After the train had been banked to Harecastle, the guard forgot to use his brake while two wagons were taken off. His van and 19 wagons ran back and hit the pilot engine at Lawton Junction, killing the guard and derailing six wagons. The driver saw the wagons approaching and tried to run ahead of them, but the Dodds' wedge motion jammed. Drivers found that the motion often jammed and sometimes two men with crow bars were needed to free it. After this accident Dodds' wedge motion was replaced on every locomotive fitted with it.

A ganger who forgot to report that a rail had been taken out for repair was blamed for a de-railment at Barlaston in February 1875. The train was only moving slowly and no one was hurt. Later in the year, on 1 November, an MS & L train was involved in a crash at Bollington on the joint line. Seven years later an MS & L empty stock train hit an NSR local at Macclesfield.

A stopping train from Stoke hit the back of a coal train outside Crewe station on 17 August 1876, slightly injuring several passengers. Far more serious was a crash on 16 January 1885 when an LNWR express from Manchester ran into an NSR mineral train shunting at Sideway. The NSR engine was wrecked and the LNWR driver killed as his locomotive overturned. The track was mangled but no passenger was hurt.

The NSR chairman remarked three weeks later that two men had made a mistake and added that it was absolutely impossible to prevent accidents altogether as long as they had to deal with the human agency. The Board of Trade thought differently, reporting signalling—not men—to be at fault. While both distant and home signals were at danger, the signalman was said to have given the 'line clear'. He forgot the presence of the mineral train and the Inspector, Lt Col W. Yolland, suggested the introduction of an electro-mechanical 'reminder' for signalmen. He thought it might be done by interlocking points with telegraph instruments so that they could not give a 'line clear' indication for any train when the signalman's previous action had been to affect 'line blocked'. It resulted in many schemes being put forward by patentees, engineers and superintendents.[2]

Later in the month an NSR excursion to North Wales was involved in a minor collision outside Chester station.

While the company never 'expected' accidents to happen to travellers, it accepted them as inevitable so far as the staff was concerned. This attitude was manifest in remarks by the chairman, Salt, in 1885 when the NSR introduced shunting poles. While he regarded them as a step towards greater safety, he admitted there was still some danger to the men. But, he added, it was a convenience and they believed the poles reduced danger to shunters. Poles allowed trains to be marshalled quicker: a skilled man was able to couple 40 wagons in four to five minutes.

An extra shunting hazard, more to goods than men, involved the sharp application of the steam brake by drivers—a practice which the management tried to stamp out by instructing guards to report drivers who used it, instead of the hand brake, for shunting. The steam brake was supposed to be used only in emergencies.

Long hours of duty were an obvious source of safety lapses, especially among older men and the company confessed in its rule book that *many* platelayers had been killed as they stepped from one line to another, or into the 'six foot'.

Foremen and gangers had to walk their lengths twice daily, once on Sundays, and in the early days they had also to check all distance signals, which were troublesome because of long connecting wires.

Typical of the long hours worked in early days were those of gatemen, who had to be on duty from at least half an hour before the passage of the first morning train, until the last evening train.

COMPENSATION CLAIMS AND FRAUD

The fear of having to pay compensation always worried the directors, especially in mid-Victorian days when courts sometimes awarded heavy damages. A woman passenger knocked down by a train in 1853 got £580 and in 1869 a man who arrived at Burslem, stayed in the waiting room until other passengers had left, and then fell down a hole where part of the platform had been taken up, got £1,500—even though the company contended that a porter had warned him of the excavation. A traveller from Birmingham got £1,000 in 1878 because a train jerked and his head 'was brought into collision with the side of the carriage'.

The directors were indignant about claims totalling £590 made by passengers of a train which was in collision in fog near Stoke in December 1878. The chairman was later to comment:

> At the time there was no loss of life, no serious injury, but at the same time we all know that people begin to feel ill some little time after these accidents, and whether imaginary or not, is not for me to say; but at all events claims are often made some time after an accident of that sort has taken place.

Not all cases, though, went against the company. It successfully defended an action brought in 1880 by a woman who had travelled from Blythe Bridge to Normacot, where the train slightly over-ran the platform. She claimed £1,000 damages, alleging she was thrown when the train jerked forward as she was climbing down to the platform ramp.

Salt said in March 1884 that it was impossible to say what amount a man might claim. He might only pay 6d or 1s for a train ticket, and yet, because of injury, claim £1,000 compensation. From 1880-90 the company paid £400 a year in insurance premiums to guard against loss from injury caused to passengers, but from 1890 it paid £900 a year to cover 'any accident that is likely to happen'.

The carriage of three marble mantelpieces created a classic case of insurance under the Railway & Canal Traffic Act of 10 July 1854. A customer called Peek wanted to send the mantelpieces to London. He got a notice from the NSR stating that it would not be responsible for the loss or damage to

> any marbles, musical instruments, toys or other articles which, from their brittleness, fragility, delicacy, or liability to ignition were more than ordinarily hazardous, unless insured.

Peek asked the NSR to collect the mantelpieces, but they were taken only as far as his local station, where they stayed during insurance discussions. Peek eventually forwarded them uninsured but sued when they were damaged through getting wet. The NSR contended they were absolved from liability because Peek had signed a special contract. Several courts disagreed with the different contentions and eventually the case went to the House of Lords, which ruled in Peek's favour.[3]

That case was isolated, but the NSR was continually paying compensation for broken pottery: difficult goods to carry in wagons with stiff springs. In 1879 the bill was £323; ten years later it rose to almost £5,000.

There was also a slow but steady increase in crime. It was noted on 14 January 1851 that a wedding cake had been collected from a station by an impostor. But that was minor crime and six years later when the board heard that seven men had been caught stealing cotton twist at Stoke, it ordered the case to be 'carefully prosecuted'. In 1878, Meadows, the station master at Tunstall, disappeared with takings of £300. His fate was recorded by the chairman who stated two years later that: 'in an unfortunate moment he came back to the district and was caught'. After that the NSR insured itself against thefts by servants.

In summer 1880, a shareholder called Roach asked why so many stations were being broken into. The chairman replied that the total stolen was less than £100 and said it was impossible for the company to start police duties. At Newcastle, where it was supposed that they had an efficient police, the office had been broken into. He could not see how the company could always guard against such occurrences.

The company lost £7,000 in 1888 through forgery from an unexpected source, a trustee who forged the signature of a co-trustee on the transfer of company stock. The NSR found itself liable to pay, although Salt protested:

> We are perfectly innocent parties, unable to protect ourselves or the company. The only satisfaction we take is that a serious forgery of this kind seldom occurs.

The case had national repercussions and led to the passing of the Forged Transfer Act in 1891.

FARES AND TICKETS

The framework of passenger fares and luggage charges was laid down in the company's original Acts, which provided for maximum fares of 2d first class; 1½d second and 1d third, although specials, or extra trains, were exempt from those limits. Luggage allowances were 100lb, 60lb and 40lb.

In July 1852 the company was successful in piloting through the Railway Clearing House a scheme to replace company cyphers on tickets with information on routes, useful to passengers and ticket collectors. It was quite a radical change for it involved putting the initials of the issuing company on the front of tickets. The man responsible was Charles Cooper, the passenger superintendent, who later joined the LNWR and became district superintendent, Manchester.

Annual contracts were first issued between NSR stations and Manchester in July 1853—£1 a mile first class; 17s 6d second. In the same month, day tickets (5s first; 4s second) were issued between Manchester and Alton, on three days a week.

While many fares remained static, first class fares had risen to 2½d a mile by 1862, a level higher than the national average since the GER and MS & L were the only other companies charging at this rate. Most charged less, although eight minor companies had a first class rate even higher.

Contract facilities were extended as better relations developed with the LNWR and in 1866 the issue began of annual season tickets from local stations to those on the LNWR—charged at that company's rates.

For some time children at local schools got free train passes, but it seems the NSR board knew nothing of the system for once it heard of the practice it ordered it to be stopped at once, the decision being taken on 26 May 1868. The NSR wanted—and needed—every penny it could get and even ten years later its highest local fare was under 10s and the average was ninepence.

Other non-payers continued using the line after children were banned: fare dodgers. Apart from the loss of revenue, there were difficulties in dealing with offenders when they were caught. Staff were warned in the 1865 rule book:

> The power of detention is to be exercised with great caution, and never where the address of the party is known, or adequate security offered for his appearance to answer the charge. When it shall be necessary to detain any person, such detention shall not continue for a longer period than is absolutely necessary, but he shall be conveyed before a Magistrate with as little delay as possible.

The next rule stated:

> The power of detention for OFFENCES is limited to the person of the Passenger, and does not extend to his luggage; but the luggage may be detained for the fare in case it is not intended to proceed against the Owner for a penalty, such luggage being subject to a lien for the amount of the fare.

Station masters were also warned that it was *intent* which constituted an offence. The power of detention should be exercised with caution and discretion as

> cases may frequently occur of persons travelling unintentionally beyond the distance for which they have paid their fare, or even against their wish; and to their inconvenience.

The suggestion in the first rule that 'he' shall be conveyed before a magistrate points to none of the gentler sex ever being thought guilty of such conduct.

The value of money in Victorian and Edwardian days is underlined by the fact that in 1908—sixty years after its inception—the NSR still had a 1d fare, although it was now restricted to children aged between 3-12 travelling third. By now the second minimum was 2d and the first, 3d. The short distances run by NSR trains were reflected in the fare structure. Returns between local stations were available only on the day of issue, except those bought at weekends, which could be used up to Monday evening. Returns from NSR stations to Derby, Burton, Crewe, Stafford and Market Drayton had a seven day availability.

Changes and innovations to try and attract more passengers were made all the time, and in 1908 ticket availability was improved to allow two days between local stations up to 20 miles apart and eight days for those beyond. Any booking to stations on another system more than 12 miles from point of departure was valid for six months.

Boys of Market Drayton Grammar School were offered reduced fares in summer 1911 and while the company admitted that the idea did not pay, it hoped the gesture might attract builders to the area. They were also looking out for other areas where building might develop.

In assessing contract rates for first and second class travel, no charge was made for distances under half a mile. Besides ordinary contracts calculated by distance, special ones were available in suburban areas: Burslem—Tunstall and Waterloo Road; Fenton—Longton; Hanley—Etruria and Burslem; Meir—Longton; Stoke—Fenton.

Half price contracts were offered to under 12s and pupil-teachers, scholars, students, apprentices, clerks and messengers up to 18, birth certificates having to be shown before the issue of the first contract.

The country commuter was not forgotten:

> For the convenience of those desirous of living in the Country during the summer and autumn months, monthly contracts are issued from Pottery stations and Newcastle to certain country stations.

There were special fares for golfers going to play on the NSR course at Rudyard.

Special arrangements were made to extend trains during the hunting season and unlike others taking horses with them on journeys, hunters did not have to give 24 hours notice. A passenger who hired a horse box did not always end his expense there, for if he had luggage in excess of personal allowance (150lb, first; 120lb, second; 100lb, third), he had to pay excess unless:

> the charge amounts to as much as the charge for a Horse, in which case the rate for one or more Horses must be charged, according to the number of stalls occupied.

In its basic fare structure, the NSR followed standard practices, allowing concessionary rates for equestrian performers, theatrical and operatic parties and commercial travellers. Concessions were first given to commercial travellers in 1880 after a long campaign by them against heavy charges for excess baggage. They had contended that their journeys helped to develop subsequent traffic in different areas.

All classes of concessionary travellers could take with them up to 3cwt of personal luggage, first class; 2cwt, second and 1½cwt, third.

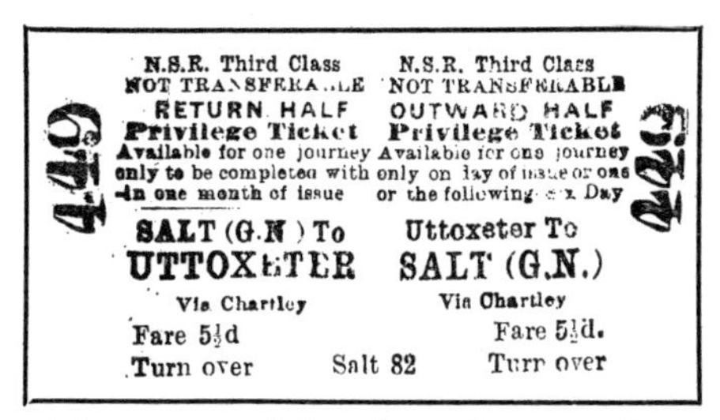

Privilege monthly return ticket issued to employees at reduced fare

There was another, and much used, type of special ticket: those for market travellers, introduced on 8 March 1881. It allowed farmers and their wives taking produce to market up to 28lb of baskets carrying eggs, butter, fruit or other produce at their own risk.

For the company it meant risks of another sort as Walker[4] noted when he suggested an antidote for people who thought the Potteries were purely industrial. He commended a run down the Churnet Valley, particularly on Wednesdays—market day at Leek and Uttoxeter.

> These places are fine examples of country markets conducted in the good old fashioned way, where the process of 'smacking hands' over the price of a cow is duly observed, the bargain usually being sealed in pots of Imperial measure. The village stations en route each supply a good compliment of marketers —chiefly farmers' wives—and as their luggage averages two or three large baskets of eggs, butter and live fowl per head, the state of the compartment can be imagined.

The importance of market traffic was reflected by the issue of an eight page booklet on *Market and Weekly Workmen's Tickets*. It was issued free, unlike ordinary time tables which then cost 1d. There were plenty of markets to which trains ran, or to which the NSR issued cheap tickets: Ashbourne, Bucknall (for Hanley), Burslem, Burton, Chatterley (for Tunstall), Cheadle, Congleton, Crewe, Derby (NSR and GNR), Hanley, Harecastle, Leek, Longton, Macclesfield, Market Drayton, Newcastle, Newport, Norton Bridge, Rugeley, Sandbach (Wheelock), Silverdale, Stafford, Stoke, Stone, Tunstall, Uttoxeter, Wellington.

Among the most unusual tickets were those for bicycle insurance, costing 1d, introduced in co-operation with insurance companies in 1920. They were not widely used, judging by the experience of one cyclist who collected a sequence of 24 tickets issued at Tutbury during the twelve months to April 1927. There is no record, either, of the use made of a privilege extended to a few: of riding in any goods guard vans they chose. It could be done only by the holders of gold or silver passes.

White was the colour used to distinguish first class single tickets, and yellow and white, returns. Ordinary second singles were cerise; returns, blue and cerise. Third singles were green, and returns, drab and green.

GENERAL REGULATIONS

The NSR, like many companies, constantly found itself needing to revise bye-laws, by which it protected its property and travellers using it. The original bye-laws of 12 February 1848 were first amended on 15 February 1866 by The Lords of the Committee of Her Majesty's Privy Council for Trade & Foreign Plantations. Nine in number, the laws provided, among other things, for a 40s maximum penalty for several offences. They included non-payment of fare; of travelling in a higher class than that for which a ticket was held—quite a common practice according to the directors' comments from time to time; smoking in carriages or on stations, and intoxication.

The last of the bye-laws laid down:

> Dogs will not be suffered to accompany Passengers in the Carriages, but will be conveyed separately and charged for.

By the time the bye-laws were revised, vandalism was becoming a problem and it was laid down that a passenger found cutting the linings, removing or defacing the number plates, breaking windows or causing other wiful damage, would forfeit £5 and pay for repairs. Passengers who accidentally broke windows also had to pay 8s 6d on the spot, or have their names taken.

Smoking was also becoming a problem and it was suggested to station masters that they should use 'all gentle means' to stop passengers smoking in carriages or on stations if others complained of annoyance. If a person refused to stop smoking, he was to be removed from the company's premises.

The 1866 bye-laws did not survive long for a new set of seventeen were approved by the Board of Trade on 5 December 1874. No 16 stated that the company could refuse to carry anyone suffering from an infectious disorder. If they tried to get on a train without special permission, they could face a fine of up to 40s and be removed 'at the first opportunity' from the railway. Prisoners in charge of police, and the insane had to travel in separate compartments to those used by ordinary travellers.

CHAPTER NINE

Growth of Train Services

> Most of our runs are so short that the drivers are afraid to put on much speed for fear of running 20 or 30 miles on to somebody else's line before they stop.
>
> *W. D. Phillipps 1899*

CLASS DISTINCTION

The first trains to run in the Potteries bore all the usual marks of Victorian class distinction, conforming to the pattern of other companies. After the opening of the branch from the temporary terminus at Whieldon Grove, Stoke, to Norton Bridge, in 1848, the first train of the day, the 8 am from Stoke, carried only first and second class passengers, (or, at any rate, passengers who travelled first and second class!). The working classes—the very people who had to get to work early—had to wait for the first Parliamentary train at 9 30 am. As they were barred from the early afternoon train—1 pm from Stoke—the only one left for them was the 4 30 pm. The last train, the 6 pm from Stoke, was again limited to first and second class.

The arrival of the railway was a great wonder to everybody, but so far as the Church of England was concerned, it was a six day one, and it fiercely opposed trains on Sundays, even though it was the only day on which workers, then on a six day week, could hope to get out of town. But the opposition by the Church, and indeed, many shareholders, did not succeed in preventing all Sunday trains, although Sunday excursions, introduced in 1848 between Stoke, Stone and Norton Bridge were quickly abandoned in the face of protests by the Bishop of Lichfield and others. But the company stood firm on the need

Page 189 (above) *One of the tallest signal boxes on the Knotty, Bromshall Junction;* (below) *inside a typical signal box—Ford Green—showing crossing gates wheel*

Page 190 (top) *Class 'G' 4–4–0 No 86 newly built in 1910 with burnished buffers and coupling rods;* (centre) *0–6–0 No 66 as built at Stoke in 1877, the first with a flush firebox and the last with the safety valve casing;* (below) *Hookham's unique class 4 cylr D 0–6–0T No 23 fitted with indicator shelter for trials in 1922*

for some Sunday trains and told people who complained about two passenger trains and an early goods using the Churnet route on that day that they were 'as few as necessary'. To try and avoid annoyance, the driver of the Sunday afternoon train through the valley was instructed to suppress whistling.

For the rest of the week, the Churnet had four daily passenger trains, allowed up to 1h 25m for the 32 miles from Macclesfield to Uttoxeter. They ran through to Derby in an overall time of 2h 20m.

There were five daily trains between Crewe and Derby, Macclesfield, Burton and Norton Bridge, while the Stone—Colwich line had two. Crewe—Derby trains were allowed just under 3h for the 52 miles, including, generally, an appreciable waiting and refreshment time at Stoke. The mid-morning service (1st and 2nd class only) stood for 35m. A Parliamentary train on this route stopped for just 2m!

Improvements in operating methods and motive power brought improvements in services, despite the handicap of trying to fit in with services run by neighbours. In 1874 the Knotty showed commendable enterprise in trying to develop a through coach service between Liverpool & Nottingham once the Midland opened its Willington line in May of that year. The line ran from Stenson Junction, just north of Willington, to Swarkestone Junction on the Ashby line, and a link from there (via Weston-on-Trent) ran to Sheet Stores Junction, thus providing an avoiding line south of Derby. The Knotty was given running powers and built 6 composite coaches for the Liverpool—Nottingham link.

Six years later the Knotty complained that it was being forced into running fast trains between Crewe and Derby because of current competition between the LNWR and the Midland, but its efforts must have satisfied the LNWR for when it started a Birmingham—Derby express service from 1 May 1885, connections were made at Burton for Uttoxeter. When the LNWR extended trains to Burton over the Ashby & Nuneaton Joint line from 1 July 1890, through workings were introduced between Ashbourne and Nuneaton, extended to Rugby from 1 November. On 1 April of the following year, the Churnet Valley service was augmented by a through one between Macclesfield and Rugby, via Uttoxeter and Burton.

From 1 July this service was further extended to link Manchester and Rugby.

In summer 1892 the NSR received another 'bonus' from the LNWR with the opening of the new west departure platforms at Euston, the 10 55 am 'Tourist Train, Special Express' for North Wales (18 July-31 August), Shrewsbury, the Cambrian line and North Staffordshire, being one of six trains 'appointed' to use the new platforms.

EXCURSIONS

Once Bank Holidays became established, the Knotty did all it could to exploit the potential tripper market and on 10 August 1878, it ran a record number of excursions. Nearly 1,000 people were taken to Liverpool (where many of them saw the sea for the first time); 700 went from Leek to Derby and Nottingham over the GNR; 900 went to Manchester from the Churnet Valley, but a similar train from the Potteries did badly and was 'only a train of 10 coaches carrying 400 people'. Two excursions went to London, one carried 500 passengers to St Pancras; the other ran to Euston. Other trippers went that August Bank Holiday to Birkenhead and Birmingham, Matlock and Buxton.

In later years excursions were not always as popular and those to London for the Coronation of King George V in 1911 were poorly filled. Royalty did not often visit the Potteries, but there were occasions. On his first visit to Britain in June 1873, the Shah of Persia went to Liverpool and then travelled via Crewe to stay with the Duke of Sutherland at Trentham. The next day, 27 June, the Shah returned to Crewe to be shown round the works by Webb, and then spent a second night at Trentham. The next morning he travelled to Euston. Seven years later the Prince of Wales and Prince Christian travelled to Trentham by train.

LNWR EXPRESS WORKING

When the LNWR started routing some London—Manchester services through the Potteries, the Macclesfield—Colwich section became the Knotty main line, even if it did insist that the title remained with that between Derby and Crewe. The NSR could afford no delays in handling the expresses for it was laid down that it was to be 'fined' £1 for every minute which they lost while on the system.

Between Macclesfield and Colwich, the Knotty operated its fastest services. In 1914, and again in 1921, the 12 43 pm Macclesfield—Stoke was allowed only 27m for the 19.8 miles, an average of 44mph. At first glance, a casual traveller catching this express at Manchester London Road and noting a little tank standing at its head might have thought he was looking at the station pilot. If he did, he would have got a shock for once the whistle blew, this little tank pulled smartly away with the heavy express, heading for the first stop at Stockport. It was not an unusual sight, for up to grouping the 12 10 pm was often in charge of a tank over the $37\frac{1}{2}$ miles to Stoke. It was a tough assignment for beyond Stockport lay a severe slack round the curve at Cheadle Hulme and then a steady climb to Macclesfield. Here an 0–6–2T was waiting to bank the train to the Moss. Then the tank was away with its 12 or more coaches for the run to Stoke, where an LNWR tender engine took over for the longer, yet less strenuous road to Euston. The noon express was worked by several Knotty types. Apart from the 4–4–2 tanks, there were occasional 4–4–0 or 0–6–0; from 1916 'F' 0–6–4Ts. At times the LNWR provided a pilot as far as Congleton.

To go back a few years to late Victorian days, the service was a little slower, as could be seen from the July 1896 timetable.

Up		am		pm		pm	
Manchester		8 30		12 00		5 30	
Macclesfield Hibel Road		9 02		12 35		6 06	
Congleton		9 18		—		6 18	
Stoke	arr	9 35		1 05		6 37	
	dep	9 38	9 44	1 09	1 17	6 39	6 44
Lichfield		10 11		—		—	
Rugby		10 56		2 25		7 55	
Euston		12 55		4 15		9 45	
Stafford			10 13		1 44		7 12
Wolverhampton			10 51		2 14		7 49
Birmingham			11 20		2 45		8 25

Down		am		pm		pm	
Euston		7 30		12 00		4 00	
Rugby		9 44		1 53		5 50	
Lichfield		10 40		2 36		6 33	
Birmingham			9 55		1 00		
Wolverhampton			10 35		1 32		6 13
Stafford		11 14			2 25	—	7 00
Stoke	arr	11 42		3 18	3 04	7 14	7 38
	dep	11 44		3 22		7 17	7 58
Congleton		—		—		7 37	8 30
Macclesfield		12 13		3 48		7 43	8 51
Manchester		12 45		4 20		8 15	9 55

Euston—Manchester expresses of 1898 mainly had restaurant cars and stopped at Willesden, Rugby, Lichfield, Stoke, Macclesfield and Stockport. The evening express from Manchester, now put back to 6 15 pm, was allowed 181m for the 145¾ miles from Stoke to Euston with the only stop at Willesden. There was no difference in the overall timings of expresses routed via Crewe or Stoke: all were allowed 4h 15m.

In Edwardian years, the early morning down express, which ran via Stafford and Stone, left Euston 20m earlier to reach Manchester nearer mid-day. The 12 15 pm carried a luncheon car to Rugby and the evening train included a through coach to Colne. The service was:

Euston	7 10	12 15	4 05
Stoke	11 00	3 39	7 08
Manchester	12 05	4 45	8 15

The up service was 'pitched' at times a little later in the day:

Manchester	8 30	12 10	5 35
Stoke	9 41	1 15	6 43
Euston	12 25	4 00	9 50

The 8 30 am carried a Buxton through coach from Nuneaton; those from Colne and Bolton (Great Moor Street) were attached to the midday express. Passengers on the evening service had to wait for a meal until a car was attached at Rugby (7 57 pm).

A through coach service from Euston to Buxton via Ashbourne was introduced from 1 October 1899 when the 11 am from Euston slipped a coach at Nuneaton, which reached Buxton at 3 22 pm. The early afternoon train from Buxton (1 20 pm) carried a coach attached at Rugby to the 4 35 pm to Euston, due 6 25 pm.

The through coach was not shown in the NSR timetable as the company regarded the LNWR's Buxton service as competitive.

The LNWR concentrated Manchester—Birmingham services via Crewe and only a few ran via Stoke. As a result the fastest Stoke—Birmingham link was 88m for 42 miles, including a change at Stafford. Through coach services via Stoke were a little slower. Trains ran intermediate to the Euston services:

Birmingham	9 15	12 15	3 30	6 50
Stafford	10 30	1 20	4 24	7 41
Stoke	11 00	1 57	5 25	9 00
Manchester	12 05	3 52	6 44	11 05

Manchester	8 30	12 10	5 35
Stoke	9 37	1 14	6 43
Stafford	10 14	1 54	7 20
Birmingham	11 10	2 55	8 31

There was also a limited service between Birmingham and Stoke.

The importance attached by the NSR to the development of long distance services was illustrated when Stockton Brook station was opened on 1 July 1896. All trains were booked to stop, but the 12 30 pm SO from Leek called only to pick up London and Birmingham passengers, who went forward from Stoke at 1 1 pm. There was also a service—if you could call it that—between Stoke and Walsall, via Colwich. It ran once a day and waited at Rugeley for 70m.

The magnificence and charm of country stations between Stone and Colwich, which made them among the most pleasant in Britain, was never matched by their passenger figures and they were comparatively little used. Yet they had a useful service which formed part of the pattern between Macclesfield and Colwich and Stafford. Four stoppers ran on weekdays between Macclesfield and Stafford (reduced to one on Sundays), and it was augmented by two locals between Stoke—Stafford and Macclesfield—Colwich. There were also three Stoke—Colwich weekday locals, four on Saturdays. The only Sunday service was a local Stoke—Stone. In the reverse direction there were four Stafford—Macclesfield, three Stafford—Stoke, four Colwich—Stoke, one through to Crewe; two Stone—Stoke.

When he made his remark, quoted at the beginning of this chapter, about the rather humorous possibility of trains overshooting the system, Phillipps need not have worried about those on the main line between Derby and Crewe. For the service was always so sparse, if adequate, that any overshooters from the main line would have caused little inconvenience to other companies. Typical was the pattern of July 1896 when there were no more than five through trains each way, more than halved to two on Sundays. The first left Crewe at 7 20 am and did not reach Stoke until 8 10 am—and that in an age when most people started work early. The train took 1h 33m from Stoke to Derby. The rest of the service was:

	Weekdays					*Sundays*	
Crewe	11 00	1 35	4 14	6 45	8 45 /	8 00	5 45
Stoke	11 43	2 13	5 21	7 30	9 26	9 10	6 29
Derby	1 10	3 20	6 05	8 56	–	11 20	8 10

Reverse timings were much the same. The rather liberal timings were tightened over the years and by 1908, 15m had been knocked off the mid morning train from Crewe, re-timed to leave at 11 15 am.

Integrated into the main line service were through summer expresses to Llandudno, mainly extensions of the Derby—Crewe locals. The 11 am daily from Derby (NSR)[1] was normally made up of three coaches from that station, one from Nottingham MR and another from Nottingham GNR.

A sixth coach from Burton joined the train at Uttoxeter. At Stoke, the train detached a coach for the Cambrian Coast, which ran forward 4m later at 12 10 pm to reach Crewe at

12 37 pm, Whitchurch 1 29 pm, Aberystwyth 5 pm and Barmouth 5 35 pm. The Llandudno express ran non-stop through Crewe to call at Beeston Castle, Chester, Rhyl (2 1 pm), Colwyn Bay and Llandudno (2 50 pm). On the return journey starting at 4 10 pm, the train called at Prestatyn and Chester and, on home territory, at Harecastle, Etruria, Stoke, Uttoxeter and Tutbury. The working was balanced by an LNWR train over the same route between Derby and Llandudno. Through coaches at this period used both the Midland and GNR routes between Nottingham and Derby.

GNR SERVICES

One of the services that helped to make Uttoxeter among the busiest passenger stations was that which the GNR maintained between Nottingham and Stafford through Derby. It had a service of six weekday trains and two on Sundays. In NSR terms this was not an important service, yet for years it was given an enhanced status by being placed first in the NSR public timetables. It was shown as a through service between King's Cross and Stafford via Peterborough. A footnote advised passengers that at Marchington, three trains:

> Stop to set down Passengers from GN Stations and to pick up for Stations West of Uttoxeter. Passengers wishing to alight must advise the Guard at the preceding stopping Station.

The most intensive GNR service over NSR metals was that on the Burton branch on which it ran eight through trains from Derby (Friar Gate) alternatively with the Knotty locals shuttling between Burton and Tutbury. The service was increased by an extra train on Saturdays and halved on Sundays. A timetable footnote warned travellers that horses and private carriages were not conveyed *locally* on two morning trains.

Another of the Knotty's rural routes was that through the Churnet Valley, on which Leek was the only station where crowds of passengers could be expected—and those only on market days. In the sense that there was no road through the valley, the railway was the Churnet's life-line and the NSR serviced it with a basic passenger pattern of four daily trains each way, reduced to two on Sundays, but augmented on several other days. There was an extra working on Wednesdays, two on Saturdays, when there were also two locals Macclesfield—Alton, and another to Leek; one to Stoke and one Alton—Uttoxeter—Stoke.

Passenger trains carried all the milk traffic on weekdays, but on Sundays specials were sometimes run to get milk from the rich dairy areas in the valleys of the Churnet, the Dane and the Dove (served by the Leek & Manifold), to the cities, including Manchester and London. Stations like North Rode, set in a deep cutting, had chutes to get churns quickly to platforms and other milk handling facilities were introduced at key centres.

The Churnet trains connected at Rocester with the locals serving the Ashbourne branch from Uttoxeter: four on weekdays, one on Sundays. The busy market town of Ashbourne enjoyed an affluence which attracted the Midland to provide a through coach service with London. In the up direction it was attached to the 11 55 am from Ashbourne and reached St Pancras at 4 30 pm. The down through coach left St Pancras at 2 pm and reached its destination at 6 42 pm, getting Derbyshire residents home in comfortable time for dinner.

THE HUB AT STOKE

However much services were improved, curtailed or re-timed over the years, the Knotty's heart was at Stoke and its beat was the mass of local trains. Such was their concentration that in 1908 the station was handling 230 daily trains in summer. In winter the number was just four less. One of the busiest periods was the evening rush when over thirty trains were diagrammed through three platforms in an hour. While the number of trains handled at Stoke was impressive, the total of passengers was not: the estimate, including season ticket holders, was 5,870 in summer and a few less—5,484—in winter. The figures took no account, of course, of hundreds of passengers who changed there. The secret of Stoke's capacity to handle trains was that it was not a terminus, few trains ever starting or finishing there. All ran on for turning at other places like Newcastle. At the core of the local services were those of the Loop, shown in the time table as embracing Congleton and Uttoxeter and including the Cheadle branch. Many trains ran from Tunstall to Normacot, while others ran through to Uttoxeter or Kidsgrove. Thirty-eight down and thirty-nine up weekly workings provided a basic half-hour interval service. On Sundays the Loop was reduced to nine trains each way, mainly between Tunstall—Longton, although some ran to Totmonslow until Cheadle was opened.

One of the more unusual Loop workings was a returning cheap half-day excursion from Manchester (London Road), which left at 11 3 pm. It called at Longsight, Stockport, Macclesfield (Hibel Road), Congleton and Kidsgrove, before using the Loop to reach Stoke at 12 30 am and Normacot at 12 50 am. But the Loop was busiest during the day and the link was among the toughest for the men, their engines and the 80 ton rakes of coaches. For of the maximum distance of 30½ miles, fewer than nine were on gradients of less than 1 in 275. The twenty-three stations were served by all through trains, although there were in fact many which made shorter trips. The Loop service allowed many workers to get home for lunch and as one observer pointed out:

> The North Staffordshire deserves mention among those railways which have met, and in most cases stimulated, a demand for frequent and effective service of suburban and inter-district trains.[2]

Other inter-district trains radiating from Stoke were those to Market Drayton and Audley; Leek, and Congleton, through the Biddulph Valley. The Market Drayton line ran mainly through the rolling hills to the west of the Potteries, a rich farming area on the borders of Staffordshire, Shropshire and Cheshire. The five weekday trains (six on Wednesdays; two on Sundays), were rarely crowded but on Tuesdays trains were extended over the GWR Wellington—Nantwich branch as far as Hodnet for people going to market. The trains, which returned empty to Market Drayton, were run by the NSR to avoid passengers having to wait nearly two hours at Market Drayton for a GWR connection. The Potteries end of the

Market Drayton branch was rather busier than the western section because it also carried the three daily local trains over the Audley branch, and extras run on several days, and also Newcastle trains. This town had an intensive service of seventeen trains, plus an extra on market days. Another train ran as far as Silverdale and another served Keele. Another intensive service from Stoke was that over the short branch to Leek and, before doubling in 1910, the line carried fifteen trains each way, which involved smart working. In summer some trains were extended to Rudyard, but in winter this practice was restricted to Saturdays. Services were augmented on Mondays, Wednesdays, Thursdays and Saturdays, when local markets were being held.

The Leek branch was used for part of its length by the four daily trains through the Biddulph Valley—a service doubled on Saturdays. They took 40m for the short journey, one reason being the need for an engine run-round at Congleton Upper Junction. For some years Congleton people could reach Stoke over the Pinnox branch, which had an unbalanced working of two daily stoppers:

Congleton	–	2 24
Tunstall	9 45	2 52
Longport	9 50	2 57
Stoke	10 0	3 05

Just as the LNWR dominated the pattern of passenger services on the Macclesfield—Colwich route, the Manchester, Sheffield & Lincolnshire and later the Great Central, dictated and worked passenger trains on the joint line from Macclesfield to Marple. One result of this policy was that there was no second class accommodation on the trains. Although another mainly rural line, the service was gradually built up from an initial one of four weekday and two Sunday trains, to seven trains each way. Some were extended from Romiley to Woodley, Hyde or Manchester (London Road). The joint line services of which the NSR had sole charge were Buxton expresses via the Middlewood Curve and rush hour locals between Macclesfield and Bollington: two on weekdays and three on Saturdays. The Buxton express service was never very successful or impressive,

NORTH STAFFORDSHIRE RAILWAY.

TIME TABLES

MAY AND JUNE, 1908.

CONTENTS.

Price ONE PENNY

McCorquodale & Co., Limited, Printers to the Company.

Cover of May 1908 timetable

London, Birmingham (South Stafford Stations), Stafford, Stoke, Macclesfield, Stockport, and Manchester.

WEEK DAYS.

Miles from Stafford.																
L. & N. W. Railway.				a.m.		a.m.	a.m.	a.m.	a.m.	a.m.		p.m.		a.m.	p.m.	a.m.
	London (Eust) dep	...	...	...	...	...	5 0	7 10	...	...	...	...	...	10 37	...	10 37
	Rugby	...	...	...	...	...	6 56	8 56	7E15	...	...	...	...	10 58	...	12 17
	Nuneaton	...	...	...	...	...	7 19	9 19	8E 3	...	...	...	...	11 20	...	12 39
	Tamworth	...	...	...	...	...	7 38	9 43	8E35	...	...	...	...	11 43	...	...
	Lichfield	...	...	...	...	...	7 51	9 57	9E 0	...	...	...	...	11 54	...	...
	Birmingham (N. St.)	...	...	6 0	...	6 0	7 20	9 15	9E 0	9 55	...	...	...	12 15	12 40	1D0
	Dudley	...	...	...	...	...	7 28	9 30	8E40	10 5	...	...	...	12 28	12 41	1D5
	Walsall	...	...	5 55	...	6 40	7 15	9 15	9E35	9 38	...	...	...	12 20	1 8	1 5
	Wolverhampton	...	...	6 45	...	6 10	7 53	9 50	8E30	10 32	...	...	...	12 51	12 35	1 40
	Cannock	...	...	...	...	7 1	7 1	8 40	9E55	9 55	...	...	...	10 40	1 29	...
	Rugeley Junction	...	...	...	...	7 28	8 20	9 18	10E20	10 20	...	...	...	12 5	2 0	...
	Shrewsbury	...	...	...	...	...	7 40	...	...	10 10	...	...	...	11 45	...	12 35
	Wellington	...	...	...	...	...	7 59	...	...	10 26	...	...	...	12 11	...	12 55
								H C								
		a.m.	a.m.	a.m.	a.m.	a.m.	a.m.	a.m.	a.m.	a.m.	p.m.		p.m.	p.m.	p.m.	p.m.
...	**Stafford** dep	...	...	**7 25**	...	...	**8 56**	**10 30**	...	**11 15**	...	*Saturdays excepted Stone to Stoke, also Rail Motor Car (one class only).*	...	**1 20**	...	**2 25** B
...	Great Bridgeford	...	...	7 31	...	...	9 2	...	...	11 21	...		...	...	...	
5½	Norton Bridge *for E'shall*	...	...	7 37	...	...	9 8	...	...	11 27	...		...	1 30	...	2 35
Colwich Line.	**Colwich** dep	...	...	...	...	8 24	...	**Express.**	10E45	...	**Saturdays only.**		*Saturdays only.*	...	2 6	...
	Great Haywood	...	...	...	...	8 29	...		10E49	...				...	2 10	...
	Hixon	...	...	...	...	8 34	...		10E54	...				...	2 16	...
	Weston (Ingestre)	...	...	...	...	8 38	...		10E58	...				...	2 21	...
	Sandon	...	...	...	...	8 43	...		11E 3	...				...	2 27	...
	Aston by Stone	...	...	...	8 0	8 48	...		11E 9	...			1 11	...	2 34	...
9½	Stone Junction ...... M ... dep	...	...	7 45	8 5	8 53	9 16	10 48	11 14	11 35	...	1235	1 15	1 40	2 38	2 45
11½	Barlaston (Tittensor) M	...	...	7 51	8 10	8 58	9 22	...	11 20	11 41	...	1240	1 21	1 46		2 51
13½	Trentham ...... M	...	...	7 57	8 15	9 3	9 27	...	11 25	11 47	...	1245	1 27	1 52	Stop	2 58
16	**STOKE** arr	...	...	8 3	8 21	9 9	9 32	11 0	11 30	11 54	...	1254	1 33	1 57		3 6
					‡	‡	‡			‡		‡	‡			
	STOKE dep	**7 15**	**7 35**	**8 6**	**8 30**	**9 25**	**1020**	**11 3**	**11 33**	**12 18**	**1233**	**1 16**	**1 48**	**2 5**	**3 0**	...
17	Etruria (Basford)	7 19	7 39	8 10	8 34	9 29	...	...	11 37	12 22	1237	1 20	1 52	2 9	...	...
18¾	Longport (Wolstanton)	7 24	...	8 16	8 39	9 34	1027	**Express.**	11 42	12 27	1242	1 25	1 58	2 14	3 7	...
20¼	Chatterley	7 29	...	...	8 44	9 39	...		11 47	...	1247	1 30	2 3	2 19	...	...
22	Harecastle (Kidsgrove)	7 34	8F9	8 23	8 49	9 44	1034		11 52	12 32	1252	1 35	2 9	2 24	3 14	...
...	Harecastle dep	7 38	*Via* Loop Line.	...	To Crewe.	...	To Crewe.		...	12 40	...	To Crewe.	...	2Th35	3S25	...
...	Lawton	7 43		...		...			...	12 45	...		...	2Th40	3S30	...
...	Hassall Green	7 49		...		...		...	...	12 51	...		...	2Th46	3S36	...
...	Sandbach (Wheelock) arr	7 54		...		...		...	...	12 56	...		...	2Th51	3S41	...
24½	Mow Cop (Scholar Green)	...	8 15	...	...	9 50	...	...	11 58	...	1258	...	2 15	2 30	...	...
27½	Congleton	...	8 20	8 34	...	9 57	...	...	12 5	...	1 4	...	2 22	2 37	...	...
31	North Rode	...	...	C	...	10 4	...	...	12 12	...	...	...	2 29	2 45	...	...
35¾	Macclesfield (Central)	...	...	8 51	...	1014	...	...	12 22	...	To Biddulph Line.	...	2 41	2 58	...	...
...	Buxton (via Middlewood)	...	...	10 20	...	1H5	...	1A 5	2 A20	...		...	3I45	4J25	...	...
36	**Macclesfield** (H. Rd.) ... arr	...	...	**8 52**	...	**1015**	...	**11 30**	**12 23**	...		...	**2 42**	**2 59**	...	...
L. & N. W. Railway.	Stockport arr	...	...	9 20	...	1039	...	11 53	1 1	...		...	...	3 33	...	...
	Manchester (London Road)	...	...	9 36	...	1050	...	12 5	1 13	...		...	...	3 52	...	...
	Huddersfield	...	...	1045	...	1239	...	2 6	2 6	...		...	...	5 40	...	...
	Leeds (New Station)	...	...	1130	...	1 12	...	2 35	2 35	...		...	...	6 17	...	...

‡—Passengers change at Stoke.
A—Via Stockport (L. & N. W.).
B—Calls by signal to pick up Passengers for the N.S. Line only.
C—Calls by signal to pick up passengers for Manchester only.
D—*Saturdays only* during May, and *Fridays and Saturdays only* during June.
E—*Tuesdays and Saturdays only.*
F—Kidsgrove Station.
H—*11.5 a.m. Saturdays* in June.
H C—Horses and Private Carriages are not conveyed by this Train.

I—From June to Buxton. Will not run into Hibel Road Station after May.
J—Via Stockport L.&N.W. *On Saturdays* arrives 5.15 in May and 3 45 in June via Middlewood.
M—For Motor Connections to and from Trentham and Stone, see pages 24 to 27.
S—*Saturdays only.*
Th—*Thursdays only* from June.

For other Trains between Stoke and Harecastle, see pages 6 and 7.
For SUNDAY Trains see page 14.
The Times of Trains on Foreign Lines are given for information only.

London, Birmingham (South Stafford Stations), Stafford, Stoke, Macclesfield, Stockport, and Manchester.

WEEK DAYS.

L. & N. W. Railway.

Station	p.m.		a.m.		p.m.		p.m.		p.m.		p.m.	p.m.			p.m.	p.m.
London (Euston) dep	1215	*Mondays & Saturdays only.*	*10 37*	...	1 30	...	2J40	...	4 5	...	4 5	5 30	Thurs. & Sats. only commencing June	...	7B30	*8 50*
Rugby	2 17		*12 17*	...	3 14	...	3 53	...	5 45	...	5 45	6 7		...	7 48	*1053*
Nuneaton	1 12		*1 12*	...	3 37	...	3 37	...	5 25	...	5 25	5 25		...	9V[illegible]	*1116*
Tamworth	1 43		*1 43*	...	3 30	...	3 30	...	5 53	...	5 53	6 50		...	8 45	*1139*
Lichfield	2 59		*1 54*	...	4 5	...	4 5	...	6 26	...	6 26	7 1		...	8 57	...
Birmingham (New St.)	...		*2 15*	...	3 30	...	4 55	...	...	...	5 20	6 50		...	9 0	*11 0*
Dudley	HC		*2 23*	...	3 40	...	5 5	...	...	...	5 30	6 28		...	9 5	*11 8*
Walsall	...		*2 12*	...	3 35	...	4 33	...	5G16	...	5K55	6 35		...	9 15	*1030*
Wolverhampton	...		*[illegible] 48*	...	4 4	...	5 27	...	...	...	5 25	7 17		...	9 40	*1137*
Cannock	...		*1 29*	...	3 24	...	...	...	5G37	...	6K14	...		...	8 28	...
Rugeley Junction	...		*2 28*	...	4 0	...	4 58	...	6 43	...	6 48	7 18	*7 18*	...	9 20	...
Shrewsbury	...		*2 40*	...	3 10	...	4 50	...	...	...	...	5 43	...	...	8 0	*10 8*
Wellington	...		*2 56*	...	3 35	...	5 11	...	...	...	...	5 59	...	...	8 28	*1026*
									HC							

Station	p.m.	p.m.	p.m.	p.m.	p.m.	p.m.	p.m.	p.m.	p.m.	p.m.	p.m.	p.m.	p.m.	p.m.	p.m.	a.m.
Stafford dep	Express, London to Manchester.	...	*3F45*	...	4 45	...	5 55	...	Express London to Manchester.	...	...	8 0	...	...	10 15	1223
Great Bridgeford		...	E	...	...	...	E	...		...	...	E	...	...	...	...
Norton Bridge for E'shall		...	*3F55*	...	4 54	...	6 7	...		...	...	8 10	...	...	10 25	...
Colwich Line. Colwich dep		...	...	...	...	Arrives at Harecastle at 6.16	...	...		...	6 54	...	8 45	...	...	...
Great Haywood		...	...	...	...		...	...		...	6 58	...	*[illegible]*	...	...	...
Hixon		...	...	...	...		...	...		...	7 3	...	*[illegible]*	...	...	...
Weston (Ingestre)		...	...	...	...		...	...		...	7 7	...	*[illegible]*	...	...	...
Sandon		...	...	...	...		...	...		...	7 12	...	*[illegible]*	...	...	...
Aston by Stone		...	...	...	...		...	6C30		...	7 18	...	*[illegible]*	...	...	...
Stone Junction M dep		...	4 5	*Saturdays excepted.*	5 4		6 15	6C35		...	7 23	8 18	*[illegible]*	*Saturdays only.*	10 33	N
Barlaston (Tittensor) M		...	4 11		5 11		6 21	6C41		...	7 29	8 24	*[illegible]*		10 39	...
Trentham M		...	4 17		5 18		6 27	6C47		...	7 35	8 30	*[illegible]*		10 45	N
STOKE arr	3 35	Y	4‡23		5 25	...	6 33	6C53	7 10	...	7‡41	8 36	*[illegible]*		10‡51	*1248*
STOKE dep	3 39	3 42	4 30	5 2	5 32	5 56	...	...	7 13	7 20	8 32	9 0	...	1041	11 5	...
Etruria (Basford)	...	3 46	4 34	*5 6*	...	6 1	...	...	Express.	7 23	...	9 4	Thursdays & Saturdays only commencing June.	*1044*	11 8	Saturday nights and Sunday mornings.
Longport (Wolstanton)	Express.	3 51	4 39	*5 11*	5 38	6 7	...	...		7 27	8 38	9 9		...	11 13	
Chatterley		3 56	4 44	*5 16*	...	6 12	...	...		...	...	9 14		...	HC	
Harecastle (Kidsgrove)		4 0	4 49	*5 21*	5 45	7 0	...	...		7 33	8 45	9 19		*11A14*	11 19	
Harecastle dep		...	To Crewe.	...	5 50	...	...	...	...	Th[illegible]	...	9S23		Via Loop Line.	To Crewe.	
Lawton		...		...	5 55	...	...	...	...	Th[illegible]	...	9S28				
Hassall Green	...	...		...	6 1	...	...	...	...	Th[illegible]	To Crewe.	9S34				
Sandbach (Wheelock) arr	...	...	...	...	6 6	...	...	...	...	Th[illegible]		9S39			...	
Mow Cop (Scholar Green)	...	4 5	...	*5 27*	...	7 6	...	...	...	...		9 25		*1120*	...	
Congleton	3 57	4 11	...	*5 35*	5 56	7 13	...	...	7 29	...	...	9 32		*1126*	...	
North Rode	...	4 17	...	*5 42*	D	7S20	...	...	...	...	...	9 39		...	...	
Macclesfield (Central)	...	4 26	...	*5 54*	6 9	7S30	...	...	...	...	...	9 48		...	...	...
Buxton (via Middlewood)	5T40	7 I8	...	7 8	7Y58	9P55	...	...	9H55	...	...	11L19		...	...	...
Macclesfield (H. Rd.) arr	4 9	4 27	...	5 55	6 10	7S52	...	...	7 42	...	...	9 49		...	...	...
L. & N. W. Railway. Stockport arr	4 31	5 27	...		6 31	8S1	...	...	8 1	...	...	10 51	...	...	...	...
Manchester (London Road)	4 45	5 43	...		6 44	8S15	...	...	8 15	...	...	11 5	...	...	...	...
Huddersfield	5 40	7 14	...		7 43	9S28	...	...	9 28	...	...	1 30	...	...	...	...
Leeds (New Station)	6 17	7 53	...		8 13	10S10	...	...	1010	...	...	2 38	...	...	...	...

‡—Passengers change at Stoke.
A—Kidsgrove Station.
B—On *Saturdays* Passengers start at 6.55 p.m. and travel *via* Birmingham.
C—*Saturdays excepted* during May, and *Thursdays and Saturdays excepted* during June.
D—Calls *on Saturdays.*
E—Calls by Signal to pick up Passengers for the N. S. Line only.
F—*Mondays and Saturdays only.*
G—Leaves Walsall at 5.43, and Cannock at 5.57 p.m *on Thursdays.*
H—Via Stockport (L. & N. W.)
H C—Horses and Private Carriages are not conveyed by this Train.
I—Arrives 5.25 p.m. on *Saturdays* in June.
J—By Carriage slipped at Rugeley.
K—Leaves Walsall at 6.0, and Cannock 6.23 p.m. *on Thursdays.*
L—*Thursdays and Saturdays only.* Via Stockport (L. & N.W.)
S—*Saturdays only*
M—For Motor Connections to and from Trentham and Stone, see pages 24 to 27.
N—Calls to set down passengers from beyond Stafford on notice being given to the guard there.
P—*Saturdays only.* Via Stockport (L. & N. W.)
T—Via Stockport (L. & N. W.) Arrives 6.12 Sats.
Th *Thursdays only* from June.
V—Leaves at 8.15 p.m. on *Saturdays.*
Y—*Saturdays excepted.* Via Stockport (L. & N. W.)

For other Trains between Stoke and Harecastle, see pages 6 and 7.

For SUNDAY Trains see page 14.

The Times of Trains on Foreign Lines are given for information only.

being restricted to weekdays during July and August and also in May, June and September, or a combination of those months. By 1896 Buxton expresses all started from Macclesfield and only a few carried through coaches from Stoke. All called at Bollington and the 6 55 SO from Buxton also stopped at Poynton.

The full service to Buxton—equally balanced—was:

Macclesfield	8 15	10 45	3 55	2 30 SO	7 50 SO
Buxton	8 55	11 25	4 35	3 10	8 30

The trains that chugged through the south Cheshire countryside between Harecastle and Wheelock from 1893 never caused any sensations, but they provided a useful service for local people. Three ran each way on weekdays, augmented to five on Saturdays. Some ran through from Harecastle to Stoke.

Traffic in the heart of the Potteries was further intensified by the introduction, noted in detail in chapter 5 of 'Rail Motor Cars' from 1 May 1905. The up pattern was of nine weekday services; ten on Saturdays.[3]

Departure			*Destination*
Silverdale	5 0	am	Sideway
Brampton	6 33		Trentham
Silverdale	7 30		Trentham
Newcastle	11 27		Trentham
Newcastle	1 15	pm	Trentham
Silverdale	3 10		Sideway
Silverdale	4 20		Trentham
Newcastle	5 35		Sideway
Silverdale	6 38		Sideway
Silverdale	9 0	SO	Trentham

The 1908 timetable showed rail motors as the only services stopping at halts between Trentham and Silverdale. Audley and Stone were the general limits of rail motor operation and however much they were intended to match tram competition, they could hardly have made much impact if frequency was the yardstick, and even if regarded as supplementary to steam services. Their 1907 total was 52,453 miles: that of their competitors, the trams, was over 1,500,000.

But the NSR seemed undeterred by trams and stated in

summer 1910 that to a very great extent, they had made up the leeway caused by this competition by 'careful management and by saving every penny'.

HOLIDAY AND WAKES TRAFFIC

The holiday vision for many people in the Potteries in Victorian days was a golden day beside the summer sea at one of the resorts of North Wales. So they ensured that the Llandudno expresses remained always as the backbone of the regular holiday services, but people were encouraged to travel elsewhere. They were offered cheap weekly or fortnightly excursion rates to the most popular resorts of Lancashire, the Lake District, the Cambrian Coast and other parts of Wales, the West of England, London and Scotland.

Summer holidaymakers to the Isle of Man and Blackpool had through coaches which, in 1908, were attached to the 9 45 am Stoke—Crewe on Mondays and Saturdays. They reached Liverpool at 11 20 am and Blackpool (Talbot Road), at 12 11 pm.

The Stoke Wakes in the first fortnight of August always provided a heavy burden for the NSR because of their size. While the Lancashire Wakes are perhaps better known, those of the Potteries are the biggest in Britain for people in a group of towns with inter-related industries, taking their holidays together.

Workmen's Train (Rail Motor Car) Cresswell to Stoke.

		a.m.			a.m.
Cresswell	dep.	5 23	Longton	dep.	5 40
Blythe Bridge		5 28	Fenton		5 44
Meir		5 33	Carter's Crossing		5 46
Normacot		5 37	Stoke	arr.	5 48

The Car connects with the 5 52 a.m. Train Stoke to Tunstall.

L.&N.W. and Midland Railway Companies.

These Companies have made numerous alterations in the Train Service for April, affecting the connections with the North Staffordshire Railway Company. Passengers intending to travel between the N.S. and the Systems named are advised to consult the L.&N.W. and Midland Railway Companies Time Tables.

W. D. PHILLIPPS,
General Manager.

Railway Offices, Stoke Station,
March, 1908.

HARRY LOCKETT, PRINTER, HANLEY.

Part of timetable supplement for April 1908 showing Carter's Crossing, not in main timetable

During the Wakes and throughout the summer too, Knotty ran local excursions for:

> The valleys of the Manifold and its tributary, the Hamps, are, in point of beauty, among the most precious possessions of Staffordshire.[4]

That was the opinion of Charles Masefield in 1910. The Leek & Manifold Railway was then six years old and still something of a novelty for many tourists.

For just over three months (1 June—5 September), expresses ran from Stoke at 1 5 pm on Saturdays; 2 pm Thursdays. Calling only at Bucknall, Milton and Endon and using the Leek Brook curve, they reached Waterhouses in 50m and passengers joined a waiting connection for the 40m journey to Hulme End. The return excursion left Hulme End at 8 pm both nights.

These specials supplemented the basic L & M service of four trains each way, to which a fifth was added on Mondays and Thursdays and a sixth on Saturdays.

WARTIME SERVICES

The biggest effect of the war conditions was the reduction of passenger services, ordered by the Government in 1917, but many small economies were made long before that. In the month following the declaration of war in August 1914, the Saturday expresses between Stoke and Buxton were withdrawn. One is left with the impression that this was not so much an act of patriotism, but a welcome excuse to get rid of an unprofitable service.

The NSR joined other companies in cutting back passenger services from 22 February 1915, and axed some fifteen trains, plus a number of others restricted to certain days. They included a Saturday afternoon return working from Stoke to Market Drayton, and a Saturday evening rail motor service on the Loop between Hanley and Tunstall.

Through services suffered, too, and the LNWR re-routed the 4 pm Euston—Manchester via Crewe, detaching through coaches for Stoke at Rugeley, where they were attached to the 6 41 pm all-stations which took 52m to Stoke and so added nearly 40m to the overall journey time. The fastest pre-war

Page 207 *Shed scenes:* (above) *The straight shed at Stoke about 1933 with class 'D' 0–6–0T No 1570, formerly* NSR *57, prominent on left;* (below) *Alsager shed about 1918 with class E 0–6–0 No 66 after a second rebuilding in 1905. Compare with the centre plate on page 190*

Page 208 (above) *Steam rail-motor car No 1 of 1906;* (below) *Leek & Manifold trial train at Hulme End 1904 with 'J. B. Earle'*

timings of 2h 41m between Stoke and Euston fell to 3h 21m.

In pre-war years timetables ran to over 30 pages and cost 1d. By 1921 they had been extended to 40 (including 32 pages detailing trains), and cost 3d. Bradshaw, then costing 6d, and using much smaller type, condensed NSR services into 8½ pages between those of the LNWR and the Midland Railway. It excluded from the NSR section the GNR Derby—Stafford route and the MB & M Joint line was shown under the GCR—and not as a joint line. A footnote under Poynton stated:

> Top Stn, New Road; stn for Lyme Park; 2¼ miles from L & NW Station.

There was no such distinction in the Knotty timetable. Bradshaw recorded trains to Newcastle on three different pages. One gave the local service between Trentham Park and Leycett (motor car trains), calling at all halts. Through trains to Market Drayton or Harecastle, via Audley, were given in a second table, and the third gave a summary of all trains Stoke—Newcastle. Bradshaw only showed halts in footnotes and no separate timings were given for them.

Services never given in Bradshaw were strike specials, run in times of emergency, virtually on a day to day basis in the light of the number of men who were prepared to go on working. Services gained in intensity as strikes lengthened, as was demonstrated during one of the last in Knotty days, which took place in October 1919. On the first day only a handful of trains ran on the main line and that from Stoke to Rushton, via Leek. The next day, 2 October, two Silverdale—Market Drayton trains ran and by 6 October there was a service on the main, Churnet and Ashbourne lines, although on the Loop the only link was between Stoke and Tunstall.

RUNNING POWERS AND GOODS TRAFFIC

The extensive running powers of the NSR were one of its most unusual and renowned features for they gave it a regular identity in places far outside the Potteries. The most splendid example was the Derby—Llandudno link of 118½ miles, on which NSR stock ran further than it could on its own system.

Less than half the mileage (44½) was on the NSR: the majority (67½ miles) was over the LNWR and the small balance (6½ miles) over the Midland. Passenger services also ran to Manchester, Walsall, Wolverhampton and Buxton.

Far more important was the busy goods network developed between Derby, Egginton or Burton, to Liverpool (Edge Hill), via Crewe and either Runcorn or Warrington. This service ran twice daily and there were others between Burton—Manchester, via Leek; Stoke—Macclesfield—Manchester, augmented by a third working to Edgeley; Alsager or Stoke to Bushbury, via Norton Bridge; Stoke or Alsager to Northwich.

Alsager was the starting point of a daily mineral working to Wellingborough, with conditional 'up' stops at Swadlincote, Coalville and Woodville. Other extended workings took NSR engines through Crewe to Mold Junction; south from Colwich to Rugby; and from Market Drayton to Wellington.

LNWR workings over the Knotty began with the Manchester—London goods link via Stoke, established from 1 July 1853, and in later days LNWR workings grew to include: Sideway—Rugby; Stoke—Bushbury; Alsager—Birmingham (Windsor Street); Llandudno Junction—Alsager; Crewe—Bushbury and Rugby, via Stoke; Heaton Norris—Bushbury; Liverpool—Nottingham (via Egginton); Manchester—Rugby; Parsley Hay—Burton; and Nuneaton—Leeds.

The NSR only exercised running powers over the GNR to Nottingham with excursions, and to Netherfield and Colwick with goods. It did not exploit those to Burton station, Leicester, Pinxton, Stafford, Peterborough 'or elsewhere', which it obtained by an agreement of 21 August 1896.

In return the GNR got access to Stoke and other places, although not, it seems, to Macclesfield or Market Drayton for a request for access to these towns made three years later was rejected by the NSR. The 1896 agreement provided for locomotives to be stabled at Stoke and Alsager, Peterborough and Colwick, at 10s a week. Water was to cost 1 shilling a tank. The GNR carried goods to Stoke and also over the Burton branch.

The GWR gave the Knotty power to run into Market Drayton station with all traffic and on to Hodnet with passengers and cattle and to Wellington with goods. The Midland had powers to reach Stoke from Burton and Willington, but they were left unused in later days. The GWR carried goods to Stoke via Market Drayton.

Running powers were jealously watched by different companies and when the Midland gave the LNWR access to new branches at Burton, it laid down that it was not to carry traffic through to the NSR.

On the Macclesfield joint line, NSR goods workings only went to Middlewood, the GCR taking charge of any traffic beyond.

The NSR goods services were fed by traffic initiated, collected and delivered by teams based on seven major centres: Derby, Nottingham, Burton, Market Drayton, Crewe, Ettiley Heath (for Sandbach), and Norton Bridge (for Eccleshall). The importance attached to the Burton traffic was underlined by the company having three goods agents there: the largest number in a single town. From Burton the NSR carried not only beer, but timber, plaster slabs, engineering and chemical products. Traffic was marshalled at Stretton Junction, Horninglow Bridge sidings and station yards.

At Derby, the NSR had a town office (13 Corn Market), and agents at the passenger station and its own goods station. Other agents sought traffic in Manchester and the staff network was strengthened by private agents at Birmingham, Wolverhampton, Leicester, Liverpool and Runcorn Docks. The NSR asked traders to make sure that goods 'should be ordered by the North Stafford Route'. The exhortation was more strongly pressed in advertisements offering extensive storage for wines and spirits at the company's bonded warehouses at Hanley:

> It is requested that Firms, when sending Wines and Spirits intended to be kept in these Stores, should be particular in ordering them to the care of the North Staffordshire Railway Company.[5]

The company also carried a less potent traffic: milk. It never reached such proportions that it was regarded as a major source of revenue, but milk traffic was lucrative and must have made many a rural passenger train profitable.

PRIVATE TRAINS

The Knotty was proud of the way it adapted its lines to encourage people to travel, and of the fact that regular passenger services ran over all but a few miles of the system. Such were its good relations with local pits, steel and other works, that it even allowed, indeed encouraged, these private companies to run their own trains over its lines. The trains were an operating and economical convenience to the major firms and to the NSR which was paid for the traffic and did not have to provide a service to handle it. On the sections used by the private trains, NSR boxes were provided with a list of locomotives authorised to work over the system and of men authorised to work private trains, all locomotive crews having first to be passed in NSR rules.

Besides private workmen's trains, there were local shunting movements and those which worked over short stretches of the main NSR lines. Dr Hollick[6] relates how working began unofficially and included an instance in 1852 when the Shelton Iron Company ran an engine from Etruria to Wheelock and back. The NSR board ordered that should never happen again! They wanted to know what was going on.

Customer participation was greatest in the Biddulph Valley, where two companies ran their own trains over the branch. Chatterley—Whitfield introduced workmen's trains between Whitfield colliery and Biddulph on 3 November 1890, and until the opening of Chell halt in 1912, they started from the pit yard. In 1919 the trains were extended to the newly-opened Mossley halt, and ran there until the service ceased about 1923.

The Whitfield company also ran mineral trains to Ubberley from June 1896 and to Botteslow Wharf on the Longton, Adderley Green and Bucknall Railway.

Robert Heath ran mineral trains after the opening of the Biddulph Valley Ironworks at Brindley Ford in 1866, works which, incidentally, made iron for the Menai and Forth bridges, as well as industrial locomotives and wrought iron wagons. Based on Heath's Junction, these trains ran until about 1930, mostly to Brunswick Wharf at Congleton, where Heath's had half the yard for their coal traffic.

One of the biggest companies, the Midland Coal, Coke and Iron Company, formed by amalgamations on 4 January 1890, ran passenger and mineral trains from its headquarters at Apedale to Newcastle, and mineral trains to Knutton, Pool Dam and Newcastle, where half the goods yard was reserved for them. The workmen's trains—'the Apedale Paddy'—were made up of a private engine and NSR 4-wheel coaches. They ran from Newcastle and called at Brampton Road and Liverpool Road halts after their opening in 1905.

The Pool Dam line was also used by trains operated by the owners of Silverdale Ironworks, which ran trains for many years between Silverdale, Knutton Forge and the canal wharf. The Talke branch was worked for many years by Sneyd engines and the NSR did not start regular workings until it bought most of the line in 1904. A daily goods was worked to Bradwell by a Talke engine until 1931.

On the neighbouring Chesterton branch, a mining company of that name ran twice daily trains a short distance to Hem Heath Colliery. Another limited working served Florence Colliery. This was the terminus of an NSR early morning workmen's service, the 4 57 am from Silverdale. This ran to Trentham and was extended to the pit, being pulled over the pit branch by one of the private locomotives.

A workmen's service operated by contractors was that over the Churnet Valley line from Leek during the building of the North Staffordshire County Mental Hospital at Cheddleton between 1895-9. The sub-contractors of the Waterhouses branch, Lovatts of Wolverhampton, also used Leek as a starting point for trains which they ran between 1901 and 1905 to the branch brick works at Wall Grange.

The most complex of local shunting movements by private trains involved locomotives at the Staffordshire Chemical Works at Bradwell, between Longport and Chatterley. Company drivers were instructed in NSR rules so they could run a short distance along the main line to reach the company's up sidings. This arrangement continued for many years, but a more limited one was at Harecastle, where a pit engine worked on the Loop at Kidsgrove Junction from 1893-5.

CHAPTER TEN

Locomotives & Rolling Stock

> There was a lot of old drivers used to have their own engine you see. They was very proud of them . . . and everything had to be absolutely, just to perfection.
>
> *Charles Edward Dawson*—NSR *driver*

The locomotives polished by the early drivers were often curious machines and that was due to unusual reasons. Until 1874 responsibility for the locomotive stock rested with the engineer. There were four holders of the post up to that time. None had much practical experience in running a locomotive department and however eminent they might have been in civil engineering, they had eccentric ideas about locomotives. Throughout this period Robert N. Angus, as second in command, had somehow to keep locomotives running, no matter what the whims of the different bosses.

Angus had been apprenticed to the Liverpool locomotive builders, Bury, Curtis & Kennedy at the same time as J. E. McConnel, Alexander Allan, Benjamin Connor and Robert Sinclair. He joined the NSR to take charge of Stoke Works on 1 September 1847, as 'Locomotive Foreman'.

His first chief was S. P. Bidder who by February 1847 had ordered forty-three locomotives costing about £2,300 each. After being succeeded as engineer by Forsyth in the following year, Bidder continued to exert influence on locomotive orders in his new position of general manager, which he held until 1853. Forsyth then became engineer and general manager for ten years and from 1863-5, engineer alone. He next became consulting engineer for several years, and influenced some of the work of the new resident engineer, James Johnson.

Bidder had a partiality for Stephenson patent long-boiler type of locomotive. The engines he chose were 2–4–0s with all their wheels, including 5ft 6in drivers, in front of the fire-box. This made them unsteady above 20-25mph: a fault aggravated by the outside cylinders being placed in front of the leading wheels. There was little locomotive men could do but suffer, for twenty-seven out of the first thirty-three original passenger engines suffered from these defects. They were built in four batches which differed only in detail.

Ten 0–6–0 goods engines built by the Vulcan Foundry Company of Newton le Willows also had long boilers, but their cylinders were placed inside and their drivers were smaller. In contrast six 2–2–2 passenger engines built by Sharp Brothers of Atlas Works, Manchester, were of conventional design and were the makers' most successful standard class, supplied to many railways. Inside cylinders were 15in by 20in and driving wheels 5ft 6in.

With one exception, all the 43 locomotives were delivered in 1848-9: it is recorded that six arrived at Stoke 'under steam' from Norton Bridge on 15 March 1848.

The next purchases were of five second-hand locomotives from contractors building the line: four long-boilered 0–6–0s from S. M. Peto and Company; and a 2–2–2T of unknown origin from Price & Leishman. The latter was not numbered but referred to as the 'ballast locomotive'. The rest of the stock was numbered up to 47 more or less in the order in which they were delivered. The only named engine was the Sharp 2–2–2 No 1 *Dragon*, which hauled the ceremonial first train. It was named after a local packhorse. Individual engine numbers are given in appendix 5.

BOILERS: LONG AND OVAL

Ten passenger and six goods engines were ordered in 1849. The goods locomotives, more long-boilered 0–6–0s, were built in 1849-50 but five were sold at cost price to the Midland Railway in 1851 and given the numbers 205-9. The sixth was sold to the contractor of the Dutch Rhenish Railway. Six 2–4–0 passenger locomotives were built by Kitson, Thompson & Hewitson in 1850. They had outside bearings for the leading axle. They were converted to 2–2–2s by 1852 and were modelled on the other four engines which had inside bearings to the driving axle and outside bearings for the carrying wheels on the famous 'Jenny Lind' principle. The cut-away outside frames were built from separate pieces. Both the last batches had *oval* boilers, which gave much trouble later. Another conversion by Angus at Stoke was of two of the Hick 2–4–0s, which became 2–2–2 well tanks with shortened boilers and a lengthened wheelbase. The firebox was placed in front of the trailing axle but outside cylinders, reduced in diameter to 14in, were retained. The engines were still unsteady at speed and one was involved in a derailment in 1861 in which the driver, fireman and guard were killed. These were the first tanks on the system. Two double-framed 0–6–0s similar to Midland engines were obtained from Kitsons in 1853 and their boiler diameter of 4ft 2in was not to be surpassed on the NSR until 1900, although according to Angus' notebook, the Worcester goods engines of 1866-7 had 4ft 4in diameter boilers. The next 0–6–0s built by Vulcan in 1855 were again inside framed, long-boilered types.

Up to 1859 coke was the main fuel used, the first orders having been placed in February 1847. After successful experiments with coal using a brick firebox arch for better combustion and to reduce the smoke nuisance, twenty-seven locomotives were converted to coal burning in 1859; a further thirty-five in 1860 and the last two in 1861.

Because of shortage of money no locomotives were ordered between 1855-60 and when the board agreed to the purchase of two goods engines on 29 March 1860, it laid down that they were not to cost more than £2,300—less than the price paid for some over ten years earlier. Selected were two more Stephenson double-framed 0–6–0s. Two goods tanks were obtained in 1862. They also had double frames, long boilers, flat-sided saddle tanks and coal bunkers at the firebox side, which made them look ungainly. Both were similar to engines then being used in north eastern England and on the Turin & Genoa Railway. Their wheels were small, 4ft 0in diameter.

In 1864-5 four double-framed 0–6–0 goods engines were supplied by the newly-established firm of Hudswell, Clarke & Rodgers. The design seems to have been based on contemporary goods engines of Sacré and Sturrock for the MS & L and GNR in that very long fireboxes were used having a sloping grate over the rear axle with an area of 23½sq ft. Cylinders were 16in by 24in and the wheels 5ft 0in.

When Percy Morris succeeded Forsyth as general manager in 1863 he immediately called for an outside opinion on the locomotive stock and consultants who reported in 1864 described them as 'a parcel of long-boilered locomotives'—and recommended their complete renewal. The man appointed to carry out the work was James Johnson, who became the NSR resident engineer (again with locomotive responsibilities) in 1865 after sixteen years on the GNR. He was the father of Samuel Waite Johnson, destined to achieve fame as locomotive superintendent of the Midland Railway. However it was left to the long-suffering Angus to work out the rebuilding details.

The consultants' report had stated that forty-six locomotives needed reconstruction since they were unsuited to traffic. They included the six Sharp singles, now getting too light for the main line traffic, the twenty-five long-boilered 2–4–0s, which were very unsatisfactory, and the four old goods engines bought from Peto. The oval boilers of the ten Kitson singles were also causing trouble.

A new boiler was designed for these rebuilds. It was 4ft 0in in diameter with a raised firebox casing. The barrel length was varied to suit the different classes. The engines also needed new frames, often with the wheelbase altered to allow the firebox to be placed in the normal position in front of the trailing axle. It meant the rebuilds were virtually new engines. While only four were completed in 1865, thirteen were rebuilt in the next six months.

The Kitson 2–4–0s of 1848 and two Sharp singles were rebuilt as tanks and the other four Sharps renewed as 2–4–0s with double frames like the singles. Eight of the remaining long-boilered 2–4–0s were renewed as 2–4–0s with the new, shortened boiler. Eight other locomotives were sent for rebuilding to Hudswell, Clarke & Rodgers, which gave them new works numbers. Four Jones & Potts 2–4–0s were renewed similar to the Stoke process. According to Hudswell records they included the old wheels and other parts. The other four, the Peto 0–6–0s had new 5ft 0in wheels. Two were converted to saddle tanks with rear bunkers while the other pair remained tender engines. The old Peto engines were not all broken up by Hudswell for one, or possibly two, were sold to a contractor, Moss of Stafford, who re-sold one to the LNWR on 18 April 1873 as part payment for another LNWR engine. Given the LNWR no 1858, this was cut up at Crewe on 4 May. The main passenger engines, the Kitson singles, were rebuilt at Stoke in 1869-71 when they were given new boilers and 6ft 1in drivers to make them more capable of fast running. In 1870, the four Vulcan goods of 1855 were converted to 0–6–0STs. While retaining their long boilers, they had bunkers at the side of the firebox and looked like an inside frame version of the Stephenson saddle tanks of 1862.

While Angus continued modernisation, Johnson ordered new stock of double-frame 0–6–0s, similar to earlier ones but with slightly bigger cylinders, received from three makers in 1865-67. The first two batches had long fireboxes, the Worcester batch of normal design. They were later rebuilt as Longbottom's class 'F'. A small contractor's type locomotive was bought from Hudswell in 1866. It was an 0–6–0ST with wheels of only 3ft 0in. In 1868 Stoke built three identical ones getting some parts from Hudswell.

THE WEDGE MOTION DEBACLE

Johnson, whose reign lasted five years until 1870, was later accused of doing unpopular things. The chairman, Pearson, commented that 'he had queer views and attached fireboxes not suited to the district, which had to be removed at great expense'.

The departure of Johnson did not mean the end of unusual design, for his successor, who was once again the company engineer, was Thomas Weatherburn Dodds. He was the son of Isaac Dodds, one time locomotive superintendent of the Sheffield & Rotherham Railway and more noteworthy as the inventor of Dodds' wedge motion and founder of the engineering firm, Dodds of Rotherham, which built a number of engines in the forties and fifties with the wedge motion. Thomas Dodds took out a new patent on 9 March 1871 and fitted the motion to eleven engines which he built the following year.

Before that he added an 0–6–0ST to stock in 1870. It was a five-year-old built by Dodds. No other details are known; there is a suggestion that it may have been on the NSR since 1866, but it was not numbered until 1870.

Dodds found the most urgent need was for goods engines and two, of conventional design, were completed at Stoke in 1871 and others contracted: ten from Vulcan Foundry in 1872, which had wedge motion; six from Beyer Peacock in 1874, which had link motion. Another four were built at Stoke in 1875-7. These twenty-two engines were later to become Longbottom's 'E' class.

Meanwhile, other locomotives had been bought: eight slightly smaller 0–6–0s from Sharps in 1873-4. They were the maker's standard 'off the peg' inside frame design, already supplied to the Cambrian, Furness and other companies, and indeed the first two delivered to the NSR had originally been ordered by the Furness. The remainder were built to NSR order and had a different boiler tube arrangement: class '69'.

Dodds displayed some originality when he set about meeting passenger needs with an inside frame 2–4–0. The first, no 19, built at Stoke in 1872 had 6ft 6in drivers, the largest on the line, and also wedge motion. The neat cab had a large rectangular side window with a drop light like those fitted to carriage doors. It was a type of cab introduced the previous year on one of the rebuilt Kitson singles, no 25. Two other 2–4–0s under construction were greatly modified for they were built at a time when memories were still fresh of the 1873 accident in which a light engine was unable to get out of the way of a runaway train at Lawton Junction because its wedge motion jammed at the crucial moment. The motion often jammed and it was only possible on occasions to re-start a locomotive after a pinch bar had been placed under the wheels.

The wedge motion debacle led to a change of policy and of supervision. Dodds was asked to resign and agreed, but a few weeks later in February 1874 he withdrew his resignation suggesting improvements in locomotive and coaching stock. The directors refused to consider his request and Dodds left the NSR on 31 March.

The board decided the time was ripe for a practical man to take charge and the new post of locomotive superintendent at last brought to Angus the recognition he deserved. He was destined to hold office for less than two years, yet it was time enough for him to make his mark. He removed all wedge motions and substituted Stephenson valve gear.

It is related that soon after his appointment on 1 April, Angus met F. W. Webb and the Duke of Sutherland on Stoke Station. Webb remarked: 'I suppose you'll be wanting to borrow engines?' Angus replied: 'If I do, they won't be LNWR ones!' The Duke commented: 'That's one for you, Webb!'

So the two remaining 2–4–0s had link motion when they were turned out at Stoke in 1874. Driving wheels were reduced by 4½in and the usual bent-over weather boards replaced the cosy cab of no 19 (class '38').

The 2–4–0s took over most of the main line work from the Kitson singles which, with one exception, remained in service for several years being withdrawn progressively between 1882-6. The same wheel arrangement was also favoured for local passenger work and designs with smaller wheels, 5ft 6in, were built in tender and tank varieties, both with outside cylinders.

Three small-wheeled tender engines built at Stoke in 1874 were supposedly renewals of the old outside cylinder 2–4–0s, but it seems likely that little more than the wheels were used. Cabs had a neat little round side window similar to Sacre's MS & L engines, but later they were replaced by standard ones (class '7').

Five tank engines built in the same year had many characteristics of Sharp's, which built three and supplied parts for Stoke to build the other two. They had, for instance, Sharp style cab roofs, bent over to form front and rear weather boards, open at the sides (class '9').

All Dodds & Angus engines featured raised fireboxes and shapely brass safety valve covers.

Two inside frame 0–6–0s completed at Stoke in 1875 were identical to earlier engines with raised fireboxes, safety valve casings and weather boards. In the same year, Angus got four 0–6–0STs from Stephenson's. They were virtual replicas of the 1862 engines, except for cabs which were open at the back.

Also built in 1875 were three 2–4–0s of class '38' by Dubs of Glasgow with cabs without side windows, subsequently a standard fitting for tender engines.

CLARE AND THE TANK ENGINE

The next locomotive superintendent, C. Clare, was also in office for a comparatively short term, from the end of 1875 until his death in 1882. In 1876-7 he completed at Stoke two more 0–6–0s of the type built by Dodds and Angus. Unlike earlier engines they had fireboxes flush with the boiler and so set a new standard. Although they retained the old style of lock-up safety valves, they were the last before a switch to Ramsbottom valves.

As the rebuilding policy continued, shareholders were told in 1877 that the locomotive stock was then in 'as perfect a condition as it is possible for any railway to have its stock'.

Next rebuilt was a double-frame 0–6–0 in 1877, followed by nine more in succeeding years. Extensive rebuilds were carried out on two Hudswell 0–6–0STs in 1880-1, (class '59') which were given 4ft 0in wheels—1ft 0in smaller than their original ones. This made them much more useful for shunting. The tanks received Clare's own form of cab with virtually no sides and a flat roof, domed in the centre like Stroudley's. The narrow cabs left plenty of room for the driver to lean out over the rectangular lower panels.

Locomotives were run hard and in summer 1877 mileage was reported to have increased by 30,000, while expenditure had dropped £1,604. The running cost was then about tenpence a mile, another figure which showed a drop.

New construction at Stoke in Clare's period was concentrated on tanks for the growing local passenger services. Most new engines from now forward were built at Stoke and all had flush fireboxes and also Ramsbottom safety valves, until the introduction of Belpaire fireboxes in 1910.

The first new engines, class 'A', were 2–4–0Ts with side tanks, similar to those of Angus, except for different cylinder and wheel sizes (4ft 6in). Eight built between 1878-81 had Clare's dome-roof cabs, and this was retained for the next batch, class 'B', in which wheel diameter reverted to 5ft 6in.

Ten were built in 1881-2. Later these engines and the '9' class with Sharp cabs, were given more modern cabs with cutaway sides and arched roofs.

Clare also built two more 2–4–0 tender engines, classified 'C' and named after the deputy chairman and chairman:

54 *John Bramley Moore*
55 *Colin Minton Campbell*

They were the only 'names' since by 1882 *Dragon* had lost its name.

THE LONGBOTTOM ERA

On his death, Clare was succeeded by Luke Longbottom, who was to hold office for twenty years and become the longest holder of the title of locomotive superintendent. He was also carriage and wagon superintendent, which had previously been a separate post. Apprenticed to Fenton, Murray & Jackson, Longbottom later served with two other Leeds locomotive builders: E. B. Wilson & Company and Kitson, Thompson & Hewitson, and then became locomotive superintendent of the North Western Railway. When that was absorbed by the Midland in 1852, he moved a short distance to be superintendent of the Kendal & Windermere Railway. When that was absorbed by the LNWR he became District Locomotive Foreman at Tebay and Preston before joining the NSR.

Although he retained many of the design features of his predecessors, Longbottom introduced a new colour. Up to 1882 locomotives had a bright green livery lined with a black band edged white, used in the same positions as the black-edged yellow lining now adopted in 1883. The Staffordshire Knot emblem was placed on tender or tank sides and on the large splashers of passenger engines. Longbottom introduced Victoria Brown—a rich, red brown, lined in black, yellow and vermilion. Buffer beams were painted in the usual red with a half-inch black border and quarter-inch yellow line as on the frames. Guard irons were painted buff and the cab interiors were vermilion with black edging. Buffer-beam numbers were gold with brown shading while number plates had brass figures and edging with a red background and the Knot emblem in gold with blue shading.

Longbottom perpetuated the designs of Angus and Clare, adopting their 4ft 0in diameter boiler as standard, although lengths still varied to suit each class. His first task concerned the 'A' tanks. Their 4ft 6in wheels had proved too small for passenger work and from 1888 five were rebuilt with 5ft 1½in wheels and their old wheels used in the new 0–6–0 tanks which became class 'D'. This was one of the most successful and popular of all classes and became the biggest. The original engines had cylinders 16¾in x 24in, but from 1894 17in cylinders were fitted.

Longbottom also built more of Clare's 'B' and 'C' class passenger engines. Nine 'B' 2–4–0Ts were built in 1886-95 and like class 'D' they had Longbottom style cabs with a plain arc roof, open at the sides. Class 'C' (2–4–0) additions were confined to two engines built in 1884.

Between 1884 and 1896 most inside-framed 5ft 0in 0–6–0s were rebuilt as class 'E' with 17in cylinders and new boilers. Class '69' Sharp 0–6–0s were rebuilt 1888-9, this time with 16½in cylinders. Most of the double-frame engines (nos 82-99) became class 'F' when fitted with 17in cylinders and new boilers between 1888-97. Older engines had been re-boilered in 1877-82 (nos. 78-81, 100-103).

Older 2–4–0s were also rebuilt: no 19 in 1886 and the '38' class in 1888-94. They got new boilers and 17in cylinders, as did later 'C' class engines so that apart from no 19 with its 6ft 6in wheels, all 2–4–0s were virtually identical. Small-wheel 2–4–0s with outside cylinders also got new boilers and standard cabs without side windows. (Class '7'.)

Of the outside-cylinder 2–4–0Ts (of class '9'), two were rebuilt in 1894, receiving 16½in cylinders, new cabs and standard boilers. The other three were rebuilt in 1899 as 2–4–2T with enlarged boilers and other features. In 1898-9, three class 'A' tanks with large wheels were similarly rebuilt as 2–4–2Ts with 17in cylinders. They had had standard boilers from building.

Three locomotives were sold for industrial use in 1888-90. Two Stephenson 0–6–0ST of 1862 (nos 56 and 57) went to the Kidsgrove Steel, Iron & Coal Company in March 1888 and were named *Ada* and *Marion*. One was sold about 1910 to

Chatterley—Whitfield Collieries and got a new name, *Sampson*. The third engine sold was also a Stephenson saddle tank (no 47 of 1875). In May 1890 it went to the Madeley Coal & Iron Company, via a dealer (Turner, Kidsgrove). It was named *Pioneer* and was destroyed by a boiler explosion on 1 November 1895.

By 1895 some NSR locomotives were beginning to prove too small to handle heavier trains. Boilers of at least 4ft 3in diameter were now being fitted by many other British companies. Longbottom realised the NSR, too, needed bigger boilers. So that any larger ones could be used on existing classes without major alterations, the boiler decided upon was a modest 4ft 2in, but pressure was raised by 10lb to 150lb.

The first class built with the larger boilers was one of 0–6–0 goods which appeared from Stoke in 1896: the first for nineteen years and the first tender engines for twelve years, a gap which reflected the extent to which the Knotty was becoming a line of tank locomotives. Eight of the new class '100' 0–6–0s were completed up to 1900. The next new class, the 'DX' 0–6–2Ts, were enlargements of class 'D' with longer fireboxes and bunkers over a radial truck, as on the 2–4–2Ts. A new cab with cutaway sheets as on tender engines, was fitted to these tanks and also to some rebuilds of classes 'A', 'B', '9' and '58'. Rails were added to increase the capacity of bunkers and tenders.

Rebuilding older engines with 4ft 2in boilers started in 1897 and continued until 1913. All small-cylinder engines were given new ones of 17in: class 'B' in 1897-1908; older class 'A' from 1903. Three additional engines were converted to 2–4–2Ts with enlarged bunkers: nos 21, 24 and 61 of class 'B' in 1900-1. Class 'D' was rebuilt 1900-13 and nos 58-59 in 1909. All class 'E' tender engines except nos 76 and 77 were rebuilt in 1899-1911; class '69' (except no 65) in 1903-11; classes 'C' '38' and '19' 2–4–0s (except no 15), in 1901-8. None of the outside-cylinder engines of classes '7' and '9' or the double frame class 'F' got 4ft 2in boilers.

This comprehensive rebuilding programme robbed Stoke of some of its building capacity and for the first time for 25 years orders were placed with private firms when extra 0–6–0 tender engines were needed in 1900. This was a period when

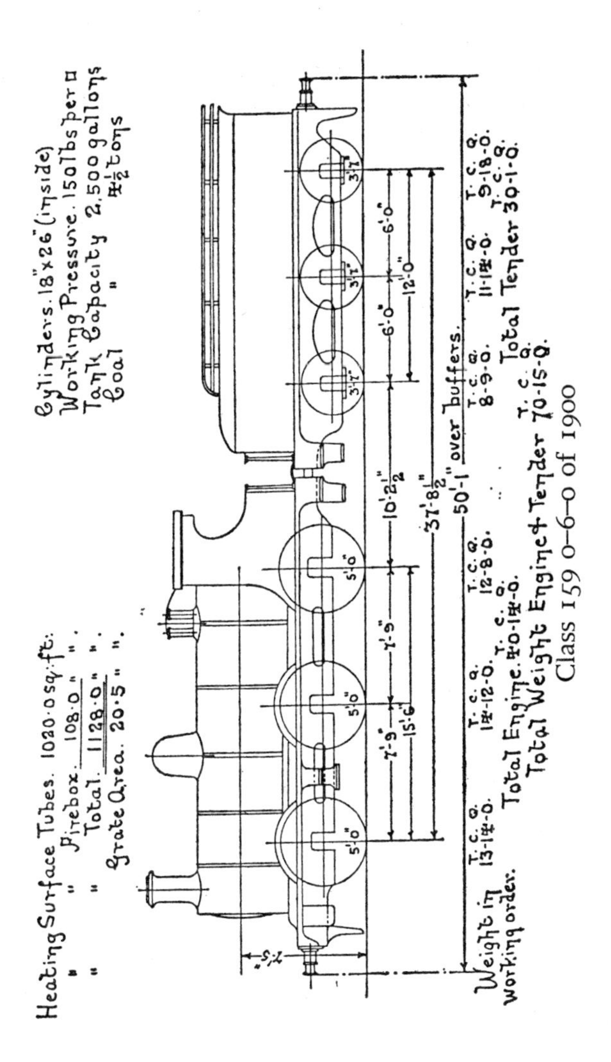

Class 159 0–6–0 of 1900

big increases in train loads caused an engine famine on many railways and resulted in private builders quoting lengthy delivery dates. Several companies bought foreign engines and Longbottom was unable to get quick delivery of more '100' class but he found that Nasmyth, Wilson & Company of Patricroft, Manchester, had on offer six 0–6–0s ordered but not required by the Furness Railway. They were larger than the '100' class having 18in x 26in cylinders and 5ft 0in wheels, but were suitable for the Knotty and they became nos 159-164. They heralded a new look having, for the first time on tender engines, cabs without rectangular lower side sheets and the tenders were wider with springs below the platforms. In later years their cylinders were increased to 18½in.

As still more 0–6–0s were needed, four veterans were purchased from the LNWR in April and May 1900. Not being expected to last long they were numbered straight into the duplicate list no 114A-117A. They dated from the sixties but had been rebuilt to 'Special DX' class in 1883-7. The last had been scrapped by 1916. The duplicate list was an accountancy expedient to allow new engines to be charged to revenue as a replacement for a locomotive which did not have to be scrapped. Duplicate locomotives were written off at nil value and not counted as assets. The list at the end of 1902 included 13 engines. Some were quickly scrapped but an old saddle tank, no 58A, first duplicate listed in 1899, was destined to be rebuilt ten years later and not scrapped until 1927.

The 177 standard-gauge locomotives in stock at the end of 1902 consisted of seventeen classes.

There were three narrow-gauge locomotives working the 3ft 6in gauge lines of the Caldon Low quarries. *Bobs* (after Lord Roberts) was built by W. G. Bagnall in 1901; *Toad* and *Frog* by Henry Hughes & Company, 1877. All were 0–4–0ST with 2ft 3in wheels and outside cylinders 7in x 12in.

JOHN HENRY ADAMS

Longbottom was succeeded as Locomotive, Carriage & Wagon Superintendent by John Henry Adams, appointed in April 1902. Born in 1860, he was the third son of William Adams and was apprenticed on the Great Eastern at Stratford under his father in 1877. He moved to Nine Elms when his father became Locomotive Superintendent of the LSWR. He fired for nine months, drove for fifteen on LSWR goods and passenger workings and then spent a year with the Leeds hydraulic engineers, Thanet, Walker & Company. He became locomotive superintendent of the Donna Thereza Railway in Brazil in 1887 and returned to England in January 1899 as assistant works manager at the Ashford works of the SE & CR.

Once he joined the NSR he persuaded a friend at Ashford, John A. Hookham, who since 1900 had been locomotive superintendent of the same Brazilian railway, to join him at Stoke as works manager. He did so in October 1902, when the Brazilian railway was taken over by the Government. Another Ashford man enticed to Stoke was A. J. Tassell, who became chief draughtsman.

Like Longbottom, Adams changed livery and replaced Victoria Brown with Madder Lake, a more delicate red than the Derby Lake of the Midland.

This was also not very different in shade from the original claret. Madder Lake was a rich crimson closely resembling the British Standard colour no 0-007: Afghan Red. It was made from cochineal (a red dye obtained from the dried bodies of a Mexican scale insect), which, in 1914, was obtained from Docker Brothers of Birmingham at 16 shillings a pound.

Lining out was simplified, boiler bands becoming black edged in pale yellow with a thin vermilion line outside. Panels were lined with a pale yellow band edged with vermilion. Wheels also were Madder Lake and lined in yellow. Wheel rims, tyres and centres were black. Buffer beams were red lined in gold and black, while buffer shanks were lake. Cab side numbers were in separate brass figures. The Knot was substituted by the coat of arms.

The first engines to receive the new livery were six 'L' class 0–6–2Ts built by Vulcan Foundry in 1903. They were notably larger than Longbottom engines. New features included a drumhead smokebox resting on a saddle as on Churchward's new GWR engines and Field's automatic relief valves for the cylinders. This batch had the leading sandboxes separately lined out from the leading splashers: subsequently they were lined as one unit. The engines also had safety valve casings in Worsdell's North Eastern style, which was not repeated on other engines.

For the opening of the 2ft 6in gauge Leek & Manifold Railway, Kitson's designed and built two 2–6–4Ts in 1904. Originally in brown livery, they were soon repainted Madder Lake.

When the 6ft 6in 2–4–0 no 19 of 1872 was rebuilt in 1905, it was given a boiler of 4ft 4in diameter and bigger cylinders.

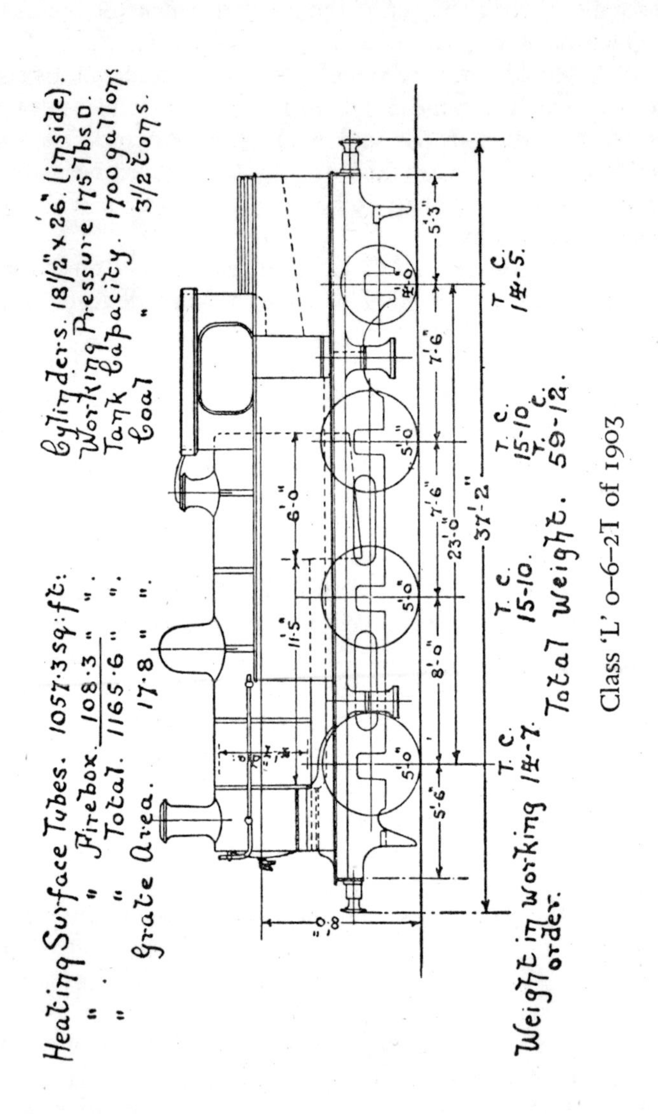

Class 'L' 0–6–2T of 1903

Two more of the class were built new the following year and differed slightly from no 19, which had retained its frames and other parts. They were the last of several thousand 2–4–0 tender engines built in Britain. All three had new tenders and were used on Derby—Llandudno expresses.

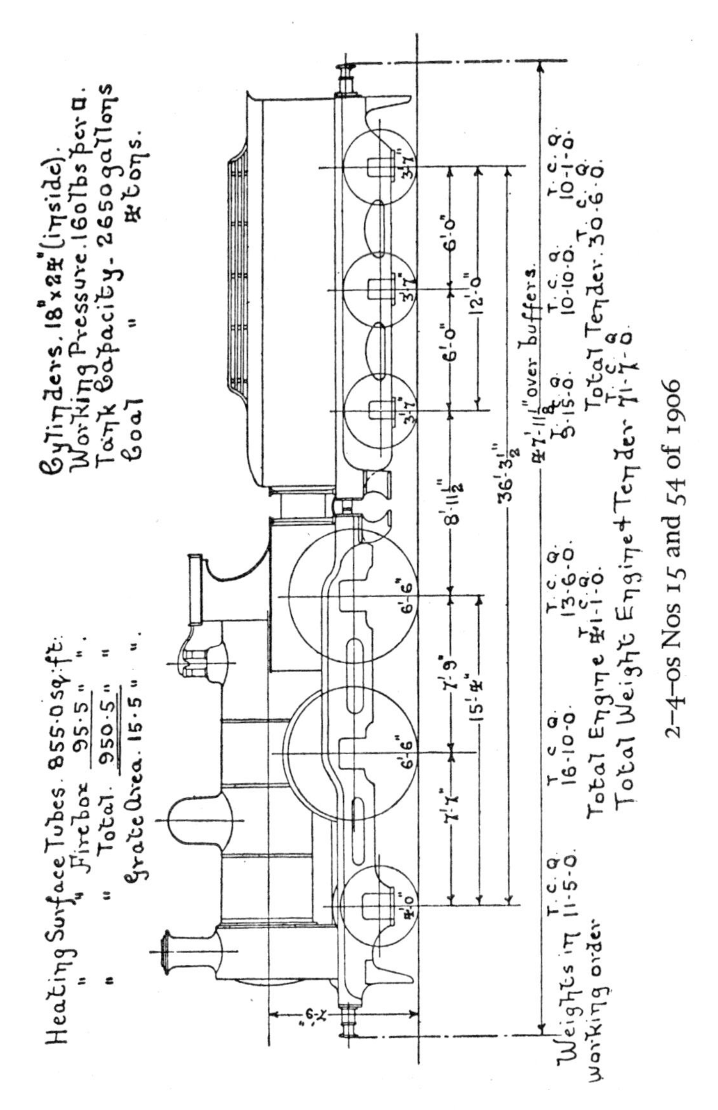

2–4–0s Nos 15 and 54 of 1906

The three steam rail motors obtained for the start of services in 1905 were bought from Beyer, Peacock. They were of the maker's design with horizontal outside cylinders mounted between the axles, driving forward on the leading wheels. Two innovations were outside Walschaerts valve gear and

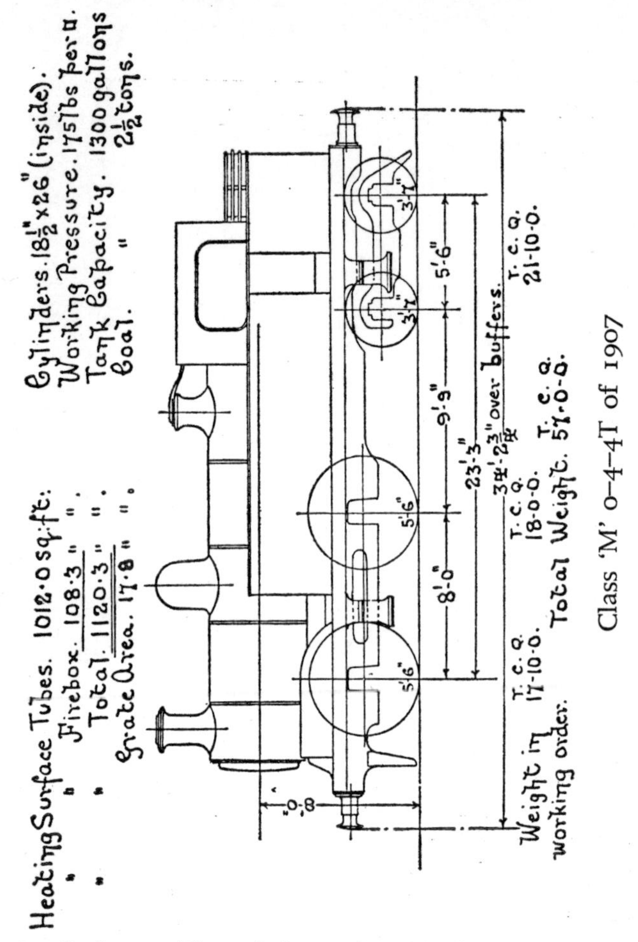

Class 'M' 0–4–4T of 1907

Belpaire fireboxes. The whole engine was boxed in a cab-like structure with just the smokebox and chimney protruding.

The year 1907 was notable for the advent of an 0–4–4T version of the 'L' class for local passenger trains. Consisting of five engines, built at Stoke, class 'M' had a new form of cab roof which curved round to join the cab sides in the style recently adopted by the Midland. It was soon to be copied by the SE & CR. The bogie was of a well-known type designed by Adams' father. Two class '100' variants were turned out at Stoke, also in 1907. They differed mainly in the abandonment of rectangular lower cab-side panels and the fitting of Adams style chimneys, narrower at the top than the base. The engines were classified 'New 100'.

More 0–6–2Ts built at Stoke in 1908-9 differed from the Vulcans by having new cab roofs and higher bunker sides. Eight 'New L' class initiated a practice of building locomotives in batches of four or eight and they were followed by four goods engines from Stoke in 1909. Designated class 'H', they were an 0–6–0 tender version of the 'L' class. Although they had drumhead smokeboxes, they were fitted with older type cabs with arc roofs. They also had new standard tenders of larger capacity provided by solid fenders instead of coal rails.

The next year Adams introduced another type new to the NSR: four Stoke-built 4–4–0 tender engines. These had larger boilers with Belpaire fireboxes, rounded cab roofs, drumhead smokebox and shapely Adams chimneys which gave these engines—class 'G'—a fine, modern appearance. They had the raised footplating over the coupled rods as on the 2–4–0s of 1906, which they displaced on the Llandudno trains.

The 'Llandudnos' were the only trains that the NSR could not operate with tanks (although the 'F' 0–6–4Ts were sometimes used), and the 4–4–0 tenders were designed to carry enough coal and water to avoid an outward stop. The locomotives were serviced at Llandudno Junction, where the staff admired the footplate layout: traditional NSR right-hand layout—the opposite to LNWR practice. The North Western men thought the wheels were too small for really fast running, but then there was nothing on the Knotty to equal the glorious straights and sweeps of the Coast line. Yet they ran the 52½ miles Crewe—Rhyl in 62 minutes.

Four more class 'H' 0–6–0s built at Stoke in 1910-11 got class 'G' boilers reduced in length, and Belpaire fireboxes of an intermediate size: 6in longer than those of class 'M', six inches shorter than the 4–4–0s. They were also fitted with the now-standard cab with rounded roof.

Stoke's next engines were the superb class 'K' 4–4–2 tanks, turned out in 1911-12. Basically a tank version of the 4–4–0s, they differed mainly in having a Schmidt superheater and piston valves above cylinders, increased to 20in diameter. This resulted in the boiler being pitched much higher than the tender engines, giving the tanks a most impressive appearance. As with most other early superheated engines, the boiler pressure was reduced, to 160lbs. Later it was raised to 170lbs. Eight tanks were ordered but one, no 38, was turned out as a tender engine instead and classed 'KT'. It differed from the other 4–4–0s by having a straight footplate and longer cab and other features first used on the Atlantic tanks. Yet another innovation on no 38 was 'pop' safety valves. All eight engines had mechanical lubricators.

Stoke built eight 'New L' 0–6–2Ts in 1913 and unlike the previous engines, they had saturated Belpaire boilers, identical with the second batch of class 'H' 0–6–0s. They also had feed-water heaters consisting of exhaust-steam condensers in the side tanks, which were lagged. There were also hot-water injectors and pumps.

Eight more tanks, 0–6–4s of class 'New C', had the same 5ft 0in size driving wheels as the 'New Ls', but the larger superheated boiler of the 'K' tanks, which made them powerful mixed traffic engines. The superheater was a Robinson type and boiler pressure was 170lbs. Other features included condenser type feed-water heaters with hot water injectors and pumps, anti-vacuum, bye-pass and 'pop' safety valves and mechanical lubricators.

HOOKHAM: DESIGNER AND INVENTOR

Adams designed a passenger version of the 0–6–4Ts but died suddenly in December 1915 and it was left to Hookham, as his successor, to build them. Hookham, who had remained works manager at Stoke since 1902, started work with the London, Chatham & Dover as a pupil under Kirtley at Battersea works. After a spell as a draughtsman with several private firms, he returned to the LC & D and moved to Ashford on the formation of the SE & C. He was the grandfather of Dame Margot Fonteyn De Arias.

Eight tanks of class 'F' were built at Stoke between 1916-19, the long period being due to wartime difficulties. They differed from earlier 0–6–4Ts in only three respects: they had larger drivers, a second mechanical lubricator and no anti-vacuum valves.

More unusual was a small four-wheel battery electric locomotive built at Stoke in 1917 and used for shunting at Oakamoor copper works. Its total length was only 19ft 8in, it weighed only 17 tons and its separate motors, geared to each axle, used only current of 250 volts. Yet it worked the Oakamoor sidings until they closed and now, happily, is preserved in Knotty livery at Shugborough Museum.

Difficulties in the late war, and early post-war years, forced the NSR to buy shunters from a private builder in 1919: the first outside order since 1905, purchasing from their neighbours, Kerr, Stuart & Company, two standard 'Argentina' 0–6–0 side tanks with outside cylinders and extended smokeboxes. Class 'KS', they were drafted to Stoke goods yard.

By 1920 Stoke works were back to full strength and a backlog of repairs had been wiped out. This situation led to the building of four more 0–4–4Ts and the first of a batch of eight 'New L' 0–6–2Ts. The former, 'New M', were little different from the earlier ones, receiving only longer bunkers and 'pop' safety valves. All but one of the 0–6–2Ts were similar to the 1913 batch, although they were not fitted with feed-water heaters and lagged. Instead they had exhaust steam injectors and pop valves. The exception, no 25 of 1921, had a superheated boiler, while retaining the slide valve motion of her sisters. A mechanical lubricator acting through a groove in the slide valve was later found unnecessary. Hookham used this engine for a series of tests during 1921, making comparisons with saturated engines nos 18 and 72 to see if it was practical to rebuild existing locomotives with superheaters without the expense of fitting new piston valves. Until now slide valves had been considered unsuitable by British locomotive engineers for superheated engines owing to the difficulty of adequate lubrication due to higher temperatures causing excessive wear in the valves. Hookham, using the mechanical lubricator, found he could provide adequate forced lubrication for the slide valves during the trials. He also found cast-iron packing for the piston rod and valve rod glands would stand undue wear. This was a much cheaper packing.

This was not the first time Stoke had experimented with glandular packing: in 1900 Longbottom sent a fitter to America to investigate the use there of soft metallic packing. On his return, he conducted trials with 2–4–2T no 12.

For the 1921 trials the boiler pressure of no 25 was reduced from 175lbs to 160lbs and its blast pipe orifice increased a quarter of an inch. It was estimated that to justify the cost of a superheater without the fitting of piston valves, a saving of £60 a year would have to be made in fuel consumption.

Economies were made, more on goods than passenger trains and it was also found that the superheater temperature dropped considerably during long stops. Hookham read a paper on his findings to the Institution of Locomotive Engineers in 1922.[1] Afterwards, Gresley, who had been present, asked for Hookham's designs and some were sent to Doncaster in May 1922. It led to Hookham's iron packing being almost universally adopted for superheated locomotives and the LNER in particular achieved some fine successes superheating engines with slide valves, notably some of the larger GNR Atlantics.

Packing was not Hookham's sole contribution to locomotive engineering. He experimented with oil fuel (using 0–6–2T no 93) and with a new type of feed-water heater (which greatly disfigured the front end of 4–4–0 no 87), but perhaps his most interesting work was with the crank arrangement for the unique four cylinder 0–6–0T no 23 built at Stoke in 1922. Instead of having the cranks arranged for the cylinders to act in pairs so that the engine *sounded* the same as the two cylinder machine, Hookham set the cranks so that the engine gave *eight* exhaust beats per revolution of the wheels. This gave more even torque and caused less disruption of the firebed when making a rapid start.

Hookham evidently had in mind an engine for improving the suburban services, especially over the tough gradients of the Loop. But for this experiment only a small engine with limited coal and water supply was built, mainly to keep down the weight. To help achieve this, nickel steel coupling and connecting rods were used, but even so the maximum axle load still reached 19½ tons. The 'M' boiler with round top firebox was adopted as lighter than the Belpaire type, but was superheated to make up for its small size. The first trials were unsatisfactory but performance was soon improved by altering the valve events, with the maximum cut-off being increased from 50 per cent to 60 per cent. An indicator shelter was provided for technicians on the front buffer beam. The trials ended with grouping because the LMS showed no interest in the experiment. The locomotive was rebuilt as a tender locomotive '4 cyl D' and worked trip goods trains from January 1924 until withdrawn four years later.

The 1921 trials resulted in two more 'New L' tanks being fitted with superheaters, while retaining slide valves, in 1922. Construction of four more began at Stoke but they did not emerge until after grouping, although they were numbered and lettered in NSR style.

Although Hookham's fine work on steam locomotives ended abruptly at grouping, that of his principal assistant, Major H. G. Ivatt, who had been appointed works manager in 1919, continued and he eventually became CME of the LMS. Ivatt's place at Stoke was taken after grouping by William Sinclair, Hookham's chief draughtsman in latter years.

LOCOMOTIVE DEPARTMENT

In the final years the locomotive stock had changed little and grew by only 25 engines in the fifteen years up to grouping on 1 January 1923, when the Knotty handed over 197 locomotives and three steam rail motors.

The majority were shedded at Stoke. The first 'engine house' had opened there in summer 1848 and it had a turntable which had been in position since February of the previous year. This shed was soon replaced by the famous Stoke roundhouse, still standing, though long-deserted, in 1970. This magnificent building cost £16,750 4s 7d and subsequent additions added £1,097 18s 5d to the bill. Light repairs were carried out on about half of the twenty-three roads (two for access only). An overhead crane capable of a 60 ton lift circled the roadhouse under its roofed section: the centre above the turntable was open to the sky.

Stoke's final allocation was 125 locomotives, most of which were kept in the new straight shed on the opposite (up) side of the main line. It had six through roads with a shorter terminal road kept for special engines and known to the men as 'the parlour'. Alongside was a smaller shed with two through roads, which was later used for the rail motors.

Stoke was the headquarters of the locomotive department

which had 741 men, including the running staff. A separate locomotive running department was established on 1 January 1918 and shed foremen, previously responsible to the locomotive superintendent, came under the running superintendent. Alongside Stoke roundhouse there was a shed for the fire engine and a special shed for the breakdown train. The stores superintendent had his offices adjacent to the roundhouse in the original Stoke station buildings at Whieldon Grove.

Compared with Stoke's allocation of 125 engines, the next in size was Alsager—a mere 15. Other allocations were: Macclesfield—12; Derby—9; Uttoxeter—8; Burton—7; Crewe—3. Each of these sheds was in charge of a foreman. The Stoke foreman also had charge of locomotives at sub-sheds at Market Drayton and Leekbrook, which each had two locomotives; and Ashbourne, which had one; and Caldon Low and Hulme End where the narrow gauge locomotives were kept.

Knotty engines were also sub-shedded at the GNR Nottingham Colwick, where one was kept; and two each were kept at LNWR sheds at Liverpool Edge Hill, Manchester Longsight and Stafford and, at the last two mentioned, the NSR kept cleaners, as well as drivers and firemen. Cleaners were also kept at the Midland's Wellingborough shed. The Longsight allocation consisted of a single goods engine on loan from Burton, and a passenger engine from Macclesfield. Edge Hill had two goods engines on loan from Burton and the Colwick engine was a Derby goods.[2]

EARLY PASSENGER VEHICLES

An early evening in the Staffordshire countryside in Victorian days: through the dark rumbles a passenger train, easy to spot since its lights are a little brighter than any in the fields about it. Some in the string of 4 wheel, 4 compartment coaches are better lit than others—those of the first class travellers. First compartments had four oil lamps of their own, and while the seconds had some as well, the miserable thirds were sparsely, indeed barely, lit by one lamp shining down on two compartments, separated only by shoulder high partitions.

Such passenger trains were without brake vans and for

stopping, the engine driver had to rely on nothing more than a handbrake fitted only to the tender. The guard could do nothing to help in an emergency since he was perched on a carriage roof. Although trains had luggage vans from the earliest days, passengers' baggage was placed on carriage roofs under water-proof covers which had to be pulled back and replaced at most stations: leisurely schedules were not due only to small engines!

Most vehicles were typical of the periods in which they were built but two first class coupés, which were among the earliest stock, were mounted on 6 wheel underframes, rare at that time. More spartan were the open thirds. On 27 February 1849 the board decreed that all passenger trains were to be made up of first and second covered and open thirds. This was to be the last winter in which the poor had to travel in the open for in October of that year, closed thirds were introduced on all Parliamentary trains and the open stock was rebuilt with roofs during the next three years. In October 1852, Wright was reported to have converted 25 coaches at a cost of £30 each, and the following March the company claimed ownership of only one open carriage, said to be in poor condition and worth £100.

Early in 1855 the company was sued for alleged infringement of Day's patent for improved carriage wheels. The board contended that the company did not have any in use until after the patent had expired.

The year 1860 saw the start of a number of operating improvements necessary to meet higher speeds. The bell and external communication cord was adopted on 4 December for fitting to all through trains running over the LNWR, whose trains were already fitted. From this year the use of separate guards vans in passenger trains gradually became more common, the vans having a handbrake under the guard's control. Heavy trains had several vans distributed along their length. For out-of-course stops the driver whistled the guard to apply his brake. The vans also carried passengers' luggage, although as late as 1865 the rulebook still laid down that guards had to make certain that luggage was properly stacked on carriage roofs. The practice continued for several more years until coaches were built with a guard's compartment at one end, containing a brake and small luggage space. These were called *break* carriages and were mostly used on local trains on which the amount of luggage was often small.

Despite the early use of 6 wheel carriages, 4 wheeled ones remained standard for many years and were built up to the eighteen eighties. They included a 4 compartment first and second class composite, with the firsts in the centre. For the locals, including the Loop, short 4 wheel coaches, close coupled and flat ended, were built in the seventies and eighties and marshalled into sets of four, six or eight. A typical formation consisted of a brake third with two compartments, a four compartment third, a similar second and third composite, two coaches with three compartments, either all first or all second, two more all third coaches and another brake third.

The coaches had only 20ft bodies and short buffers, which increased the length by 1ft 3in (except brake ends which had normal 2ft buffers). With a wheelbase of only 12ft 0in they must have been unsteady at any speed, and to add to the passengers' discomfort the compartments were narrow, only 4ft 9½in wide, although first compartments were 6ft 5in wide. The brake ends were without look-out duckets and in the earliest vehicles of this type the guard's windows were mounted much higher in the coach sides than those of the passengers.

For main line trains rather longer 4 wheel coaches gave a better standard of comfort. Two common types were a 4 compartment composite with two firsts in the centre, each 6ft 9¼in wide, flanked by 5ft 11½in seconds, and an all third of five compartments, each 5ft 1in across. These vehicles were 26ft 0in long in the body and 30ft 4in over buffers, with turn-under ends. The wheelbase was 16ft 0in.

The communication cord was fitted to through stock from 31 August 1869 and the simple vacuum brake, as used by the LNWR, was fitted from 1883.

The 6 wheel coaches built during the eighties and nineties introduced a new look to NSR trains because panelling on the sides of coaches was taken to full depth from cantrail to the waist and horizontal panels above and below windows were abandoned. The quarter lights were now contained within larger panels instead of forming an adjunct to the panelling.

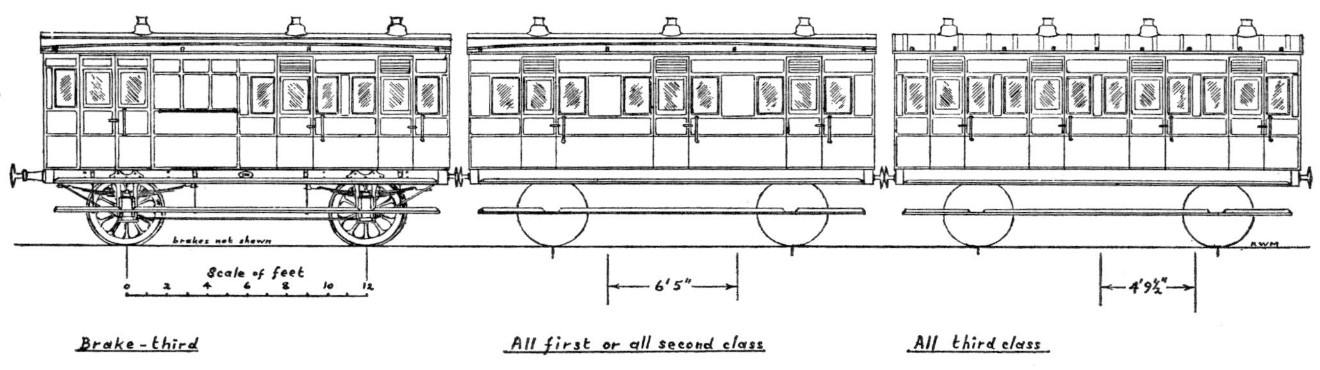

NSR four-wheeled carriages, part of a typical close-coupled local set of the 1870s

This outline lasted until grouping and enabled Knotty coaches to be instantly recognised as few other railways had similar styles, although it was in vogue on the LNWR and SECR for a short while.

The 6 wheel coaches were built concurrently in two distinct series, those for branch and suburban work having 29ft 3in bodies; those for main line use, bodies of 35ft 6in. Most of the shorter vehicles were all thirds of five compartments or brake thirds, with either two or three compartments. There were also several types of composites, including one with separate lavatories for first and second class. These were the only 6 wheel coaches with side corridors and dated from 1895. Other lavatory coaches had them adjacent to compartments. All-brake vans were built to shorter length, as was a tourist saloon of 1896 which was the first coach fitted with electric light.

Most of the longer 6 wheelers were either 6 compartment all thirds or 3 compartment brake thirds. First saloons of this length had an open balcony at each end and this made them adaptable for directors' or inspection saloons.

Family saloons, first referred to in minutes of 24 October 1877, and also invalid saloons, first built the previous year, were of intermediate size: 31ft 0in over body. Besides a spacious first class saloon, there was a second class compartment for servants. Invalid saloons had an extra pair of double doors at the first class end for loading wheel chairs.

The carriage department was faced with extra work after the ban on smoking on trains and at stations was lifted from 1 October 1868 and the company obliged to provide a number of smoking compartments, distinguished by window stickers. The story is told of a woman traveller between Manchester and Stoke who found all non-smokers full. She had to share a smoker and was surprised to notice a man on leaving the train, remove the red 'smoker' notice from the window. On getting home, she found her brother had one tucked away in his business hat. Asked how he got it, he told her: 'Friends at court, my dear!' There is no record of whether or not similar tricks were practised once 'Ladies Only' compartments were introduced on main trains as a result of a decision of 29 September 1887.

The 6 wheelers never completely ousted the 4 wheelers and several were still in use at grouping. It was normal for suburban sets to be composed of both types until the advent of bogie coaches from about 1910. A typical formation of later days on the loop was four 6 wheelers (2 brake thirds, 2 all thirds), two 4 wheel composites in the middle for first and second class travellers. The trains were strengthened at rush hours and carried special boards just under the roof with black lettering on a white background carrying the legend—for such it was: 'Loop Line Train'. Other trains had destination boards with gold letters which were placed on the guard's compartment during station stops, standing out like a finger-post.

BATTERIES AND BOGIES

The Knotty is assured of a place in railway history, if only for its pioneer work in lighting coaches by electricity. It was the largest of only three British companies—the others were the London, Tilbury & Southend and the Great North of Scotland—that switched direct from oil to electric, by-passing various forms of gas lighting which proved so troublesome in carriages of other companies.

Following experiments the Knotty decided in 1893 to install electricity in carriages as they were built at Stoke, but the decision proved to be a little premature because of fresh difficulties. Only the one tourist saloon was fitted by 1897, although the conversion of existing stock started the following year and new stock was fitted from 1899.

At first sets were lit by a crated battery fitted in a corner of the guard's van but the dynamo was unequal to the task and lights went out when speed dropped below 10mph. This problem was overcome by fitting dynamos on the slipping belt system. At best, the lighting was equal to 8 candle power for each bulb, with two bulbs illuminating first compartments and a single one in thirds, all controlled by a switch in the guard's van. The cost of installing electricity was said to be 'trifling' compared with oil and it was estimated that the increased strain on a locomotive hauling electrically-lit stock was not more than the energy produced by an extra quarter pound of coal for each carriage lit.

Enterprise was not entirely matched by speed of exploitation and while 115 coaches had been fitted by 1903, some oil-lit coaches were still running in 1910. More sophisticated was the lighting of four bogie saloon carriages built in 1909 with five clusters of lights in each, with three bulbs of 10 candle power in each cluster. Each vehicle had a dynamo and accumulator.

Six wheel coaches of both lengths continued to be built concurrently until 1905, the only change apart from lighting being the substitution of oil axle boxes for the grease boxes.

A major step forward came with the introduction of bogie coaches in 1906—although they were, of course, running on the Leek & Manifold. Five standard gauge coaches were built in 1906: for the summer Llandudno service and in winter for Derby—Crewe workings. All were 52ft 6in over buffers; 8ft 0in body width (8ft 4in over door handles; 8ft 9in over step boards and 9ft 4in over guard's duckets). The bogie wheelbase was 8ft 0in with centres 34ft 0in apart. These were standards which were to remain the same for all the company's subsequent bogie coaches.

The Llandudno set consisted of two brake thirds, one with lavatory access via a side corridor; two first/second composites with lavatories and an 8 compartment all third without toilet—unusual since many 6 wheel lavatory thirds were built up to 1905. The anomaly was remedied in 1908 when fresh stock was constructed. Each of the first compartments in the original Llandudno stock had its own lavatory.

There was a high standard of comfort. The firsts were finished in french-polished walnut and sycamore with white anaglypta ceilings. Local scenes flanked a central mirror below luggage racks. The upholstery was in blue cloth and seats had lifting elbow rests. Mahogany replaced walnut in second compartments, which were without arm rests.

Roof boards were carried—an innovation which was not practised for long. An identical five coach set was built at Stoke in 1907 and also three lavatory composite brakes for through workings from Nottingham (MR), Nottingham and Grantham (GNR) and Burton, to Llandudno. They had three third compartments with side corridor and lavatory, a first compartment and two first class lavatories arranged transversely, another first compartment and a small compartment

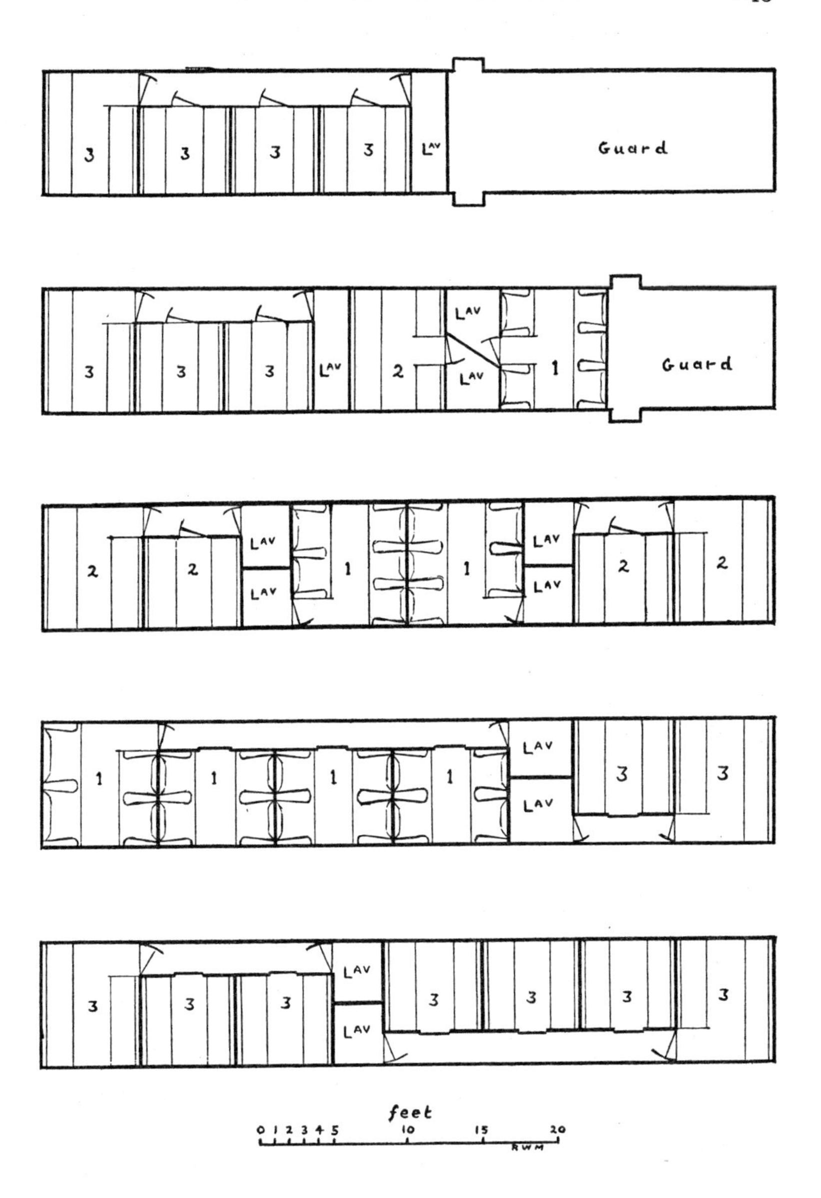

Five types of semi-corridor lavatory coach. All were built on the standard bogie underframe

for the guard, making them each self-contained units. They were of a type becoming popular on many railways.

The last 6 wheel coaches, also built in 1907, were a set of five of the shorter type, and a brake van. The latter was also the last of a line since the longer bogie vehicles were able to combine adequate luggage space with several compartments. The separate brake vans had a central ducket, a guard's door and a pair of luggage doors towards each end.

Standard milk vans continued to be built on 6 wheel chassis, to a design of 1896. Twenty-three more were built in 1906-11. After that longer chassis were used and 20 with 35ft 7in bodies were built in the years to 1921.

Further bogie coaches were built in 1908 and while they had side corridors, there were no corridor connections between coaches. The Knotty never had any because it never ran its own restaurant car trains, the 'Eustons' being entirely of LNWR stock. The 39 bogie coaches built up to 1909 had the traditional low arc roof of the 6 wheel stock, but then the pattern changed and new coaches were given higher elliptical roofs, then becoming fashionable on several railways, following its introduction on the GWR in 1904. Footboards were fitted to bogies from 1908. Among coaches with the new roofs were four 'picnic' saloons with large observation windows.

Subsequent coach designs differed only in details although a batch turned out at Stoke in 1915 had wooden underframes due to war shortage, but they were given steel frames in 1921. Post-war arrears of maintenance led to the building of a batch of 14 coaches, all thirds, in 1920 by a contractor: the Metropolitan Carriage Wagon & Finance Company, as well as other coaches.

Virtually all carriages had been equipped with steam heating by 1919. Exceptions included thirteen old 4 wheeled coaches used on miners' trains. Thirty-three coaches were fitted with through pipes for working with Westinghouse braked trains on through journeys. They included the different types of saloons. Also fitted were all horse boxes and carriage trucks, eight milk vans and three livestock vans.

There were two types of horse boxes. The older ones, of which only seven were left at grouping and withdrawn in 1924, were 19ft 10in long with flat ends and sides. The more modern fleet of 40 were 25ft 0in long and had a luggage compartment at the opposite end to the groom's. Twelve, built in 1913-14, had high elliptical roofs. At grouping the Knotty had a stock of 53 milk vans, including four 4 wheelers. There were also ten vehicles converted in 1917 from 6 compartment 6 wheel thirds into aeroplane vans with end doors. They were designed for use as milk vans if the transporting of aeroplane parts declined after the war.

Carriage trucks were all 4 wheel types and only four were covered. Twenty open ones were of two lengths. At grouping there were also 16 parcel and brake vans and thirty-nine miscellaneous, including livestock, or fatstock vans and a prize cattle van with a compartment for the herdsman. There were also four L & M coaches with their distinctive balconies.

PASSENGER LIVERY

Throughout its existence the Staffordshire Knot remained the company's emblem, emblazoned in gold with blue shading, which stood out well against the claret livery of the first coaches. Claret remained popular for a long time but gradually tastes changed, and in 27 July 1875 the board decided to change coaching livery, except on branch trains, to Victoria Brown and white. From about 1882 waist panels were repainted white, LNWR style. Lining was in gold and lettering was also gold edged in blue all round. The door louvres were painted alternatively in red and gold. Under-frames were chocolate. This style was retained until 1896 when coaches were painted Victoria Lake overall. While white looked smart, it suffered badly because of the chemically polluted atmosphere of the area. The lettering of gold edged with blue and gold lining was retained.

The next change, introduced by Adams in 1903, was to Madder Lake. The lining and lettering were also changed, lining changing to yellow with red edging and the lettering (including the Knot) in transfers of gold and red. The class of the compartment was shown on the door waist panel, while coach numbers were on the next to the end waist panel. Roofs continued to be lead white but under-frames were now black.

There was one more minor change before grouping: the

waist panels of doors to first class compartments being painted cream for people to easily distinguish them.

GOODS ROLLING STOCK

Early in 1847 S. P. Bidder reported that sample goods vehicles had been ordered from three 'highly respected and experienced carriage builders'. By 15 July 1848 further orders amounting to 690 trucks, goods, coal and cattle wagons and horse boxes had been placed. Besides the horse boxes, at first included in the goods stock, there were 618 goods, cattle and mineral wagons and 59 covered vans in use at the end of 1849. They had cost £57,843. During the next two years 141 more wagons were taken into stock.

The stock was built to a loading gauge requirement which allowed loads of up to 8ft 6in wide, 13ft 5in high from rail centre and 11ft 6in high at the side. The dimensions meant that in width the NSR was slightly more restricted than many railways, notably the LNWR, which allowed another 6in. Apart from the Leek & Manifold system, the only other restriction on the NSR was at Newcastle goods yard, where height clearance was reduced to 11ft 8in.

The early open wagons were of only 4 tons capacity and by 1870 they were being replaced by 6 tonners. Some 500 old wagons had been replaced by then, but the stock was allowed to get into a poor state of repair and during 1874 no less than 360 out of 700 wagons were under repair at some period of the year. Despite this, there was evidently sufficient for traffic needs for in 1871 the NSR got £4,078 6s 2d in fees for wagon loan. The repair position improved slowly and by 1877 the number in need of attention had dropped to 40.

Around this time there was a big increase in the number of goods vehicles and in 1882, when the stock totalled 5,037, only a few 4 ton vehicles were left. The new stock had spring buffers, although it was to be many years before 'dumb' buffer wagons disappeared. Much of the new stock was built at Stoke, as well as by contractors.

The latter included goods 'break' vans built by the Gloucester Wagon Company in June 1874. A curiosity of all NSR brake vans was the half boxed-in veranda end and a small window in the side. Later the window was increased in length and on the final 20 ton version it was replaced by two small windows each side of the vehicle. The 1874 vans were 19ft 0in over buffers with a 9ft 7in wheelbase. The veranda was 4ft 0in wide, although the doorways were only 2ft 6in. The tare weight was 11 tons 10 cwt.

Repairs carried out at Stoke in the first half of 1885 included 33 wagons 'renewed' and 337 given heavy repairs. The 6 ton wagons were now steadily replaced by those of 8 and 10 tons capacity. The stock at the end of 1892 was: 6 ton wagons—2,426; 8 ton—2,373; 10 ton—118; goods vans—103; cattle trucks—64; timber trucks—197; brake vans—78. Total—5,359.

This rose to 6,413 by 1907, of which about a quarter were 6 ton wagons, then being replaced by 10 and 15 tonners. A few 6 tonners survived to grouping. Some of the older 8 ton wagons were converted to carry two more tons—a practice that continued during the first world war. In 1916 Stoke also built 17 new 10 ton and 28 tipper wagons.

At grouping 6,612 goods vehicles, including 364 service stock, were handed over to the LMS. The majority, 5,354, were goods and mineral trucks with wooden bodies and wood solebars. Most 8 ton wagons had fixed sides of two planks. These were up to 1ft 9in high and with an overall length of 19ft 0in or 20ft 6in over buffers: 3ft 0in more than the body. There was also a three plank side door type with sides 6in higher and raised curved ends. There were also a few fixed side three plank wagons for sand traffic.

The 10 ton open wagons had mostly 2ft 3in high sides of three planks. There were a few 15 ton coal wagons with seven plank 4ft 2in sides. They were 21ft 11in long. Hopper wagons of 15 ton capacity had side and bottom doors. The remaining 6 ton wagons at grouping were 18ft 0in long. For many years NSR open wagons had inside strapping giving a neat appearance.

The 345 covered vans were mostly of two similar designs with conventional outside frames and double hinged doors. Basic lengths were 19ft 6in or 21ft 3in. A few of the larger type were fitted for silk traffic from Leek, Macclesfield and Congleton. Carriage type wheels, couplers and buffers increased the length by 1ft 0in and they were vacuum braked. The 66

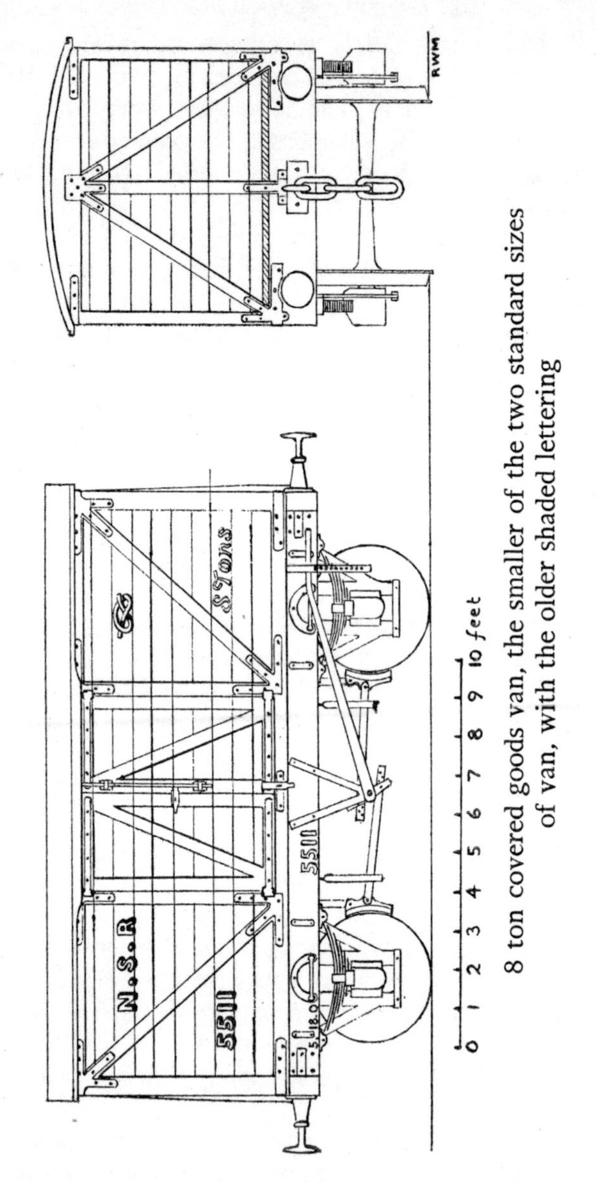

8 ton covered goods van, the smaller of the two standard sizes of van, with the older shaded lettering

cattle trucks were 19ft 0in long, 7ft 11in wide. They had vertical iron bars instead of the bottom two side planks. The remaining goods vehicles—356—were mostly timber trucks, some of short 7ft 0in wheelbase. Twin timber trucks, perma-

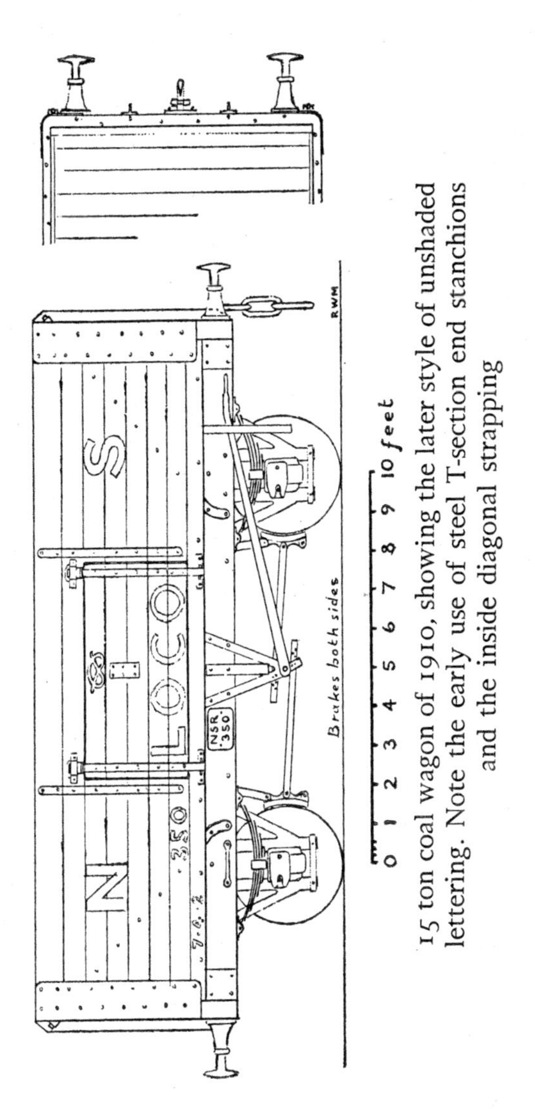

15 ton coal wagon of 1910, showing the later style of unshaded lettering. Note the early use of steel T-section end stanchions and the inside diagonal strapping

nently coupled, had halves with wheelbases of 9ft 0in. Identical were twin boiler trucks with blocks shaped for 4ft 0in diameter boilers. Single boiler trucks had longer wheelbases of 20ft 0in and were 34ft 0in long overall. Similar vehicles, called rail trucks, were fitted with conventional bolsters. They included a 6 wheel version. Other special vehicles included 4 wheel well trucks and furniture trucks to carry removal containers. There were four types, differing only in detail. Bogie vehicles included two long—55ft 1in—trolley wagons with a 32ft well, and two 44ft 0in bogie bolsters built in 1921. There were also 127 goods brake vans of two main types.

The company extensively used Spencer's patent cylinders for springing buffers and draw gear.

Service stock consisted of 223 locomotive coal wagons, mostly 15 ton capacity; 88 low-sided ballast wagons of various types; 53 miscellaneous vehicles, including 7 cranes and 7 mess and tool vans.

Goods livery was a purplish red oxide with white lettering, including the Knot motif, shaded in black. Solebars, headstocks and corner plates were black; roofs, lead white. The company was among the last railways to introduce large initials for its goods stock and did not do so until 1912. Before then the initials NSR (with only two full stops) some 6in high were used on the left side of vehicles. On open wagons the number, of the same size, appeared on the right and the Knot in the centre. The same size number was repeated on the solebar, just left of centre. From 1912 just the two initials NS were used, unshaded, one at each end of the vehicle, now about 1ft 2in high, with a small knot, generally central. The numerals remained in small size and were placed as usual lower down on the left side.

Narrow gauge Leek & Manifold bogie goods vehicles included one bogie van, 2 low-sided open wagons, and 4 transporter wagons for carrying standard gauge wagons. There were also about 100 4 wheel wagons on the Caldon Low tramway. These had low fixed sides, mostly two plank, flush with the solebars which were extended to form dumb buffers. The wheels had inside bearings while brakes were fitted on the north side only.

The entire NSR wagon stock was small when compared with the fleets of private owner wagons which worked over the system. Each of the pits, ironworks and other undertakings had their own stock and so did distributive traders. These vehicles carried personal livery and names splashed in large letters for advertisement. Most unusual of the private stock were the wagons of Robert Heath and Low Moor, which had wrought iron bodies. They were of 10 and 12 ton capacities. Other private stock included animal vans of Barnum & Bailey's Circus, whose central English depot was at Cliff Vale, Stoke. Although built locally (with bogies by Krupp of Essen), the vans had an American appearance with peak roofs. They were fitted with automatic couplers except at the end of rakes. They were painted in an eye-catching livery of bright yellow with red letters proclaiming 'Barnum & Bailey—Greatest Show on Earth'. Three vans were sold to the Chatterley—Whitfield Railway in 1910 and used to carry miners to the pit in a Paddy train which ran from Pinnox Halt. Careful experiment by the colliery authority found that each van would hold 125 men.

STOKE WORKS

If there was nothing remarkable about the company's works at Stoke, they were at least efficient and progressively geared to match the needs of the system in the building and repair of locomotives and carriages and wagons. Located near the down side of the main line at Stoke Junction, they lay on a 12 acre site well below rail level and the only connection was over a single spur off the Leek branch.

Modernisation of the equipment was often dictated by finance available and, occasionally, by experience. After the fire which destroyed the roof of Stoke station in 1868, a number of fire precautions were thought necessary at the works. Partitions were raised to divide up the roof and double iron doors were fitted between the saw mills and the smithy and between there and the carriage shops. In the same year, £220 was spent adapting two arches of Stoke viaduct as a shop for repairing and tarring wagons. Shortly before the first world war, the works employed nearly 900 men: 483 in the locomotive section: 391 in the carriage and wagon department.

The main locomotive erecting shop (1 on plan on page 252), had three roads and was serviced by two overhead electric cranes of 30 tons capacity. The second erecting shop (2) had three roads and was used mostly for tenders. As its roof was low, some work, on tanks for instance, had to be carried out in the yard outside.

The main machine and fitting shop (3) originally had a

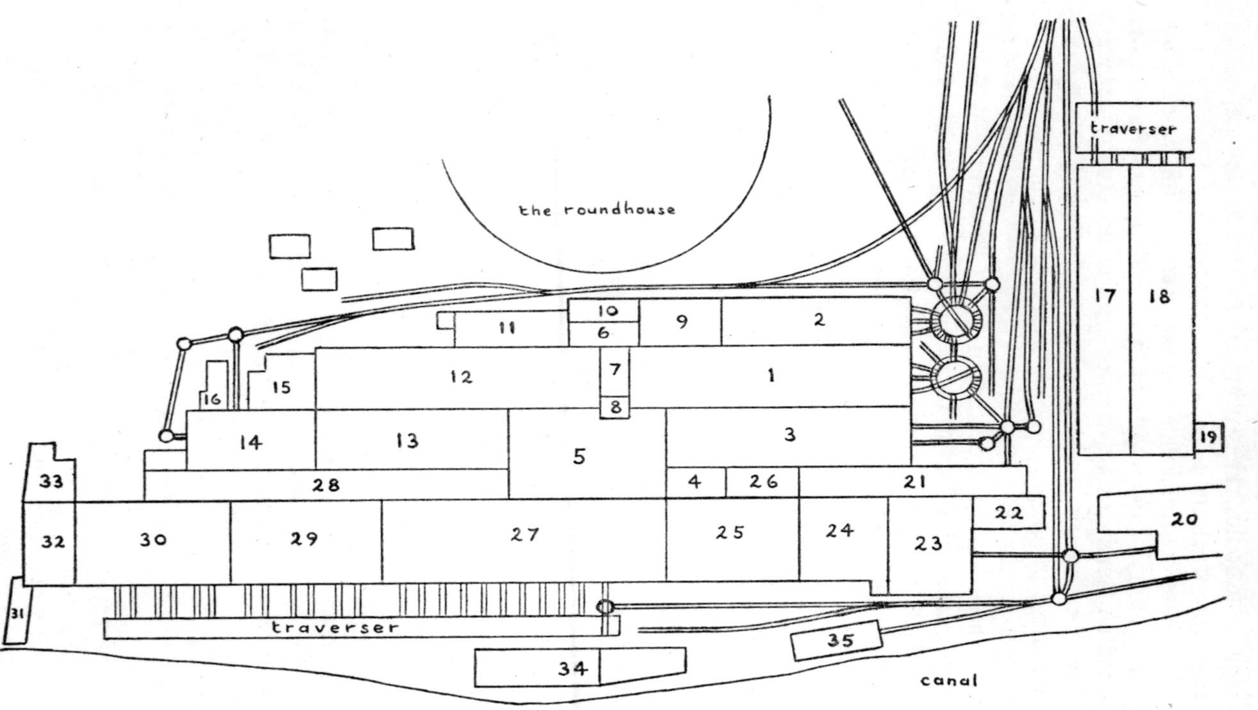

NSR locomotive, carriage and wagon works, Stoke (see page 251)

service road down the centre with a series of turntables connecting with the adjoining erecting shop. All were later removed and the machine shop spilled over into part of the erecting shop. The equipment included the usual planing and milling machines, lathes and drills. One of the old lathes was adapted for machining smokebox saddles when they were introduced by Adams in 1903. A characteristic of the works was the operation of machinery by compressed air. On the locomotive side there were 13 pneumatic hoists, many on swinging run-ways and jibs. Their maximum lift was 6 tons and they were simple and reliable, air being controlled by two hanging chains. All were built in the works.

The tool and gauge store (4) was also used to store shop drawings. The new machine shop (5) was an extension of the main one. The boilerhouse (6) was adjacent to the engine house (7) which drove the locomotive machinery through overhead shafting and belts. In the engine room there was a vertical engine of 1849 which drove shafting by *wooden* toothed gearing. The works office (8) was at first floor level between the engine room and the new machine shop. The permanent way shop (9) machined point blades. The two-storey joiners' shop (10) had the pattern makers accommodation above. The coppersmiths and brass foundry was next door (11). The large smithy (12) included 4 steam hammers. Wheels were tyred in this shop. The old boiler shop (13) and the 107ft long new extension (14) had hydraulic riveters and a press of 240 tons pressure for forging throat plates etc. The engine room and boilers for the hydraulic press were at (15), adjacent to the oil recovery plant, wash house and drying room (16).

The new carriage shops (17 and 18), were in a separate building on the south side of the works, reached by a traverser on the east side. Until these new shops were built, Stoke works were unable to handle bogie stock as access to the old shops was over a small turntable. From 1906 carriage construction was concentrated in the new shops, but some repair work was also carried out there. Their boiler house (19) made them independent of the works for power. Also separated from the main buildings were the timber sheds (20) alongside the canal which was used to deliver timber, being discharged in a dock just south of the shops.

The main buildings included a new wheelwright's shop (21) and the saw mill (22). The new body shop (23) built horse boxes and carriage trucks and repaired 4 and 6 wheel stock in later years. The metalwork fitting shop (24) was adjacent. The smithy (25) had 3 steam hammers and was supplemented by the small smithy (26), where tyres for road vehicles were handled.

The wagon shop (27) and its extension (28) mostly built new wagons, the large wagon repair shop being on the opposite side of the main line. The old body shop (29) handled new construction and repairs to roofed goods vehicles. Some repairs were also done in the old paint shop (30). Access to wagon shops was over a turntable and traverser running along the canal side where there was also the trimmers' shop (31).

Offices in a two-storey brick building included the mess (32), and the main entrance (33), which had an office for the issue of privilege tickets. Two canal side buildings housed the wheelwrights' and general joinery shops (34) and the carriage and wagon boilerhouse (35).

CHAPTER ELEVEN

London, Midland & Scottish Railway

Goodbye to days of Knotty fame,
Engines bearing drivers' names.
The loss for some was hard to take,
Golden sovereigns hard to make.

Amalgamation song from
The Knotty[1]

CHANGE AND ECONOMY

Profitable as it may have been and able to pay 5 per cent, the Knotty took only sixth place as a constituent of the LMS, well behind the LNWR, MR, L & Y, Caledonian and Glasgow & South Western Railway.

Broadly, it gave little to the LMS—and gained little from it, and the system handed on at nationalisation was, apart from a few limited economies, much of 1923 vintage. One of the first of these was the cessation of locomotive building at Stoke Works, only four being completed between grouping and the closure of the works on 31 December 1926. The run down, however, continued until the following July. Staff were transferred to Derby or, in the main, Crewe, and a works train was introduced between the Stoke area and a special halt opened in Crewe Works beside what is now the engineering apprentices training school.

On grouping, the MB & M Joint Line passed to the control of the LMS and LNER, under an LMS Act of 1 August 1924. The secretary was James McLaren at Marylebone, who had been appointed joint secretary of the LNER on grouping.

The LMS took over the Caldon Low quarry, but according to its figures, it made a profit only until 1925.[2] One reason had been the closure of the Brunner Mond works at Sandbach in 1920. ICI later started quarrying at Tunstead, near Buxton, instead. The Sandbach works had used much of Caldon's daily output of 1,000 tons of limestone. In 1923 expenditure on Caldon by the LMS totalled £42,000 and net receipts were £3,000—compared with a loss of £1,180 in the last year of NSR operation. The quarry was leased to a Sheffield firm in 1934, and the three narrow gauge locomotives were scrapped in their shed in May 1936 still in NSR livery.

Links between the railways and the quarry were renewed on 12 July 1938 during a ceremony to mark the start of rebuilding Euston. From the shareholders' room, the LMS chairman, Lord Stamp, remotely fired a blast at Caldon to bring down about 100,000 tons of limestone, including the foundation stone for the station.

The LMS also inherited the T & M canal system which, in 1922, had lost £7,342. The Knotty hotels were also merged into LMS ownership.

Economies in services followed the usual pattern of either the withdrawal of passenger trains from a branch or the closure of individual stations. The earliest economies, carried out in 1923, were the closure of two of the rail motor halts at Sideway and Brampton, followed by Knutton and Hartshill & Basford in 1927.

These latter closures were, of course, in the year following the general strike in which the railways throughout Britain lost ground to road transport. One example of the trend was in the village of Bosley, near Macclesfield, whose life-blood up to then had been the Churnet line. The strike forced farmers and traders to consider other transport, especially for perishable traffic like milk. After the strike several local traders did not return to the railway.[3]

It was a pattern that was to be repeated and 1927 brought the first branch economy, the Biddulph Valley losing regular passenger trains on 11 July. The new owners had not taken long to realise that the line had little passenger potential. As once was said: 'The siting of the stations could never have been said to be of much use to the inhabitants of the Biddulph Valley, but as a mineral line it was a very different matter'.[4] The line remained healthy for mineral traffic long after the industrial decline set in the valley, which included the closure of the Biddulph Valley Ironworks at Brindley Ford in 1928.

Another factor that led to a decline in local rail traffic was the reversal by the LMS of the NSR policy of allowing private trains to run over its lines. What had been a welcome source of revenue to a small company like the Knotty, was a nuisance to a giant like the LMS, but it showed some tolerance in enforcing the ruling, and Heath's trains continued to Brunswick Wharf, Congleton, until about 1930.

The Trentham branch closed to local services in September 1927 but remained open for excursions. There was no freight. The closure of the Sandbach branch to passengers followed on 28 July 1930: how different its passenger fortunes might have been if the Liverpool extension had been built! The Audley passenger services ceased on 27 April 1931 and the Talke branch was closed beyond High Carr Tileries in 1931. Once the Audley line had been among the busiest on the NSR, receiving traffic from an unbroken line of pits between Talke and Silverdale. In the industrial depression after the first world war they suddenly became ' worked out ' and closed, although the more likely reason was that they were more difficult than many to mechanise because of geological faults. Talke pit closed on 14 January 1928, putting 1,000 men out of work and five more local collieries closed in 1930.

The Audley passenger economies paved the way for others on the Market Drayton line and Madeley Road was also closed on 27 April 1931. So sparse was its traffic that it was equipped with signals so that trains need make only special stops when passengers actually presented themselves. The section between Silverdale and Pipe Gate was singled on 7 October 1934. The Audley Junction was moved east from Keele to Silverdale and the double track worked as single lines with the loop at Keele becoming part of the Audley line. The 6¾ miles between Silverdale and Pipe Gate became a single block section—the longest on the Knotty system. Pipe Gate continued to handle occasional race specials.

Further south, the tunnel on the Cheadle branch, the source of so much trouble, was eliminated by the re-alignment of the branch on 26 November 1933, although part of the old line at the Cheadle end was retained to serve New Haden Colliery.

LEEK AND MANIFOLD DECLINE

The LMS got rid of another unprofitable legacy by the closure on 12 March 1934 of the ever-ailing Leek & Manifold Light Railway. Up to 1921 the total capital spent on it had been £68,000; the accumulated loss was then £14,000 and was growing at £2,000 a year. It was against this background that Parliament forced the LMS to buy it for £30,000 and it became the company's only public English narrow gauge line.

Closure was surrounded by sentiment and the spirit of the occasion was caught by a reporter who wrote of events after the last train reached Hulme End:

> The driver and fireman rake out the glowing fire of the locomotive and run it into the shed. The guard locks up the last gate. Tomorrow he walks four miles to Hartington for a train to his next job at Uttoxeter.

Locomotive no 1 ran along the line, collected the stock and after it reached Waterhouses, a tarpaulin was thrown over it—and there it remained for three years. It was to enjoy a final moment of glory before being taken for scrap. Demolition contractors used it to haul a standard gauge transporter wagon with a track lifting wagon.

The L & M closure took the legs from under the Leek—Waterhouses passenger service and it finished once the ramblers had gone home at the end of the following summer, the last train running on 30 September 1935. There was controversy over the L & M's future when the LMS put it up for sale. Councils at Cheadle and Leek wanted the trackbed converted into a road. A committee formed by local people supported the idea claiming that the need for transport in the Manifold Valley was just as urgent as it had been before the railway. They also asked:

> What justification is there for excluding motorists as a body? There are many lovers of the countryside who are not young and strong, and yet get health and pleasure by viewing the beauty spots. The fact that they are unable to walk long distances cannot justify their exclusion.

The day was won by the ramblers and other bodies who pressed for the railway to be turned into a footpath. When Staffordshire County Council agreed, the LMS made a gift of the trackbed. It was concreted over at a cost of £6,000 and opened officially on 23 July 1937. Station buildings and name boards survived for a time. The victory, though, turned out to be partial for in 1953, the section from Redhurst to Butterton, through the tunnel, was converted into a road.

Elsewhere, changes went on all the time. Stoke goods depot was improved in 1931 and two years later the electricity supply for the passenger station was switched from the original independent NSR supply to that of the city.

BUS COMPETITION

As buses and cars gained more and more hold on traffic, train services were reduced: those of Market Drayton, Cheadle, Ashbourne, Leek, and on the Loop and Stone—Colwich lines, all suffering heavily. The latter line and the Cheadle branch both lost their Sunday services.

Bus competition not only hit trains, but trams as well. Pirate bus services which began running on competing routes soon made inroads into tram services and they did it so effectively that the Potteries lost their trams on 11 July 1928. As the bus fleets expanded, the Potteries' Electric Traction changed its name to embrace the Potteries Motor Traction of today, but unlike many big bus companies, the railways had no shareholdings in it. The buses were at once able to develop routes planned for trams, but never built. Trains remained in favour for long distance travel although there was no marked speed up.

The importance of Stoke was recognised by the Railway Air Services Limited when it substituted the city for Manchester in 1935 when Manchester was linked with other Railway Air Services by the newly created Manx Airway. In 1935 the RAS 'main line' of scheduled flights, as it was called, stretched from London via Stoke to Liverpool, Belfast and Glasgow. It was maintained all the year round by just two aircraft: de Havilland 86 4-engine biplanes called *Mercury* and *Jupiter*.

THE SECOND WORLD WAR

The war years 1939-45 were ones of marked activity and a few minor economies. The LNER withdrew passenger trains between Derby and Stafford on 4 December 1939, a few days before the Battle of the River Plate. RAF specials continued to use Stafford Common. The 1½ mile tip of the Waterhouses branch beyond the junction to Caldon quarries was closed on 1 March 1943 and Waterloo Road station on the Loop closed in October of that year. The war finally dashed what slender hopes had remained of extending the Trentham branch to Pool Dam and in 1940 the large bridge just outside Trentham station was dismantled for badly-needed scrap. The branch to Trentham became busier than ever because the Hall became the headquarters of the Bank of England Counting House, evacuated from London. There was also a daily goods up to the end of the war.

A few months after D-day a number of stations had their names altered. Harecastle (for Kidsgrove) became Kidsgrove Central. Kidsgrove was renamed Kidsgrove (Liverpool Road), and Kidsgrove Halt remained unaltered.[5] Local signal boxes were also renamed: Harecastle Junction became Kidsgrove (Central), Harecastle (Kidsgrove Junction) became Kidsgrove (Liverpool Road) Junction. All the changes took place from 2 October 1944.

A new halt called Wedgwood was opened outside the pottery company's modern works between Trentham Junction and Barlaston on 1 January 1940 and is still open today. Ministry of Supply factories were opened in several parts of the Potteries and one at Radway Green on the Crewe branch was served by sidings and an island platform for workers' trains.

More significantly, a branch of almost 1½ miles was opened to serve a ROF factory built at Swynnerton, tucked away in the wooded, rolling country between the Potteries and the west coast main line. The Cold Meece branch, as it was called, was a ghost line veiled in wartime secrecy and while it carried 3,000,000 people a year—an average of 8,000 a day—it never appeared in a public timetable. And though it served a huge factory, it never carried freight: that was handled from

Badnall Wharf on the Stafford—Crewe main line, which also provided access to $8\frac{3}{4}$ miles of factory lines.[6]

The Cold Meece branch, double tracked, was opened on 5 August 1941 from Swynnerton Junction, nearly 2 miles from Stone on the branch to Norton Bridge. It ran to a 4-platform brick terminus with engine run-round roads in the middle of the two groups. It was also used by thousands of Americans travelling to a USAF base established at Cold Meece. The factory continued production after the war and trains continued until this was phased out in 1958, the last scheduled train running on 27 June.

In its heyday, Cold Meece had handled workers' trains (a maximum of 5 in 25m), serving all parts of the Potteries from starting points at Cobridge, Longton, Silverdale, Newchapel and Blythe Bridge.

POST-WAR ECONOMIES

The return of peace brought the return of economies and one of the earliest was the withdrawal of stopping trains between Stone and Colwich, an $11\frac{1}{2}$ mile stretch which by November 1946 had one of Britain's sparsest passenger services. One of the last LMS cuts was the closure of the Jamage branch in 1947 after the shut down of Jamage and Rookery collieries.

Nationalisation not only gave the old Knotty system a new owner, the Trent & Mersey Canal got the same one as well: the British Transport Commission.

LMS LOCOMOTIVE POLICY

What happened to the NSR locomotives under their new ownership? At first, very little. Passenger engines, including the 0–6–4Ts, remained in red livery, albeit the LMS style with large numerals on the tender or tank sides. Goods engines were, however, repainted plain black. Many engines were fitted with Ross 'pop' safety valves and all but one of the 'K' class 4–4–2Ts received smaller bogie wheels.

Some Knotty engines were transferred to other parts of the LMS: five 2–4–0Ts went to the North London section; a 'New

L' class 0-6-2T went to St Pancras; an 'F' 0-6-4T went to work on Stafford—Shrewsbury passenger trains; a D class 0-6-0T was sent to Birkenhead Docks and 'K' tanks were used on passenger links between Derby—Sheffield; Derby—Birmingham; and Stafford—Cannock. From 1929 all Knotty engines not already withdrawn were repainted black, although some passenger types had a red lining out. Numerals were transferred to cab or bunker sides. Some 'K' tanks went to Stockport and 'New L' 0-6-2Ts took over trains on the Manchester, South Junction & Altrincham for a time before its electrification in 1931.

The withdrawal of older engines was slow at first. It began with a 'B' 2-4-0T in 1925 and continued with four 'E' 0-6-0s the following year. Seven engines were withdrawn in 1927 and the three rail motors sold for scrap. The real slaughter started in 1928-9 when 51 withdrawals were made. Subsequently at least ten engines a year were withdrawn until by the end of 1937, only two were left in LMS stock: M class 0-4-4Ts, nos 1434 and 1436. They were finally withdrawn in March and April, 1939, and after standing at Crewe for some months, they were cut up early in the war.

One engine remained in *service* stock: the little battery electric shunter now numbered BEL 2. It continued work at Bolton's siding at Oakamoor until 1964, when it was withdrawn and preserved.

The Knotty locomotives had to be replaced, of course, and mainly this was done by bigger types: ex-LNWR 4-4-0s were used on Manchester trains straight away and some 0-8-0s were sent to Stoke for repair while the works remained open. From 1926 new LMS class '4F' 0-6-0s were sent to the Potteries and eventually there were to be more than 50 of them in the district. The heavy withdrawals of 1928-9 caused the biggest influx: 'George V' 4-4-0s; 'Experiment' 4-6-0s; LNWR 0-8-0s; five new 2-6-4 Fowler tanks; new 3F 0-6-0Ts and older L & Y and MR shunting tanks. By now Claughton 4-6-0s of both types were working Euston—Manchester expresses in succession to the LMS Compounds. In 1930, the first LMS Moguls arrived together with more 2-6-4Ts and 4F 0-6-0s and L & Y and LNWR 0-6-0s. Three years later new Fowler 2-6-2Ts were tried, but they were soon transferred away as being unsuccessful. In 1934, 'Prince of Wales' 4-6-0s replaced the 'Experiments' and some old MR 0-6-0s were also transferred to the NSR.

The 2-6-4Ts soon established themselves as the most popular on local services and in 1935-6, the first Stanier classes arrived. They were Prairie and 2-6-4 tanks, mixed traffic and Jubilee 4-6-0s. The Jubilees quickly became a success on the Euston—Manchester expresses. Three Stanier 0-4-4Ts were transferred to Stoke in 1941, but they later moved to Stockport. The new rebuilt Royal Scots began service on the Euston links in 1946 but they were never to be as successful as the Jubilees. The original Royal Scots were not allowed over the Congleton viaducts because of weight restrictions. This meant that in LMS days many of the crack London—Manchester expresses went via Crewe and of those best known in the era, only the up *Lancastrian* and the down *Comet* served Stoke. Even their balancing workings were via Crewe.

The *Lancastrian* was named in 1927 as part of the LMS policy of progressively improving express services, which in 1925 had led to the restoration of 1914 timings between Stoke and Euston. The up *Lancastrian* was a successor of the old 12 10 pm up from Manchester (London Road) in Knotty days, on which Knotty tanks did such sterling work. Timed now to leave at 12 5 pm, it picked up an East Lancashire portion at Stockport and, calling at Macclesfield, took 49m to Stoke. It ran the 145 miles to Euston in even time. When traffic was heavy, the Colne portion was sometimes run separately via the Churnet Valley.

The down *Comet* made four stops more than its fast morning counterpart. It left Euston at 4 10 pm and called at Bletchley, Rugby and Lichfield, reaching Stoke in 170m. It was allowed another 65m to Manchester, with calls at Congleton and Macclesfield. These working times were creditable when it is remembered that while there were only five speed restrictions between Stockport and Colwich, via Crewe, with 20mph through Crewe by far the most severe, there were fourteen in the Potteries. These included 15mph through Stoke and 30mph through Etruria and Macclesfield.

Among LMS daily runs over 100 miles non-stop was a night parcels, the 12 33 am from Stoke, booked to cover the 140 miles to Willesden in 188m at a fraction under 45mph.

Every summer between 1923 and 1939 the Knotty was used by an express between the north west and the Norfolk Coast resorts, via the Midland & Great Northern Joint Railway. The Manchester portion ran through the Churnet Valley to Uttoxeter to link up with a Liverpool portion, routed via Crewe and Stoke. The LMS used the Churnet line for goods and an evening newspaper train: the 9 50 pm Manchester—Euston, often made up of only one van.

Stoke remained—and remains—the hub of the NSR system and in LMS days local quickly followed local under an operating pattern much the same as the olden days. The key to both was the same: Stoke was not a terminal station, but a run through. The locals were controlled by calling-on arms on home signals, which replaced special distant arms operated from the platforms and placed between the home signal and the distant for the box ahead.

SHEDS AND SALES

The old Knotty sheds lost some of their identity when in 1926 the LMS reorganised all those they had inherited. Stoke and other depots all got the same no: 40 carried on a small metal plate behind the cab and later on the smokebox door. Reorganisation in 1933 introduced the more universal system of numbers and letters.

Three sheds were included in the Crewe district: Stoke (5D), Alsager (5E), and Uttoxeter (5F), while Macclesfield (9C) was placed under Manchester Longsight. The code remained standard until BR adopted national codes based on LMS practice.

Once working patterns became settled, economies began in shed operation and the NSR ones at Crewe and Burton closed shortly after grouping when their locomotives were transferred to the LNWR sheds. When Derby shed was closed, the engines were transferred to the MR shed. Colwich shed closed soon after grouping and later economies included Market Drayton on 27 April 1931, Leek Brook on 2 January, 1932, and Ashbourne on 14 November 1932.

The premature withdrawal of many NSR locomotives in prime condition was due to a standardisation policy of the

LMS, which did not consider it economic to maintain small classes, however good the engines might have been. Seven Knotty locomotives were sold for further service. The first, no 75 (LMS 1603), one of the Kerr Stuart 0–6–0Ts of 1919, spent many years at Nunnery Colliery, Sheffield. The other six were all 'New L' class 0–6–2Ts. The first, no 158 (LMS 2253) went to Longmoor Military Railway and was named *Marlborough*, no 207. It was re-numbered 70207 during the second world war and in 1948 it was sold to the National Coal Board, going to Coatbridge Colliery, where it worked until September 1949. It was then sold to a local firm and dismantled for scrap. Three more of the tanks were sold to Manchester Collieries for work on the extensive Bridgewater Collieries Railway, where they were later joined by two of the superheated variety, nos 1 and 2, actually built by the LMS in 1923. Sale dates and new names were:

22	LMS 2264	sold	June	1936	*Kenneth*
72	2262		January	1937	*Sir Robert*
69	2257		May	1937	*King George VI*
1	2270		October	1937	*Queen Elizabeth*
2	2271		October	1937	*Princess*

The new nameplates were fixed to the bunker sides. All ran virtually unaltered at first, retaining smokebox number plates. Some kept their 5D shed plates and exhaust steam injectors. *Queen Elizabeth* still had LMS on the tanks and 2270 on the bunkers. The two superheated engines were later fitted with new saturated boilers by Hunslet (as were some others), *Princess* in March 1946 and *Queen Elizabeth*, a year later. The latter was the first to stop work, being partly dismantled for spares in 1951. By June 1953 only the boiler and frames were left. The frames were still at Walkden in 1962. *Kenneth* ceased work by May 1962 and was cut up in March 1967; *Sir Robert* stopped working late in 1963 and was scrapped in March 1966; *Princess* was repainted in NSR livery and went to the Stoke centenary celebrations. On return, it kept its livery and was fitted with a new chimney in 1961, which rather disfigured its appearance. It was out of use with a condemned boiler early in 1966 before preservation. *King George VI*, built Stoke

1913, went on to achieve the distinction of being the last Knotty engine to work. Rather confusingly it was renamed *Sir Robert* in August 1965, being turned out at Walkden in NSR livery with its new name painted on. It stopped working in 1969 and was cut up on 19 September of that year after unsuccessful attempts to preserve it.

COACHING STOCK CHANGES

The new livery adopted by the LMS for carriages was virtually the same as the old Knotty colour, although numbering was different. NSR passenger vehicles were placed in the batch 14701-14992 in date order, without regard to type. Thus all coaches built during 1907 were numbered 14862-86. Some 50 older vehicles on the NSR duplicate list were given duplicate numbers in the same LMS series and prefixed 'O'. Vans, carriage trucks and horse boxes numbered in passenger stock were given LMS numbers 6001-6149, again with 44 duplicates prefixed 'O'.

The new owners quickly swept away the remaining 4 wheel coaches and in the ten years following grouping, one-third of the NSR carriage stock was withdrawn, mostly the older 6 wheel coaches and vans built before 1901. At least one 4 wheel coach got a new lease of life when the chassis was rebuilt into gas-holder wagon no 13782 with two longitudinal cylinders. The original axleboxes and Stoke works plate were retained. In 1933 the LMS renumbered all its carriage stock on a systematic basis with all the same types of vehicles grouped together (See appendix no 9).

Quite a lot of bogie coaches survived through LMS into early BR days. Several worked in the Furness district, others on the Fenchurch Street—Tilbury—Southend line, and became Eastern Region stock. Two covered carriage trucks were transferred to the Cheshire Lines system.

Probably the last 6 wheel coach was brake third no M27790 (ex 14849), built at Stoke in 1905 and withdrawn in South Wales in December 1953. It was in use as a stores van at Manningham the following year. One at least of the bogie brake thirds was converted to a push and pull driving trailer—no M58036—and used on the Burton branch. Two 7 coach sets of NSR bogies were still at Uttoxeter in 1953 and at least two coaches were still in service in November 1958.

The wholesale introduction of diesel multiple-units hastened the end of old compartment coaches and it is a pity that a Knotty example was never preserved. The body of a 6 wheel saloon of about 1892 still exists and until recently it was used as a house at Littleover, Derby. It still contained its original NSR pictures and lavatory.

CHAPTER TWELVE

Years of Decline and Development

NATIONALISATION

Nationalised. Rationalised. Modernised. Dieselised. Electrified. Such are the five headings which sum up the Knotty's fortunes since 1948. All the changes which have affected the shape of the original system have stemmed from national, rather than local, influences, just as the earlier forms of competition from trams and buses had national characteristics.

One of the first results of nationalisation was the closure of a number of offices at Stoke including that of the North Staffordshire district engineer. As the last holder of the post, N. C. Walker pointed out at the time:

> This is a unique occasion and one that is likely to remain so for many generations and probably for several hundreds of years, because, never before has a Railway Engineer's office of such age and of such traditions been brought to a complete close.

Another economy which affected the NSR only indirectly was the closure of the Stafford & Uttoxeter Railway between Stafford Common and Bromshall Junction on 5 March 1951. The track remained in situ long enough for a special run by the Stephenson Locomotive Society on 23 March 1957. Later the line was lifted.

This closure was isolated and no more took place for a while, but when they did resume, there was plenty of local opposition. Especially fierce was that against the withdrawal of the Uttoxeter—Ashbourne—Buxton trains. It was said there were no travellers first class since everybody knew everybody else. Not surprising when the average number of each train was only nineteen. The trains were said to be losing £16,000 a year but before they were withdrawn on 1 November 1954, local people were assured specials would run between Buxton and Ashbourne only if villages were cut off by snow. The economy left Ashbourne, population 5,000, as the largest NSR town to lose its trains up to that time. Ramblers' excursions continued and specials ran from Derby and Stoke via Ashbourne to local villages for well dressing ceremonies, and for Dovedale.

Two big cuts were made on 7 May 1956 by the withdrawal of passenger services between Silverdale and Market Drayton and Stoke and Leek. When the Shropshire closure was proposed, Councillor C. D. Allen of Market Drayton, who had used the line for thirty years, contended that it gave a good service locally and for London connections at Stoke.[1] Both closures were considered by the West Midlands Transport Users' Consultative Committee on 13 March 1956, when British Railways estimated they would save over £6,000 a year.

Bradshaw warned travellers that while Bucknall & Northwood station was the station for Hanley, the town was a mile away. It was not a distinction mentioned in NSR timetables, but it helps to explain the demise of the branch. It was the victim of buses. They ran on a road roughly parallel, which served the local villages more closely and their shopping centre at Hanley more directly.

Another indication of the changing pattern of public transport was the closure of the branch to the North Staffordshire Mental Hospital at Cheddleton, put up for sale in April 1960—six years after the last goods ran on 16 December 1954. Another private casualty was a 3ft gauge horse-drawn tramway used to carry peat from Macclesfield Moss to sidings beside the main line. It closed in 1966 and the sidings were later taken out on electrification.

DIESELISATION

The replacement of the steam passenger services by diesels was gradual. The main line between Crewe and Derby was converted on 16 September 1957 and at the same time diesel railcars replaced nine Loop trains. A large diesel maintenance depot was completed at Cockshute sidings, Stoke, in December of that year and besides facilities for servicing up to thirty-eight dmu's a day, it was equipped for the heavy maintenance of sets based on several smaller depots.

Diesels were introduced between Stoke and Manchester on 3 March 1958, worked by sets based on Stoke and Buxton. Up to electrification, the Stoke dmu's also ran to Rugby via Birmingham.

The first section of the Knotty to be dieselised progressively, rather than in one step, was the Macclesfield, Bollington & Marple, on which Derby lightweight units ran from 1956 until their replacement by heavier units ten years later.

Closures continued with the Cold Meece branch, already mentioned. That was a line used only by passengers: the economy that followed it was of the Newfields branch, which carried only freight and it closed on 3 August 1959. The branch was subsequently lifted, as was the Grange freight branch, officially abandoned on 29 October 1961. Its fate was rather different from most lines. The Grange goods wharf had been sold to Stoke Corporation on 28 October 1953 and then the branch was used as a back-shunt for the Shelton steelworks. As they were extended, the branch was obliterated and a new line and junction put in with the main line.

The Newfields and Grange closures attracted little attention, but plenty of publicity surrounded the demise of the Burton—Tutbury branch and 'Tutbury Jennie', withdrawn on 13 June 1960, after hope faded that the dieselisation of the main line would increase branch traffic. Economy was not new on the branch: the three intermediate stations had been closed on 1 January 1949. Latterly, the trains had carried an average of a dozen passengers and lost £7,000 a year.

In the mid-fifties, the writer of the official guide of the Macclesfield Rural District Council still felt able to describe North Rode as an 'important railway junction'. But its days were numbered and by the time the Burton closure had taken place, a public inquiry had been held into the fate of the Churnet Valley line. Since the withdrawal of the Stoke trains in 1956, Leek had lost its status as a junction and become only a wayside station on the Churnet—its original status in 1848. No longer were there market day crowds to jam the platforms dangerously—but there were plenty of objectors to their closure. Over 120 went to the inquiry of the West Midlands TUCC in February 1960. They included officials of all the local authorities in the area, the National Farmers' Union, representatives of both sides of industry, and ramblers who used occasional Sunday specials from Manchester.

The trains were said to be losing £22,000 a year and alternative buses would do just as well for the area of Leek, a town with a population of some 19,000 people. The objectors felt the buses would overload roads already dangerous and often blocked by snow in winter. They claimed diesels could provide a train service that was economic. The Minister of Transport agreed with British Railways, but he upheld the insistence of the TUCC that workmen's trains should continue between Leek and Uttoxeter, mainly for the Oakamoor & Froghall copper works.

The last regular passenger trains ran through the Churnet Valley on bonfire night 1960 and they received noisy farewells at Rudyard, scene of so much Knotty enterprise half a century earlier. The section from Oakamoor to the Uttoxeter triangle was officially closed from 4 January 1965. Further economy followed at Uttoxeter on 31 January 1966 when the west-north and north-east curves of the triangle were closed for through running. Part of the former was retained as a station siding and part of the latter for the use of an oil company's trains. Dismantling between Uttoxeter and Oakamoor was completed a few months later. Late in 1968 the Churnet platform tracks and locomotive shed roads were lifted and the platforms converted into a car park for race-goers.

THE BEECHING REPORT

The Leek—Uttoxeter passenger service had been listed for withdrawal in the Beeching Report of 27 March 1963, together with the Potteries Loop, the Stoke—Silverdale, and MB & M service through to Manchester. The Cheadle branch was shown among lines where the withdrawal of passenger trains was considered before the Report was prepared. Passenger services on all other main NSR routes were recommended for modification.

The NSR passenger and freight patterns that emerged from the survey showed reasonably healthy main lines and rather ailing branches. The Derby—Stoke—Macclesfield lines and the Norton Bridge 'branch' had the highest passenger density of some 50,000 a week; the Stone—Colwich section had 5,000-10,000 but all other lines, including Stoke—Crewe had under 5,000 weekly passengers.

Stoke had receipts of over £25,000; Leek and Uttoxeter and one or two other towns, had receipts of between £5,000-£25,000. Every station between Leek and Uttoxeter; Stoke—Stone and on other lines, had under £5,000.

The Derby—Crewe and Norton Bridge—Macclesfield lines were shown as carrying some 100,000 tons of weekly freight about half routed via Colwich. The Sandbach branch was also carrying a similar tonnage. The Churnet and Market Drayton lines were handling up to 10,000 tons a week, but other routes were below the 5,000 ton level. The Manchester—Stoke—Birmingham route was classed as favourable to rail freight still being carried by road. Stoke was proposed as a Liner train terminal, lying on the routes between Manchester and London and the Midlands.

MORE CLOSURES

The last pre-Beeching economy, a few weeks ahead of the Report, brought the final demise of the Audley branch. Goods traffic was withdrawn from 7 January 1963, but this was little more than a 'paper' withdrawal for not only was this thirty-two years after the end of passenger trains, but several after the end of anything like a regular goods service over most of the branch, although for a short time in later years open-cast coal mining brought a reprieve through the building of sidings at Diglake for workings at Bignall Hill.

For about two years before closure, only an occasional goods ran to Audley and none went beyond. The last traffic was handled at Leycett in 1959, this was some two years after the closure on 21 September 1957 of Madeley Colliery at Leycett, the last of the once famous local pits. Jamage colliery had closed in 1941, but the branch from Diglake remained open officially until 1947 handling coal still screened at Jamage. The track was in situ for another six years.

Passenger trains were withdrawn from the Cheadle branch on 17 June 1963, but it continued to be used for a while by occasional excursions and still handles a busy freight link.

Economies in the Biddulph Valley network—Knotty and private—continued for years and accelerated in the sixties. The curve between Brown Lees Colliery and Black Bull station was covered by the Victoria Colliery tip in 1960. About this time traffic ceased to use the Packmoor Wharf, terminus of the Turnhurst Colliery line since the closure of the pit in 1914, but the line continued in use as a wagon store. Heath's line to Birchenwood closed in 1965.

Two years earlier the Biddulph Valley branch had lost its northern outlet through the closure of the spur between Congleton Lower and Upper Junctions on 1 December 1963, when the Upper Junction was taken out as a prelude to electrification. It had been used by coal trains bound for the Manchester Ship Canal until 25 September.

A new connection was put in between the Biddulph line and Whitfield Colliery to allow the complete closure of the Pinnox branch from 17 February 1964 three days after the running of the last Whitfield train. Pinnox Junction was removed just over two years later on 15 May 1966. The Biddulph line was further cut back by the closure of the northern tip between Victoria Colliery, Biddulph and Brunswick Wharf, Congleton, from 1 April 1968. Kidsgrove became the rail-borne coal depot for Congleton after this economy took place.

The southern section of the Longton, Adderley Green & Bucknall Railway between Millfield Junction and Park Hall, closed on 23 December 1963, had shrunk already through the widening of the ¼ mile gap by which the line was split in 1895. This had been achieved by closing a section of almost ½ mile between Park Hall and Weston Coyney. The L AG & B finally passed into history a few months later with the closing of the northern section between Botteslow Junction and Adderley Green on 6 July 1964.

Closures more sweeping in concept had taken place on 2 March 1964. They involved the stub of the Market Drayton passenger services, which had continued between Stoke and Silverdale after the early economy; and of the Loop passenger service. In case it comes as a shock to readers to think of the end of a line which once carried over 70,000 passengers a week, it is worth stating that it was perhaps surprising that the Loop survived so long. A survey in summer 1956 showed that one mid-morning train was carrying four passengers, three of them railwaymen travelling free. No wonder there was a drastic reduction in services at the start of the winter timetable on 17 September of that year. By 1967 Etruria—Waterloo Road was all that was left of the famous line—and that only for freight. It finally closed on 31 July 1969. Cobridge Tunnel was filled in and after track and bridge lifting, the area was left with a number of ugly brick abutments and overgrown embankments: features which while familiar in the Potteries, do nothing to improve the landscape.

The quickly changing pattern of economies in recent years is vividly illustrated by the fortunes of the Market Drayton branch. After the end of passenger trains in 1956, it continued to carry three daily goods to and from Stoke. Once Basford Hall marshalling yard was modernised and coal and other traffic in the Potteries concentrated at a few points, the branch became busier than ever. To aid electrification work, all traffic from Stoke and places to the south was routed to Madeley and then over a chord line, opened on 9 June 1962. It was laid on an embankment built during the building of the Market Drayton branch ninety years earlier, but not opened. A run-round loop controlled by a new box at Madeley was built on what had been the up line to Stoke until the branch was singled in 1934. Traffic from north of Stoke continued to reach Crewe via Harecastle.

But on 8 March 1966, the Market Drayton branch was closed completely between Newcastle Junction and Brampton Sidings: the hilly 1½ mile section and the Hartshill tunnels were filled in with coal waste, together with the site of Newcastle station. Newcastle Junction was severed on 13 March as a prelude to electrification. A few days earlier, on 8 March, the section west of Madeley to Market Drayton (Silverdale

Junction) was closed. The section had not been used for some time and while this was the official date, the line was not regarded as closed until 9 January 1967. One reason for the delay in lifting the line was indecision over plans for a large marshalling yard at Walcot, near Wellington. It was overtaken by the development of block trains and so fell the concept of using the Market Drayton branch as a feeder for traffic between the yard and the Potteries.

When the branch was finally severed, Newcastle goods depot stayed open to handle road traffic via Stoke. After through trains from Stoke stopped using the Madeley chord, it remained open as a bi-directional route to Brampton Sidings, mainly for coal from Holditch and Silverdale Collieries and waste metal handled in the sidings themselves. The chord also provided the only access to the Pool Dam branch in the eighteen months between the Newcastle closure and its own on 11 September 1967.

The chord was not the only major engineering work on the branch in recent years. When the M6 (Birmingham—Glasgow) Motorway was being driven through Staffordshire, the branch was carried across it on a bridge said to have the longest reinforced concrete beams in Britain: 297ft long and stressed by steel cables to just over 60 tons.

Several economies have been carried out at Burton. The ½ mile southern tip of the Tutbury branch between Horninglow and North Stafford Junction was closed on 4 April 1966, leaving the NSR fly-over as the only access to sidings at Stretton. These included the ½ mile stretch of the Tutbury branch between Horninglow and Stretton, which was retained as a single siding until 30 January 1967. Complete closure of the section between Stretton and Egginton Junction, including the GNR curve, followed on 6 May 1968.

ELECTRIFICATION

It was left to electrification to give the Potteries what the Knotty promoters always intended it should have: a firm place on the main line between London and Manchester. Today that has been achieved by the routing of many of the intercity expresses via Stoke.

The Harecastle—Crewe branch and the Loop were never planned for electrification according to the Minister of Transport, Mr Ernest Marples, in a Parliamentary statement of 30 November 1961. By then the Loop was in its death throes after rejection by a bus-and-car using public, and the Crewe branch and the remainder of the old 'main line' between Stoke and Derby were handling mainly freight to and from areas outside the Potteries which required all-through diesel haulage.

The inter-city expresses run over almost 2½ miles of new main line forming the Harecastle diversion, a £1,000,000 project which was the most spectacular of all the changes brought by electrification. It was conceived after initial surveys showed that clearances were insufficient for the installation of overhead wires in the main (south) tunnel of 1,763 yards at Harecastle and in the two shorter ones: middle, 180yd and north, 130yd. All were in poor condition and it was estimated that £30,000 a year would have to be spent on them, with the engineers having weekend possession for between twenty and thirty *years*.

As the land lying above the north tunnel was shallow, it was easily opened out, but the others were far too deep: there was 70ft of earth over the middle tunnel and up to 180ft above the main one where it burrowed under the wooded Harecastle ridge. A new tunnel parallel with the existing ones, as at Woodhead, was ruled out as being too costly. Singling the lines through the old tunnels would have restricted traffic too much. The diversion was the best answer as it could be taken through a shallow valley a little to the west and then under the ridge—73ft deep at that point—by a tunnel of no more than 220yd. But there were other complications. The route of the diversion meant altering two small reservoirs and diverting Chatterley Sidings and the Chesterton branch (from 18 October 1964); reconstructing a road bridge; building two new ones, two footbridges and an under-bridge.

Parliamentary powers were obtained in 1962 and the contract for the work was let in the same year. Harecastle North tunnel was quickly opened out and boring of the new one started in October 1964. Break-through was achieved on 25 February 1966, but not before two old shafts were encountered: that of an old mine and of the 1824 bores made by Telford in building the second and wider of the Harecastle canal tunnels. The shafts were bridged over and one reservoir, Bath Pool, was drained while it was reduced in width and a railway cutting built alongside. It was also elongated by 100yd to maintain its water capacity. The other reservoir, Nelson Pool, was replaced by a covered one.

Chatterley Sidings were modified and the junction of the Chesterton branch altered from a north facing one situated just south of the entrance to the old main tunnel, to a south facing one stemming from the line at Bradwell Sidings at the southern extremity of the diversion. The diverted branch was destined to have only a short life for once Parkhouse Colliery closed it lost its livelihood and official closure followed on 9 June 1968.

One advantage gained from building the diversion—total length 2 miles 850yd—was that it allowed electrification work, which would have been difficult in the tunnels, to be carried out without interfering with the 210 trains daily then using the section. It also helped in the erection of and maintenance of the overhead equipment.

The diversion, landscaped to match one of the more pleasant and green areas of the Potteries, included a maximum up gradient of 1 in 80 between the main and the old north tunnel, and a climb of 1 in 100 for down trains approaching the ridge. There was a sentimental journey of a last train through the south and middle tunnels on 26 June 1966 and the deviation was then brought into use.

Overhead equipment stretching for 134 miles was erected between Colwich and Cheadle Hulme and the contractors worked from a main depot at Crewe and subsidiary ones at Alsager, Weston and Stockport.

Apart from the deviation, electrification work in the Potteries was similar to that elsewhere, involving the deeper ballasting of track, the alteration of lay-outs, rebuilding of bridges to give clearance for the wires, and lengthening platforms to take longer trains of standard formations. Four-aspect colour light signals replaced semaphores and a new power box opened at Stoke on 17 July 1966 was built on the site of an old carriage shed demolished in the thirties. It lay on the up side just north of the station. The box controls the heart of the Knotty, from Colwich and Norton Bridge to Grange Junction, where another new box was built. Others were erected at Kidsgrove Central and Macclesfield.

The main line junction at Norton Bridge was drastically altered and a new box built on the up side of the main line to control part of the stretch between Stafford and Crewe, the entry and exit to the Stoke line, and the up and down NSR goods loops at the approach to Norton Bridge.

All electrified lines were track circuited, fitted with AWS equipment and, in places, long-welded rails.

In renovating stations, the best of the distinctive Knotty architecture was preserved wherever possible and it was enhanced in places like Stone and at Stoke, where modernisation of the ticket and other offices to present travellers with the right image of the 100mph era was carried out without loss of 'historic atmosphere'.

Stoke platforms were lengthened to handle the 12 coach locomotive-hauled expresses. The biggest alteration was the removal of the down middle road between the platforms to allow the erection of overhead gantries.

Associated developments included the closure in 1962 of the engineers' depot to make way for a new postal sorting office, a station car park, opened 1966, and the demolition, in March 1968, of the rifle range.

The transition from steam to electric traction was commemorated by a 17ft long mural in ceramics and other materials on the up platform at Stoke. It was unveiled on 5 November 1969.

The most dramatic station work took place at Macclesfield where Hibel Road station was closed on 7 November 1960 (coincident with the end of the Churnet passenger trains), and replaced by a practically rebuilt Central station, renamed simply Macclesfield. Platforms were lengthened to handle 15 coach down trains and 13 up, and a loop was retained for the MB & M locals. Thus did Macclesfield get a single station, something that it had wanted for nearly a century.

Main line electrification at Crewe embraced the Knotty's up and down goods loops and the spur from NS Junction into Basford Hall sidings. The NSR sidings are now almost derelict although those on the down side are used by the civil engineers for track storage.

The Potteries electrification was completed after that of the LNWR main line and electric services began from 2 January 1967 when schedules were run to pre-electric timings. The switch to high speed services in both the NSR and Birmingham areas began on 6 March, the date of the reopening of the Stone—Colwich section, closed for conversion since 7 September 1964.

Stoke's importance as an ever-growing passenger centre led to it being among eighteen main stations throughout Britain where, from autumn 1969, passengers have been able to book tickets using a credit card.

Stoke became the biggest division in the London Midland Region covering not only the Potteries, but the whole of North and mid-Wales, taking in Aberystwyth. Its boundary points included North Rode and Goostrey, Waverton, near Chester, Shilton, on the London—Crewe main line, and Sudbury on that to Derby.

The number of railmen in the Potteries has dwindled over the years but occasionally their voice is heard nationally, as happened late in 1969 when it became known that a newspaper was paying the wife of the train robber Ronald Biggs, many thousands for her story. NUR members at Leek protested against publicity given to her and the other wives of the robbers.

FREIGHT DEVELOPMENT

A new freight terminal opened at Stoke on 9 May 1961 cost £750,000 and was built on the site of an old rubbish tip. It was the first purpose-built concentration depot under the London Midland Region modernisation plan and it took over traffic from the original Knotty depot at Stoke and eight others: Hanley, Longport, Longton, Newcastle, Leek, Congleton, Stone and Stafford.

Nearly a mile of sidings were laid to accommodate 200 wagons under cover and 77 more outside. Traffic is collected and delivered by 100 vans, some radio controlled. The depot handles mainly pottery goods, ale traffic and general sundries, the latter a class of traffic also concentrated at Uttoxeter.

Following Beeching, the British Railways Board published in February 1965 its plans for *The Development of the Major Railway Trunk Routes*. It estimated that in 1984, Stoke will be receiving 1,500,000 tons of freight a year and dispatching 600,000 tons. It was estimated 450,000 tons of freight will be from London; 400,000 tons from Corby; 250,000 tons from Banbury; 100,000 tons from Cardiff and 50,000 tons from Bristol, Burton, Carlisle, Exeter, Newcastle-upon-Tyne and Plymouth.

Half of that dispatched was envisaged as destined for similar areas. Half will go to London and of the balance, 100,000 tons will be sent to Leicester and 50,000 tons to Doncaster, Stockton, Newcastle and Edinburgh.

Stoke, it is thought, will be handling 10 trunk trains a day: 6 from London, 2 from Corby and others from Banbury and Leicester. It will be dispatching 7 trunk trains—2 each to London and Corby and others to Banbury, Leicester and Newcastle.

At electrification the National Coal Board was the biggest customer of the Stoke division, radiating traffic from a dozen pits including a new one at Wolstanton. Other major freight hauls included block iron ore trains from mines in Northamptonshire and Oxfordshire to Shelton steel works.

BR OPERATING

Nationalisation had little immediate effect on locomotive workings or train operation. The final pattern of passenger services over the Loop was of heavy engines and light trains and a 30mph limit was laid down for 2–6–4 tanks climbing from Kidsgrove to the summit. During diversions for routine engineering works and later, electrification, main line trains used the northern section of the Loop between Kidsgrove and Tunstall, but, apart from dmu's they were barred south of there. This meant they ran over the Pinnox branch, a routing which allowed locals to make the usual calls at Longport. But the diversion was messy for trains to and from Crewe because of reversals necessary at Kidsgrove and Harecastle. Before the Stone—Colwich section was closed for conversion, it was used for trains diverted by Sunday engineering work between Colwich and Stafford. Stoke—Macclesfield trains were diverted through Crewe during similar work north of Harecastle.

Holiday specials and excursions provided some of the most interesting workings in later years, especially as they got more varied as more and more lines closed and fresh routings were necessary.

What an amazing line the Knotty was! Not only did it have a branch (Sandbach) on which passenger trains were not introduced for nearly half a century after opening, but it had one on which regular excursions ran for 30 years after the end of local services, Trentham Park (renamed Trentham Gardens, 7 October 1946).

Up to the outbreak of war there were summer excursions every Sunday. Post-war excursions were mainly from the Midlands but the branch remained open long enough to pass into the diesel age: the last excursion before official closure from 1 October 1957 was an eight-car dmu from Birmingham.

Trentham was the most popular destination of excursions *into* the Potteries, and North Wales was one of the most popular destinations for specials *from* it. Holiday traffic was heaviest during the Stoke Wakes each August, but there was a service tailored to meet the demands outside it. For those who returned home on Saturday 23 July 1960, for instance, there was the choice of several trains, including a special from Butlins, Pwllheli, which left Penychain at 8 45 am for Stoke. It was timed to pass Rhyl on the up fast line at 11 27 am, and to overtake a little later the 11 5 am Rhyl—Stoke, which used the slow line to call at Prestatyn and then ran to Chester, Crewe, Alsager, Kidsgrove Central, Longport and Etruria. The 12 55 pm Llandudno—Leicester Central ran non-stop between Crewe and Tutbury, where it detached the last two coaches for Burton.

It was followed by the 1 40 pm Llandudno—Derby Midland, which called at Prestatyn, Chester, Beeston Castle, Crewe, Longport, Etruria, Stoke, Longton and Uttoxeter. Finally there was the 5 10 pm Llandudno—Stoke, calling at Prestatyn, Chester, Crewe, Alsager, Kidsgrove Central, Longport and Etruria.

These workings, roughly balanced, were to remain in vogue

for the following two years. They included a 10 coach special to Llandudno from Ford Green, most southerly of the stations on the Biddulph branch, closed to regular passenger trains in 1927.[2] Nationalisation also produced a Sunday Nottingham GN—Llandudno booked service worked by a class 'B1' 4-6-0 throughout (and by Uttoxeter men from there).

The Stoke—Leek branch was used by football specials from after the end of regular services in 1956 until 23 April 1960. For the Wakes, selected stations were re-opened a week early for people to get train, luggage and regulation tickets. Workings in 1961 included a special from the Silverdale line to Blackpool, routed via Stoke, Leek and the Churnet Valley to Macclesfield to avoid reversal. Specials which originated on the Loop had to be banked. Another operating problem was caused by the opening of the Harecastle deviation before the end of steam operation for their exhausts damaged the overhead system. It meant that diesels had to be drafted to haul them over the deviation.

Because of the nature of the route, the Potteries were rarely considered when faster services were planned. As a result none of the services in the summer 1955 reached 60mph, the magic figure for Britain's crack expresses, just as 100mph is today, even the down *Comet* failed to qualify though by only 1m, still being allowed 146m for the 145 miles Stoke—Euston.

The introduction of diesels between Stoke and Manchester on 3 March 1958 was marked by a speed-up in the service and in its intensity, 8 trains being added to provide an hourly service, dovetailed into the Manchester—Buxton service, to give Stockport—Manchester shoppers a half-hourly service.

By summer 1964 the Knotty passenger network had shrunk to the size it remains today, with the exception of the MB & M locals and the fag end of the Churnet service, still maintained between Leek and Uttoxeter. The local timetable gave brief details of local *bus* services and details, under the heading 'Road—Rail Co-ordination', of schemes for the alternative availability of tickets. The links between the Potteries and the traditional holiday resorts were reflected by 'Bargain Holiday Fares', ranging from 16s between Stoke and Prestatyn to 30s for a Blackpool return.

The running down of branches as a prelude to closure led

to a number of operating restrictions. From September 1952 (possibly earlier), Diglake signal box on the Audley line was open only as required, while the other intermediate one at Leycett was open only between 8 40 am and 3 50 pm. One of the last instructions issued for the Adderley Green branch warned drivers that they must be prepared to stop 'in the event of level crossing gates being across the railway'.

Lingering death was not confined to branches: Macclesfield Shed (9C) got a reprieve when it was decreed that workmen's trains had to continue between Leek and Uttoxeter after the closure of the Churnet. Instead of closing at the same time as Macclesfield Hibel Road station, it remained open to service engines which ran light to Leek, but closed on 11 June 1961 when dmu's took over the service of 2 up and 3 down trains Monday—Saturdays.

INTER-CITY EXPRESSES

British Railways made sure well in advance that everybody knew about the high speeds that would be possible with electrification. Yet what people did not perhaps realise was the sort of point to point timings that would be necessary to achieve 2h 40m schedules between London and Manchester through the Potteries. The hilly, twisting, congested nature of the Potteries route, even with the deviation, made it impossible to reach the 100mph mark locally and an 85mph maximum was fixed between Colwich and Macclesfield, restricted to rather less in places and down to 30mph through Stoke. The effect of the restrictions was to allow slightly higher average speeds in the open country south of Stoke than in the congested area north of it. The fastest 1969 express between Stoke and Euston was the 19 13 hours, timed over the 128 miles to Watford in 101m—an average of 76.33mph. Three expresses were timed over the 145 miles between Stoke and Euston in 117m—an average of 74.83mph. The fastest down train was a fraction slower. The best timings between Stoke and Macclesfield were achieved by three trains timed to cover the 20 miles at 68.78mph.

The express pattern gave Stoke roughly a two-hourly link with Euston, intensified in the morning and evening peaks.

The fastest inter-city expresses were allowed 41m between Manchester and Stoke, calling only at Stockport; others called at Macclesfield and Congleton, which, together with other local stations, had an hourly basic service of emu's working between Manchester—Stoke—Stafford, and often Birmingham, allowed 59m between Manchester and Stoke with eleven stops. On the Knotty they include Kidsgrove, Longport, Etruria, Wedgwood, Barlaston & Tittensor, Stone and Norton Bridge.

Stoke's only other passenger service by then was an hourly 'main line' Crewe—Derby link, operated mainly by three-coach corridor dmu's, including, in 1969, ex-Western Region sets. They were allowed 101m for the 51 miles, including eight stops: Uttoxeter, Blythe Bridge, Longton, Stoke, Etruria, Longport, Kidsgrove and Alsager.

The sight of a dmu standing at a Cheshire station like Alsager with the destination Lincoln on its blind may seem strange, but it is correct for the units work complicated cross-country diagrams which sometimes take them to Grimsby. Although shown in the public timetable as working only between Crewe and Derby, the units regularly work forward via Nottingham to Lincoln, and provide the best service between Nottingham and Derby and Liverpool, via connections at Crewe.

Diagrams such as these mean that Stoke retains its role as a through, rather than a terminal, station. Only a few emu's and dmu's terminate there and then run on to servicing depots. There is no stabling room in the old Newcastle bay platform for besides being used by an occasional stopping train to Manchester, it is busy with parcels traffic.

In the heart of the Potteries the main line diesel and electric service is augmented by locals between Stoke and Kidsgrove. The MB & M service before closure on 5 January 1970 was maintained by trains allowed 58m for the 20 miles between Manchester and Macclesfield, compared, at best, with the non-stop inter-city expresses covering the 18 miles direct in 20m.

While the Crewe—Derby service is reduced to 5 trains each way on Sundays, journey times are cut by 25m, the trains taking a maximum of 76m through the omission of stops at Blythe Bridge, Longton, Etruria and Alsager. The closure of the four Derby line stations, and of Stone, Barlaston and Wedgwood on Sundays, leaves just six open on the whole of the old system. How pleased the Victorian shareholders would have been!

Freight operating remains as laborious as ever because of branch gradients and brakes still have to be pinned on the Birchenwood, Caldon and Biddulph lines to prevent runaways.

The NSR system is designed to carry extra heavy traffic in case of diversion and goods and crossing loops are maintained at strategic places. Signal boxes normally switched out can be quickly manned to shorten long blocks—like that of 4 miles between Radway Green and Crewe (the intermediate box here is Barthomley).

Stoke remains the natural congestion point and besides the goods lines between Stoke and Grange Junctions, the down platform road is signalled for multi-directional working.

Besides the main lines, one of the busiest for freight is the Sandbach branch, which is double-tracked for about ½ mile at both ends with a single-track section between Lawton and Elton, including a passing loop at Hassell Green. The longest of the freight arteries is that from Stoke to Caldon, via Leek Brook Junction, where the signal box controls the surviving 7½ miles of the Churnet route to Leek and the British Industrial Sand works. Both Churnet lines are worked as 'one train working', although there is less restricted working between Leek Brook and Stoke, which is largely double tracked, because of traffic via Milton Junction along the Biddulph line as far as Heath's Junction. Early in 1970 Caldon Low yard of five sidings (capacity about 100 wagons) was handling 6,250 tons of stone in 4 daily trains for either ballast or road stone. Aggregate for concrete-making pours from gravel pits around Cheadle and is carried by train. Lorries drive up a ramp built in the station yard and discharge into 21 ton hoppers destined for Liverpool and Manchester. Trains of 25 ton hoppers carry 250,000 tons of silica sand a year from Oakamoor to Port Sunlight. The Biddulph line, double for nearly a mile to Ford Green, is also 'one train' worked as is the 1½ mile branch from Kidsgrove, Liverpool Road, to Birchenwood.

The most unusual of the freight workings is that over the Madeley Chord to Holditch Colliery. It involves reversal at

Apedale Junction, and the section between Silverdale Crossing and the pit is classed as a 'through siding' for 'one train' working. Apedale is the 'junction' for a $\frac{1}{2}$ mile extension of the original Market Drayton line which is still open to Brampton Siding.

PRELUDE TO DISASTER

The sparsity of Sunday trains is not the only feature redolent of Victorian days: more serious is the continuing incidence of accidents on level crossings. There was a spectacular one during track lifting near Ashbourne station on 19 October 1964 when three loaded wagons ran away, crashed through gates at Clifton, and Norbury and Ellastone stations and came to rest, checked by a rising gradient, only a few yards short of a crossing at Rocester, where the gates had been closed to road traffic by emergency police action.

While this accident was soon forgotten it is doubtful if the disaster at Hixon level crossing will ever be. It happened on 6 January 1968 when the 11 30 am Manchester—Euston express of the usual 12 coach formation hauled by AL 1 electric locomotive no E 3009, hit a heavy road transporter carrying a transformer weighing 120 tons which was straddling the automatic half-barrier crossing as the express, carrying some 300 passengers, approached at about 75mph. Eleven people including three locomotive men were killed and 45 injured, 6 seriously.

The accident happened at a time when there was growing concern throughout Britain about unmanned crossings and ten days later the Minister of Transport, Mrs Barbara Castle, made history by ordering a formal inquiry, not through the Railway Inspectorate of her Ministry, but under section 7 of the Regulation of the Railways Act of 1871. The section had been used only once before: for the inquiry into the Tay Bridge disaster in 1879.

The Hixon inquiry was held by a Queen's Counsel, Mr Edward Brian Gibbens, who had power to enforce the attendance of witnesses and the production of documents. The main reasons for the change of procedure were that other authorities besides British Rail were closely concerned with the accident, and also because it was felt there should be an independent investigation of automatic half-barrier crossings, which had been in use nationally for only a few years. While the inquiry sat, the Hixon crossing reverted to manned operation and plans were halted for the installation of further automatic crossings.

The Inspector's report of 25 July 1968[3] showed that the crossing was converted under an order of 19 January 1967—an order which still gave legal recognition to the Knotty by virtue of its title: British Railways Board (North Staffordshire Railway) Hixon Level Crossing Order. The crossing was installed the following April, although it was manned until July 1967 when monitoring was continued from Colwich signal box. A census taken after the crash showed that each 24 hours it was used by 26 trains and about 870 road vehicles.

The report placed the blame for the accident in several quarters and said the real cause was ignorance, born of lack of imagination and foresight. It found that the immediate cause of the accident was that the driver of the huge transporter vehicle failed to comply with a notice directing him to telephone the local signalman before crossing, and drove the vehicle across the railway at 2mph when the arrival of the 75mph express was imminent. The driver's employer and the police were criticised and the origin of the accident was found to be in the failure of officers of both the Ministry of Transport and British Railways in collaboration to appreciate the measures necessary to deal with a hazard of which they were aware. It called for basic changes in the operation of automatic crossings.

When British Rail announced the possible closure of the Stone—Colwich section a little later, it stressed that it had nothing to do with the Hixon accident. The crossing, however, remained troublesome and just after Christmas 1969, the barriers failed three times in 24 hours.

The only other automatic crossing in use on the Knotty at the time of the Hixon accident was a neighbouring one at Aston by Stone. There was also another type of unmanned crossing on the Crewe branch at Barthomley. This was a gated crossing with flashing red and green lights and it was operated by motorists. The next NSR accident was on 15 October, a day before, as it happened, the Ministry of Transport announced the appointment of a designer to work on improvements to the half barrier crossings. This accident happened at Tean on the Cheadle branch, where a couple and their two children escaped serious injury when a train hit their van after it had stalled on an unmanned crossing.

Crossings were troublesome to cattle as well as people and Crewe—Derby trains were delayed for 30 minutes on 8 November 1968 while a cow was freed from the Barthomley crossing.

Although economies left little of the Churnet operational, it was the scene of a drama in summer 1969 when on 26 August it was blocked by five tons of stone which fell from a lorry after it hit the overbridge at Froghall. A man who realised a train was due got the police to stop it via Stoke control.

THE FUTURE

Four years after Beeching and after a change of government, there was a new report, *British Railways Network for Development*, published on 15 March 1967. It outlined the basic railway network which the Labour government planned to retain and develop to meet social, economic and commercial needs. It showed no change in the existing NSR pattern. Crewe—Derby and the electrified routes were to keep their passenger services. The Cheadle Biddulph and Sandbach branches and the Market Drayton line between Brampton and Madeley, were to retain their freight services, as was the Leek branch from Stoke to Oakamoor and Caldon.

The plan excluded from development the Macclesfield, Bollington and Marple and on 5 January 1970 the Manchester—Marple—Macclesfield diesels were cut back to Rose Hill, centre of a growing area of Marple.

The report was followed by a Government decision to provide in 1969 grants totalling nationally £62,000,000, to subsidise uneconomical but socially desirable lines. They included all the Knotty's remaining passenger services. That for Crewe—Derby alone totalled £346,000 in 1969. Even though the Colwich—Stone section had been designated for retention, its possible closure was announced on 11 October 1968.

As the Queen opened the new Euston, the *Evening Sentinel*, Stoke, praised British Rail, but also chided:

> Unhappily British Railways have not yet lost the habit of giving with one hand and taking away with another. It is quite astonishing to find that part of the new electrified system—admittedly only a small part—is already being regarded as redundant. The significance of this is not that the diversion would be likely to add a few minutes to the time of the journey from Stoke, but that the contemplated closure operation should take place *after* the electrification, and not before it.

The paper went on to ask:

> How much money was spent on erecting the electric equipment and raising bridges on this stretch—an undertaking that is now apparently, considered to have been unnecessary?
>
> This is far too like the kind of muddle that existed at one period during the wholesale closure of other lines—a muddle that involved, for example, the repainting of Hanley station after a decision had been made to close it.

The *Sentinel* called for representations to make sure that local passengers did not suffer through more expresses being routed through Crewe, rather than Stoke.

Truly the fears of history were repeating themselves.

These fears were kept alive for two years until the Stone—Colwich reprieve was announced by the divisional manager, Mr Frank Young, at a luncheon of the North Staffordshire Railway Association on 3 October 1970. Detailed investigations had proved the section was needed for regular passenger and freight services and as a diversionary route. Three weeks earlier modifications had been completed at the two unmanned crossings on the section at Hixon and Aston to bring them up to the higher safety standards recommended after the Hixon disaster.

The Knotty lives on!

Knottyana

Between the time this book was started and completed, the Knotty slipped a little deeper into history, yet interest in the company flourishes as never before. After death, the Knotty became, in a sense, better known because of a desire by many local people to remember something that was very much part of their lives—and their best form of transport—for many years.

The Knotty's memory was first preserved in depth by a group of local men who knew it well: a group called 'Manifold', who published *The North Staffordshire Railway* in 1952. That book is long out of print and a collector's item. In 1969 it was offered by a second-hand bookseller at 7½ guineas. In 1970, a bound copy of the company's original Acts was offered at 9 guineas.

The living Knotty is personified by the North Staffordshire Railway Association, formed in 1958 to maintain and renew friendship among old employees. The main event which it organises is an annual meeting and lunch at Stoke. By 1968 the association had 130 members, including five still working on British Railways.

The Knotty's boast that it ran passenger trains on almost all its branches was taken a stage further after nationalisation when enthusiasts ran the first-ever passenger trains over the Caldon Low and Chesterton branches. Caldon Low was reached by a railtour of the Stephenson and Manchester Locomotive Societies on 26 April 1952, hauled by ex L & Y 2-4-2T, no 50703, and piloted from Leek by a Uttoxeter 2–6–2T, no 40203. Since it was made up of brake vans and not coaches, the so-called first passenger train to Chesterton, run by the Branch Line Society and the Locomotive Club of Great Britain on 25 April 1964, was not quite that. But the branch gremlins who wanted to preserve Chesterton's reputation as a freight only line, nearly succeeded. For after slipping at its first attempt to climb the bank, 2–6–0 no 78056 had to set back to the junction and charge it. History bestowed another distinction on this special, making it the last, as well as the first, passenger-carrying train to Chesterton, for no more ran before the closure of the branch.

Leek & Manifold enthusiasts refresh memories by walking its course, pondering perhaps that the line has now been closed for a longer period than it was ever open. They may also believe that if it had survived until the present era of steam preservation, it would have had a good chance of popularity, being more accessible than several narrow gauge lines which continue to thrive.

Jubilee celebrations to mark the creation of the City of Stoke-on-Trent included a big railway exhibition in the North Western yard from 11 to 24 May 1960. It included a diesel locomotive (D 5081) and LNWR veterans from Crewe.

But the emphasis was on the Knotty and its glory. The National Coal Board loaned the 37 years old 0–6–2T no 2, then working at Walkden, near Manchester. She was restored to NSR livery at Crewe, and fitted at Crewe works with an NSR whistle. There were some 130 small evocative exhibits like the station bell that was often heard tolling across the fields around Pipe Gate station: surely one of the loneliest on the Knotty; a decorative brass lamp bracket from Norton-in-Hales; a ticket-dating machine from Keele; letters asking for jobs and a souvenir programme of the last social function held by the NSR before grouping: a last waltz, perhaps. But not quite, for in July and August 1966 the Knotty was immortalised in a musical documentary of that title created by actors at the Victoria Theatre, Stoke, Britain's first theatre in the round. They used original documents, newspapers, songs and other effects to relate the railway's fortunes in life and death. It was such a 'hit' that it was repeated in October 1967 in Stoke and at the April Festival in Florence in 1969, where it was again a great success. Extracts from the show, and some of the reminiscences recorded by old Knotty men for it, were recorded by the company on 14 September 1969 for an LP general release.

One of the documentary's creators, Peter Terson, never forgot the railwaymen he met in the Potteries and also people he met on 'The Last Train Through Harecastle Tunnel' which he took for 'The Wednesday Play' he wrote for BBC1 and which was televised on 1 October 1969. It concerned a man obsessed with railways, and the strange encounters that resulted from his trip. Interviewed about the men of the Knotty, Terson remarked: 'Their passion was so complete it made the rest of us seem trivial'. Of the last train through the tunnel, he commented: 'People stayed up till midnight just to be on that train. I felt like a king'.

The Staffordshire County Council museum established at Shugborough Hall has among its main exhibits no 2 and the battery-electric shunter, both restored to original livery. Several official photographs of NSR locomotives hang on the wall of York Railway Museum and others are at Clapham. Deposited plans for the railways in the County are in the Staffordshire County Record Office at Stafford, and other historic material is in the adjoining William Salt Library.

Considering so many lines lay outside Cheshire, there is a surprisingly large collection of deposited plans in the Cheshire Record Office at Chester. These and many other railway plans, are detailed in a useful leaflet published by the county archivist. In the sixties, Stoke became a centre for the auction of railway relics. Equipment from closed NSR stations was among goods auctioned at Stoke Railway Garage on 6 June 1964. They included platform seats bearing original station names and crest. One from the L & M sold for £8.

An organisation with Knotty connections is the Foxfield Light Railway Society, which keeps steam alive on the 3½ mile line between the main line at Blythe Bridge, and the old pit. Steam was alive, too, in the middle of 1970 at Meaford Power Station, near Barlaston, at Birchenwood and at Silverdale Colliery.

Many traces of old Knotty remain for those who have the patience to seek them out: for instance, buildings like the graceful original Ashbourne station of 1852.

The Knotty lives on beside many a winter fireside in the novels of Arnold Bennett who, as he immortalised the Potteries, portrayed the entire system. There is a pleasant description of a Burslem—Hanley train in *Old Wives' Tale*. His heart was close to the Loop and in his different books, he described the Loop's buildings, special penny timetables and the foibles of the early electric coach lighting. He wrote also of the Buxton expresses via Middlewood. The Loop trains were depicted in tiles in the Bridge Inn at Hanley and this mural of 1897 is preserved at Clapham.

In the minds of many men the Knotty remains a living railway and in their different ways, its admirers honour its memory. One was Hubert Hill, a master printer at Congleton, who died in March 1965. He left £10 to the local station master in appreciation of the efficiency and reputation of the NSR and LNWR and the safety and fabulous speed of the 9 18 am Congleton—Euston in 1900. He was then a boy aged five.

Signal lever collar

Notes to Chapters

Notes to Chapter 1, pages 17-35

1 Arnold Bennett missed Fenton out of his famous 'five towns'.
2 Hargreaves, Thomas: *Map of Staffordshire Potteries & Newcastle*, 1832. In Stoke Public Library.
3 Baxter, Bertram; *Stone Blocks & Iron Rails*, 1966, page 184.
4 Hadfield, Charles; *Canals of the West Midlands*, 1966, p 205.
5 Chaloner, W. H.; *The Social & Economic Development of Crewe*, 1950, p 14.
6 Plan deposited in Cheshire Record Office. No 65.
7 Plan deposited in Cheshire Record Office. No 99.
8 Plan in Manchester Reference Library, 625.1 M 4.
9 Osborne: *Guide to the Grand Junction Railway*, 1838.
10 Plan deposited in Cheshire Record Office, 30 November 1844. No 194.
11 This was a 'somewhat unusual fate'. See Lewin, H. G. *The Railway Mania*, revised ed. 1968, p 38.
12 Plan deposited in Cheshire Record Office, No 262.
13 Plan deposited in Cheshire Record Office 30 November, 1845. No 230.
14 'Manifold'; *The North Staffordshire Railway*, 1952, p 24.
15 Plan deposited Cheshire Record Office. No 211.
16 Plan deposited Cheshire Record Office. No 209.
17 Plan deposited Cheshire Record Office. 30 November 1845. No 263.
18 Plan deposited Cheshire Record Office. No 221.
19 Plan deposited Stafford Record Office 30 November 1845.
20 Plan deposited Cheshire Record Office. No 217.
21 Plan deposited Cheshire Record Office. No 207.
22 Hollick, J. R.; Address to Adelphic Club, Ashbourne, 12 December 1955.
23 Plan deposited Cheshire Record Office 30 November 1846. No 274.

Notes to Chapter 2, pages 36-57

1 Osborne; *Guide to the Grand Junction Railway*, 1838, p 233.
2 Hodges, William; *Law of Railways*, 1855, p 502.
3 Plan deposited Cheshire Record Office 21 April 1847. No 289.
4 Plan deposited Cheshire Record Office 30 November 1846. No 270.
5 Plan deposited Cheshire Record Office 30 November 1846. No 270.
6 Hodges, William; *Law of Railways*, 1855, p 260.
7 Davies, C. Stella; *A History of Macclesfield*, 1961, p 165.
8 Plan deposited Cheshire Record Office, 30 November 1846. No 270.

Notes to Chapter 3, pages 58-89

1 Plan deposited Cheshire Record Office, 1849. No 293. Route followed closely that of Macclesfield, Bollington & Marple line of later years.
2 Plan deposited Cheshire Record Office, 29 November 1851. No 300. Title: *A Railway from Sandbach to Birkenhead.*
3 Shrewsbury & North Wales Railway, amalgamated with the Shrewsbury & Potteries Junction Railway to form the Potteries, Shrewsbury & North Wales Railway, 16 July 1866.
4 The Newcastle-under-Lyme Canal (Lease) Act, 23 June 1864, provided for the lease to the NSR in perpetuity at reduced annual rental of £520. On 2 June 1938 the LMS got an Act to stop up part of the canal.
5 James W. Buller, MP for North Devon, was a director of the Bristol & Exeter and other companies in the West Country. He often adjudicated in railway disputes.
6 It is not known when Silverdale passenger trains first ran. The line opened on 17 April 1862, but *Bradshaw* for the following month showed only a station. No service appeared until May 1863.
7 Hollick, J. R.; *The Turnhurst Line*. A private paper.
8 The MS & L had envisaged the Macclesfield & Knutsford Railway being managed by the Cheshire Midland Railway, a company in which it had a stake. The Knutsford & Warrington Railway was to be run jointly by the Cheshire Midland and the Warrington & Stockport companies.
9 Neele, G. P.; *Railway Reminiscences*, 1909, p 309.
10 Plan deposited in Cheshire Record Office. No 445.
11 Plan deposited in Cheshire Record Office. No 462.

Notes to Chapter 4, pages 90-109

1 For further background see *Bradshaw's Shareholders' Manual* 1859, pp 202-3.
2 Steel, W. L.; *History of the London and North Western Railway*, 1914.
3 Plan deposited Cheshire Record Office. No 496.
4 *Ashbourne News Telegraph*, 21 September 1961.
5 *Railway Station Architecture*, D. Lloyd, 1967.
6 *The North Staffordshire Railway*, 'Manifold', 1952, p 152.
7 *Railway Notes*, 1911, Article by J. W. Walker.

Notes to Chapter 5, pages 110-128

1 Paish, George; *The British Railway Position*, 1902, p 268.
2 Masefield, Charles; *Staffordshire*, 1910, p 236.
3 Letter from Dr E. G. Ashton, Rotherham.
4 Smith, Ian R.; Article in *The Mancunian*, December 1968.
5 Masefield, Charles; *Staffordshire*, 1910, p 183.
6 Walker, J. W.; Article in *Railway Notes*, October 1910.
7 Davies, A. Emil; *The Nationalisation of Railways*, 1908, p 14.

Notes to Chapter 6, pages 129-145

1 'Manifold'; *The North Staffordshire Railway*, 1952, p 84.
2 Notes on apprenticeship of Thomas G. Hall, born 1877, who was a premium pupil at Stoke Works 1894-9, supplied by his son, George W. Hall.

Notes to Chapter 8, pages 162-187

1 Appendix to Working Time Book, January 1915.
2 Neele, G. P.; *Railway Reminiscences*, 1904, p 319.
3 Disney, Henry, W.; *The Law of Carriage by Railway*, 1909, pp 33, 35, 59, 101.
4 Walker, J.; *Railway Notes*, 1911.

Notes to Chapter 9, pages 188-213

1 Dr J. R. Hollick once noted: 'The Knotty had a persistent and delightful habit of calling Derby Midland, "Derby NSR" '.
2 'Wagoner'. *Railway Magazine,* November 1921, pp 291-6.
3 This was the initial rail motor service. It was soon extended to Leycett, Barlaston, Colwich and the Biddulph and Sandbach branches. An innovation was a ground-level halt at Carter's Crossing used only by an early morning workmen's rail motor (see page 205).
4 Masefield, Charles, *Staffordshire,* 1910, p 182.
5 Note in company timetables.
6 Hollick, Dr J. R.; *The Workings of the Locomotives and Trains of private firms over the North Staffordshire Railway.* Private paper, pp 25 and map.

Notes to Chapter 10, pages 214-254

1 *Comparison between superheater and non-superheater tank engines,* by J. A. Hookham, Journal of the Institution of Locomotive Engineers. No 55, 1922.
2 From notebook kept by Hookham.
No proper locomotive records were kept at Stoke until 1891. Early information is taken from builders' records, an inventory of 1859 when the plant was taken over from Wright as contractor, an 1870 re-numbering list and a boiler list kept from 1885-90. Another source is the twice annual stock returns in directors' reports. Research into early NSR locomotive affairs was undertaken for many years by the late A. C. W. Lowe and continued by the late W. J. Bell from about 1918. Between them they compiled a basic list in 1930. Based on this, W. Beckerlegge wrote articles on early locomotives in the *Journal of the Stephenson Locomotive Society,* Vol XXIV, pp 139-149 (June 1948) and pp 253-6 (October 1948). Other articles include those in the *Railway Magazine* Vol IV, pp 336-40 (April 1899) and by E. Haigh in *The Railway Observer,* Vol XI, (1939) pp 178, 241, 253, 318, 367, 372, and Vol XII, p 102. Locomotive details given extensively in *The North Staffordshire Railway* by 'Manifold', 1952, amplify earlier notes and correct some errors and misconceptions.

Notes to Chapter 11, pages 255-267

1 The words of *Amalgamation Song* were written by Christopher Martin. Tune by Jeff Parton.
2 The London Midland & Scottish Railway Company: *A Record of large scale Organisation & Management* 1923-1946; Euston March 1946.
3 Letter from A. W. Brackenbury.
4 Hollick, Dr J. R.; Private paper.
5 Alterations to NSR passenger stations are listed in *Journal* of Railway & Canal Historical Society, Vol XVI No 1. January 1970.
6 Advertised for sale 3 July 1969.

Notes to Chapter 12, pages 268-289

1 *News Chronicle*. 7 February 1956.
2 Christiansen, Rex; *Getting Them Away*. Holiday passenger traffic survey. BBC Third Programme 24 August 1960.
3 *Report of the Public Inquiry into the Accident at Hixon Level Crossing on January 6th 1968*. Cmnd. 3706.

Appendixes

I: AUTHORISATION AND OPENING DATES

	Authorised			Opened					
				Passengers			Goods		
Froghall—Caldon Low (a)	13	5	1776		—				1777
Stoke—Norton Bridge (b)	26	6	1846	17	4	1848	3	4	1848
Stoke Jc—Uttoxeter		,,		7	8	1848	7	8	1848
Uttoxeter—Burton		,,		11	9	1848	11	9	1848
Stoke—Crewe		,,		9	10	1848	9	10	1848
Harecastle—Congleton		,,			,,			,,	
Stone—Colwich		,,		1	5	1849	1	5	1849
Congleton—Macclesfield		,,		18	6	1849	18	6	1849
North Rode—Leek—Uttoxeter		,,		13	7	1849	13	7	1849
Marston Jc—Willington	2	7	1847		,,			,,	
Etruria—Shelton		,,			1	1862			1850
Knutton—Pool Dam (c)	13	8	1859		—				1850
Knutton—Silverdale		,,			5	1863		,,	
Lawton Jc—Wheelock	26	6	1846	3	7	1893	21	1	1852
Wheelock—Ettiley Heath		,,			—			,,	
Ettiley Heath—Sandbach		,,			—			12	1866
Rocester—Ashbourne	22	7	1848	31	5	1852	31	5	1852
Stoke—Newcastle	26	6	1846	6	9	1852	6	9	1852
Newcastle—Knutton	2	7	1847		5	1863		,,	
Apedale Jc—Whiteburn		,,			—		11	7	1853
Whiteburn—Apedale	2	7	1847		—		7	11	1853
Pool Dam—Newcastle Canal Basin (d)		5	1853		—				1854
Talk o' th' Hill branch (e)	28	6	1861		—				1860
Stoke—Biddulph—Congleton Upper	24	7	1854	1	6	1864	28	8	1860
Congleton Lower—Brunswick		,,			—			,,	

	Authorised			Opened					
				Passengers			Goods		
Shelton—Hanley	13	8	1859	13	7	1864	20	12	1861
Chesterton branch	29	7	1864		—			1	1866
Milton—Cheddleton Jc	13	7	1863	1	11	1867	1	11	1867
Stretton Jc—Hawkins Lane Jc		,,			—		1	4	1868
Marple Wharf Jc—Macclesfield (f)	14	7	1864	2	8	1869	1	3	1870
Extension to Waters Green Jc (g)		,,		1	7	1873	3	4	1871
Silverdale—Market Drayton	29	7	1864	1	2	1870	1	2	1870
Alsager—Honeywall Jc		,,		28	6	1880	24	7	1870
Bignall Hill and Jamage branches		,,			—			,,	
Grange branch		,,			—		29	3	1872
Hanley—Burslem	5	7	1865	1	11	1873	1	11	1873
Burslem—Tunstall		,,		1	12	1873	1	12	1873
Tunstall—Goldenhill		,,		1	10	1874	1	10	1874
Newfields branch	25	7	1864		—			,,	
Longport—Tunstall		,,		27	7	1892	1	6	1875
Botteslow Jc—Normacot Jc (h)	16	7	1865		—			9	1875
Hulme Valley branch (h)		,,			—			,,	
Goldenhill—Kidsgrove	5	7	1865	15	11	1875	15	11	1875
Keele Jc—east curve to Audley line	26	8	1880	1	10	1881	1	10	1881
Uttoxeter N to W curve	26	8	1880		10	1881		10	1881
Middlewood curve (j)				1	6	1885(k)	26	5	1885
Cresswell—Totmanslow (l)	7	8	1888	7	11	1892	7	11	1892
Ashbourne, extention to new station (j)	4	8	1890	4	8	1899	4	8	1899
Totmanslow—Cheadle (l)	7	8	1888	1	1	1901	1	1	1901
Waterhouses—Hulme End (m)	6	3	1899(n)	27	6	1904	27	6	1904
Leek Brook South—Ipstones (o)		,,		15	6	1905	15	6	1905
Leek Brook N to E curve	9	8	1899		,,			,,	

Ipstones—Waterhouses (o)	6	3	1899(n)	1	7	1905	1	7	1905
Caldon Jc—Caldon Low (o)		,,			—			,,	
Trentham Park branch	21	8	1907	1	4	1910	1	4	1910
Lines opened since 1923:									
Tean—Cheadle deviation				26	11	1933	26	11	1933
Swynnerton Jc—Cold Meece				5	8	1941		—	
Madeley chord					—		18	6	1962
Chesterton branch deviation					—		18	10	1964
Chatterley—Harecastle deviation				27	6	1966	27	6	1966

notes:

(a) Trent & Mersey Canal Railway
(b) Temporary termini at Norton Bridge and at Stoke
(c) The Silverdale and Newcastle Railway—built without powers. Authorised to convert to a public railway 13 8 1959. Leased to NSR 31 8 1860
(d) Newcastle-under-Lyme Canal Extension Railway
(e) North Staffordshire Coal & Iron Co's Railway—built without powers. Authorised to convert to a public railway
(f) Temporary terminus at Macclesfield. Joint railway with MSLR
(g) Joint railway with MSLR
(h) Longton, Adderley Green & Bucknall Railway
(j) Joint railway with LNWR
(k) Used by excursion trains Whit Monday 25 5 1885
(l) Cheadle Railway
(m) Leek & Manifold Light Railway
(n) Date of Light Railway Order
(o) Leek, Caldon Low & Hartington Light Railway

2: MILEAGE OWNED AND WORKED 1922

Lines owned:	*Double*		*Single*	
	M	C	M	C
Macclesfield—Colwich	38	53		
Stoke Jc—Burton	28	76		
Churnet Valley line	27	54		
Silverdale—Market Drayton	12	37		
Stoke Jc—Congleton Upper Jc	8	9	4	54
Waterhouses branch			8	68
Harecastle—Crewe	8	30		
Audley line	7	37		
Loop line	7	25		
Milton Jc—Leek Brook			6	46
Ashbourne branch	1	36	5	30
Sandbach branch	2	36	4	4
Marston Jc—Willington	4	38		
Cheadle branch			3	71
Adderley Green branch			3	54
Norton Bridge branch	3	52		
Newcastle Jc—Knutton Jc	2	3		48
Apedale branch			1	46
Chesterton branch			1	48
Grange branch			1	24
Trentham Park branch			1	14
Horninglow branch	1	2		
Pinnox branch	1	8		
Brunswick Wharf branch			1	4
Caldon Jc—Caldon Low				61
Newfields branch				61
Jamage branch				54
Park Hall branch				40
Uttoxeter curve		28		
Bignall Hill branch		25		
Leek Brook curve		20		
Crewe Coal Wharf branch				9
Total 203 miles 43 chains	155	1	48	42

Lines leased and worked:	*Double*		*Single*	
Silverdale & Newcastle Railway		79	1	29
Talk o' th' Hill branch			1	55
Leek & Manifold Light Railways			8	11
Total 215 miles 57 chains	156	0	59	57

Owned jointly with GCR:		
Macclesfield, Bollington & Marple Rly	10	72
Owned jointly with LNWR:		
Ashbourne joint station		33
Middlewood curve		32
Colwich joint station		17
Macclesfield joint goods station		6
Total jointly owned	12	0

3: LINES CLOSED

		Passengers			*Goods*		
Honeywall west curve		1	10	1881	1	10	1881
Park Hall—Adderley Green			—			1	1895
Adderley Green—Hulme			—		about		1900
Froghall—Caldon low			—		25	3	1920
Milton Jc—Heath's Jc		11	7	1927		*	
Heath's Jc—Congleton Lower			,,		1	4	1968
Congleton Lower—Upper Jc			,,		1	12	1963
Lawton Jc—Wheelock		28	7	1930		*	
High Carr—Talke			—				1931
Alsager—Audley		27	4	1931	7	1	1963
Audley—Keele			,,		18	6	1962
Tean—New Haden		26	11	1933	26	11	1933
New Haden—Cheadle			,,		about		1940
Waterhouses—Hulme End		12	3	1934	12	3	1934
Leek Brook—Caldon Jc		30	9	1935		*	
Caldon Jc—Waterhouses			,,		1	3	1943
Jamage branch			—		21	12	1947
Bignall Hill branch			—		7	1	1963
Chesterton Jc—High Carr			—				1955
Rocester—Ashbourne		1	11	1954	1	6	1964
Stoke Jc—Leek Brook		7	5	1956		*	
Silverdale—Madeley Road			,,			*	
Madeley Road—Market Drayton			,,		9	1	1967
Trentham Park branch		1	10	1957	1	10	1957
Cold Meece branch		28	6	1958		—	
Newfields branch			—		3	8	1959
Marston Jc—Dove Jc		13	6	1960	6	5	1968
Dove Jc—Stretton Jc			,,			7	1968
Stretton Jc—Burton NS			,,		6	5	1968
Grange branch			—		29	10	1961
North Rode—Leek	(a)	7	11	1960	15	6	1964
Leek Brook—Oakamoor (sand siding)	(b)		,,			*	
Oakamoor—Uttoxeter	(b)		,,		4	1	1965
Cresswell—Cheadle		17	6	1963		*	
Millfield Jc—Park Hall			—		23	12	1963
Tunstall Jc—Longport Jc		17	2	1964	17	2	1964
Etruria—Shelton		2	3	1964		*	

	Passengers			*Goods*		
Shelton—Waterloo Road (oil depot)	2	3	1964	31	7	1969
Waterloo Road—Birchenwood		,,		3	1	1966
Birchenwood—Kidsgrove		,,			*	
Stoke—Brampton		,,		8	3	1966
Brampton—Silverdale		,,			*	
Botteslow—Adderley Green		—		6	7	1964
Chatterley Jc—Chesterton Jc		—		18	10	1964
Uttoxeter E & W curves	7	11	1960	31	1	1966
Chatterley—Harecastle	27	6	1966	27	6	1966
Knutton Gate Jc—Apedale		—		7	10	1967
Pool Dam branch		—			,,	
Chesterton branch		—		21	6	1968
Stretton Jc—Hawkins Lane Jc		—			7	1968
Macclesfield—Rose Hill	5	1	1970	5	1	1970
Rose Hill—Marple Wharf Jc		*			,,	

(a) Workmen's service continued until 15 6 1964
(b) Workmen's service continued until 4 1 1965
— never opened for this class of traffic
* remains open

4: OTHER STATIONS CLOSED

	Passengers			*Goods*		
Alsager		*		2	11	1964
Alton Towers		†		4	5	1964
Ashbourne	1	11	1956		†	
Aston by Stone	6	1	1947	13	8	1962
Barlaston		*		2	11	1964
Biddulph		†		7	12	1964
Black Bull		†		6	1	1964
Blythe Bridge		*		13	3	1950
Bosley		†		1	6	1964
Bradnop		†		4	5	1964
Brampton	2	4	1923		*	
Bromshall	31	12	1865		—	
Bucknall and Northwood		†		4	6	1962
Carter's Crossing		not known			—	
Chatterley	27	9	1948		—	
Cheddleton		†		4	5	1964
Chesterton		—		4	6	1962
Cliffe Vale	31	7	1865		—	
Clifton		†		4	6	1956
Colwick	3	2	1958	3	2	1958
Consall		†		4	5	1964
Cresswell	7	11	1966	4	1	1965
Crown Street Δ	7	6	1949		—	
Egginton	5	3	1962	7	8	1961
Endon		†		4	5	1964
Ettiley Heath		—		4	1	1965
Fenton	6	2	1961		—	
Fenton Manor	6	5	1956		—	
Ford Green		†		6	1	1964
Great Haywood	6	1	1947	6	1	1947
Hanford Road Δ		4	1913		—	
Hanley		†		1	8	1966
Hartshill and Basford Δ	20	9	1926		—	
Hassall Green		†		1	11	1947
Hixon	6	1	1947	6	1	1947
Horninglow	1	1	1949		—	
Ipstones		†		4	5	1964
Keele		†		9	1	1967

	Passengers			Goods		
Keele Park	5	3	1907		—	
Kidsgrove Market Street Δ	25	9	1950		—	
Kingsley and Froghall		†		4	5	1964
Knutton Δ	20	9	1926		—	
Lawton		†		4	5	1964
Leek Brook Δ		†		7	5	1956
Leigh	7	11	1966	7	12	1964
Madeley Road	20	7	1931		—	
Macclesfield Hibel Road	7	11	1960	3	9	1962
Marchington	15	9	1958	6	1	1958
Meir	7	11	1966	4	1	1965
Middlewood	7	11	1960		—	
Milton		†			—	
Mossley Δ	13	4	1925		—	
Mount Pleasant Δ	30	9	1918		—	
Mow Cop and Scholar Green	7	9	1964	1	6	1939
Newcastle Liverpool Road Δ	29	2	1964		—	
Normacot	2	3	1964	4	10	1961
North Rode	7	5	1962	7	5	1962
Norton Bridge		*		22	6	1959
Oakamoor		†		4	5	1964
Pipe Gate		†		1	2	1965
Radway Green and Barthomley	7	11	1966	7	6	1964
Rolleston on Dove	1	1	1949	1	1	1949
Sandon	6	1	1947	5	9	1955
Scropton	1	1	1872			
Sideway Δ	2	4	1923		—	
Silverdale		†		9	1	1967
Stockton Brook		†		4	1	1965
Stone		*		10	8	1967
Stretton and Clay Mills	1	1	1949			
Sudbury	7	11	1966	3	5	1965
Tean	1	6	1953	1	6	1953
Trentham	2	3	1964	2	12	1963
Tutbury	7	11	1966		*	
Uttoxeter Bridge Street		10	1881		*	
Uttoxeter Dove Bank		10	1881		—	
Uttoxeter Junction		10	1881		—	
Wall Grange		†		7	5	1956
Waterloo Road Δ	4	10	1943		†	
Weston and Ingestre	6	1	1947	2	9	1963

	Passengers			*Goods*		
Whieldon Road Δ	30	9	1918		—	
Winkhill		†		4	5	1964

Δ Described in NSR timetables as halts
† Closed as per appendix 3
* remains open
— never opened for this class of traffic
Other stations were closed on the dates given in appendix 3

5: LOCOMOTIVE LIST

NSR Nos. *First*	*1870*	*Type*	*Maker's No.*		*Built*	*Re-placed*	*Remarks*
1	1	2–2–2	SB	484	1848	1891	*Dragon* Reb 2–2–2ST 1866
27	2	2–2–2	SB	551	1848	1890	Reb 2–2–2ST 1866
65	3	2–2–2	?		?	1883	Reb 2–2–2WT 1859 Aq. 1849
7	4	2–4–0	Hick		1848	1881	Reb 2–2–2ST 1851
8	5	2–4–0	Hick		1848	1881	Reb 2–2–2ST 1851
30	6	2–4–0	KTH	176	1848	1878	Reb 2–4–0ST c1865
31	7	2–4–0	KTH	177	1848	1874	Reb 2–4–0ST c1865
32	8	2–4–0	KTH	178	1848	1878	Reb 2–4–0ST c1865
45	9	2–4–0	KTH	179	1849	1874	Reb 2–4–0ST c1865
46	10	2–4–0	KTH	180	1849	1874	Reb 2–4–0ST c1865
47	11	2–4–0	KTH	181	1849	1874	Reb 2–4–0ST c1865
48	16	2–4–0	KTH	226	1850	1884	Reb 2–2–2 1851
49	17	2–4–0	KTH	227	1850	1882	Reb 2–2–2 1851
50	18	2–4–0	KTH	228	1850	1882	Reb 2–2–2 1851
51	19	2–4–0	KTH	229	1850	1872	Reb 2–2–2 1851
52	20	2–4–0	KTH	230	1850	1883	Reb 2–2–2 1851
53	21	2–4–0	KTH	231	1850	1882	Reb 2–2–2 1851
54	22	2–2–2	KTH	238	1851	1882	
55	23	2–2–2	KTH	239	1851	1886	
56	24	2–2–2	KTH	240	1851	1886	
57	25	2–2–2	KTH	241	1851	1882	
2	26	2–2–2	SB	486	1848	1882	Reb 2–4–0 c1867
23	27	2–2–2	SB	549	1848	1883	Reb 2–4–0 c1867
24	28	2–2–2	SB	550	1848	1882	Reb 2–4–0 c1867
29	29	2–2–2	SB	554	1848	1883	Reb 2–4–0 c1867
6	30	2–4–0	Hick		1848	1881	Reb from long-boiler type c1866
9	31	2–4–0	RS	671	1848	1879	Reb from long-boiler type c1866
10	32	2–4–0	RS	672	1848	1884	Reb from long-boiler type c1866
19	33	2–4–0	RS	675	1848	1883	Reb from long-boiler type c1866
22	34	2–4–0	JP		1848	1884	Reb from long-boiler type c1866
28	35	2–4–0	RS	677	1848	1881	Reb from long-boiler type c1866
40	36	2–4–0	JP		1848	1883	Reb from long-boiler type c1866
42	37	2–4–0	JP		1848	1883	Reb from long-boiler type c1866
3	38	2–4–0	JP		1848	1874	
4	39	2–4–0	JP		1848	1874	
38	40	2–4–0	JP		1848	1881	Reb from long-boiler type c1872
12	—	2–4–0	JP		1848	1866	
14	—	2–4–0	JP		1848	1865	
25	—	2–4–0	JP		1848	1866	
39	—	2–4–0	JP		1848	1865	
11	41	2–4–0	RS	673	1848	1874	
13	—	2–4–0	RS	674	1848	1868	
20	42	2–4–0	RS	676	1848	1874	
5	—	2–4–0	Hick		1848	1868	
39	43	2–4–0	HCR	57	1865	1883	
14	44	2–4–0	HCR	58	1865	1883	
25	45	2–4–0	HCR	60	1866	1884	
12	46	2–4–0	HCR	61	1866	1884	
82	51	0–6–0ST	HCR	77	1866	1880	
5	52	0–6–0ST	Stoke		1868	1879	
13	53	0–6–0ST	Stoke		1868	1880	

NSR Nos. First	*1870*	*Type*	*Maker's No.*		*Built*	*Re-placed*	*Remarks*
24	54	0–6–0ST	Stoke		1868	1882	
	55	0–6–0ST	Dodds		1865	1882	Aq. 1866
67	56	0–6–0ST	RS	1414	1862	1888	Sold
68	57	0–6–0ST	RS	1415	1862	1888	Sold
34	58	0–6–0ST	HCR	67	1866	1881	
36	59	0–6–0ST	HCR	68	1866	1880	
60	60	0–6–0	VF	383	1855	1884	Reb 0–6–0ST 1870
61	61	0–6–0	VF	384	1855	1887	Reb 0–6–0ST 1870
62	62	0–6–0	VF	385	1855	1885	Reb 0–6–0ST 1870
63	63	0–6–0	VF	386	1855	1884	Reb 0–6–0ST 1870
15	64	0–6–0	VF	279	1848	1873	
16	65	0–6–0	VF	280	1848	1873	
17	66	0–6–0	VF	281	1848	1877	
18	67	0–6–0	VF	282	1848	1875	
21	68	0–6–0	VF	283	1848	1875	
28	69	0–6–0	VF	284	1848	1873	
37	70	0–6–0	VF	285	1848	1873	
41	71	0–6–0	VF	286	1849	1874	
43	72	0–6–0	VF	287	1849	1876	
44	73	0–6–0	VF	288	1850	1888	Reb from long-boiler type 1875
33	—	0–6–0	RS	406	1844	1866	Aq. 1848
34	—	0–6–0	RS	422	1844	1866	Sold Aq. 1848
35	—	0–6–0	RS	423	1844	1866	Aq. 1848
36	—	0–6–0	RS	424	1844	1866	Sold Aq. 1848
58	—	0–6–0	RS	678	1849	1851	Sold to Midland Rly.
59	—	0–6–0	RS	679	1849	1851	Sold to Midland Rly.
60	—	0–6–0	RS	680	1849	1851	Sold to Midland Rly.
61	—	0–6–0	RS	681	1850	1851	Sold to Midland Rly.
62	—	0–6–0	RS	682	1850	1851	Sold to Midland Rly.
63	—	0–6–0	RS	683	1851	1851	Sold to Rhenish Rly.
33	76	0–6–0	HCR	69	1866	1902	Later class 'E'
35	77	0–6–0	HCR	70	1866	1902	Later class 'E'
69	78	0–6–0	HCR	35	1864	1899	Later class 'F'
70	79	0–6–0	HCR	36	1864	1898	Later class 'F'
71	80	0–6–0	HCR	39	1865	1900	Later class 'F'
72	81	0–6–0	HCR	40	1865	1899	Later class 'F'
73	82	0–6–0	HCR	43	1865	1907	Later class 'F'
74	83	0–6–0	HCR	44	1865	1907	Later class 'F'
75	84	0–6–0	N	1145	1865	1909	Later class 'F'
76	85	0–6–0	N	1146	1865	1909	Later class 'F'
77	86	0–6–0	N	1147	1865	1910	Later class 'F'
78	87	0–6–0	N	1148	1865	1910	Later class 'F'
79	88	0–6–0	N	1149	1865	1909	Later class 'F'
80	89	0–6–0	N	1150	1865	1913	Later class 'F'
90	90	0–6–0	WE	7	1866	1910	Later class 'F'
91	91	0–6–0	WE	8	1867	1911	Later class 'F'
92	92	0–6–0	WE	9	1867	1911	Later class 'F'
93	93	0–6–0	WE	10	1867	1909	Latcr class 'F'
94	94	0–6–0	WE	11	1867	1909	Later class 'F'
95	95	0–6–0	WE	12	1867	1909	Later class 'F'
96	96	0–6–0	WE	13	1867	1913	Later class 'F'
97	97	0–6–0	WE	14	1867	1913	Later class 'F'
98	98	0–6–0	WE	15	1867	1908	Later class 'F'
99	99	0–6–0	WE	16	1867	1908	Later class 'F'
64	100	0–6–0	RS	1330	1860	1896	Later class 'F'
66	101	0–6–0	RS	1331	1860	1897	Later class 'F'
58	102	0–6–0	KTH	316	1853	1897	Later class 'F'
59	103	0–6–0	KTH	317	1853	1898	Later class 'F'

NSR No.	*Type*	*Class*	*Maker's No*		*Built*	*LMS No. 1923*	*1928*	*With-drawn*	*Remarks*
74	0–6–0	E	Stoke		1871	2320	8650	1934	74A in 1919
75	0–6–0	E	Stoke		1871	2321	—	1926	75A in 1919
104	0–6–0	E	VF	642	1872	2322	8651	1932	
105	0–6–0	E	VF	643	1872	2323	—	1926	
106	0–6–0	E	VF	644	1872	2324	8652	1932	
107	0–6–0	E	VF	645	1872	2325	—	1927	
108	0–6–0	E	VF	646	1872	2326	8653	1930	
109	0–6–0	E	VF	647	1872	2327	8654	1931	
110	0–6–0	E	VF	648	1872	2328	8655	1929	
111	0–6–0	E	VF	649	1872	2329	8656	1930	
112	0–6–0	E	VF	650	1872	2330	8657	1928	
113	0–6–0	E	VF	651	1872	2331	8658	1928	
19	2–4–0	19	Stoke		1872	—	—	1920	Renewed 1905
69	0–6–0	69	SS	2342	1873	—	—	1922	69A in 1913
70	0–6–0	69	SS	2346	1873	2332	—	1927	70A in 1914
64	0–6–0	69	SS	2378	1874	—	—	1919	64A in 1913
65	0–6–0	69	SS	2379	1874	—	—	1919	65A in 1913
114	0–6–0	69	SS	2424	1874	—	—	1920	114A in 1916
115	0–6–0	69	SS	2425	1874	—	—	1920	115A in 1916
116	0–6–0	69	SS	2426	1874	2333	—	1926	116A in 1916
117	0–6–0	69	SS	2427	1874	—	—	1916	
118	0–6–0	E	BP	1348	1874	2334	—	1927	118A in 1918
119	0–6–0	E	BP	1349	1874	2335	—	1926	119A in 1918
120	0–6–0	E	BP	1350	1874	2336	8659	1930	120A in 1918
121	0–6–0	E	BP	1351	1874	2337	—	1927	121A in 1919
122	0–6–0	E	BP	1352	1874	2338	8660	1933	
123	0–6–0	E	BP	1353	1874	2339	8661	1928	
7	2–4–0	7	Stoke		1874	—	—	1897	7A in 1895
10	2–4–0	7	Stoke		1874	—	—	1894r	
71	2–4–0	7	Stoke		1874	—	—	1894r	
38	2–4–0	C	Stoke		1874	—	—	1912	
39	2–4–0	C	Stoke		1874	—	—	1912	
9	2–4–0T	9	Stoke		1874	—	—	1907r	
11	2–4–0T	9	Stoke		1874	—	—	1907r	
12	2–4–0T	9	SS	2445	1874	—	—	1908r	Reb 2–4–2T 1899
41	2–4–0T	9	SS	2446	1874	—	—	1908r	Reb 2–4–2T 1899
42	2–4–0T	9	SS	2447	1874	—	—	1908r	Reb 2–4–2T 1899
47	0–6–0ST	56	RS	2251	1875	—	—	1890	Sold
48	0–6–0ST	56	RS	2252	1875	—	—	1887r	
49	0–6–0ST	56	RS	2253	1875	—	—	1885r	
50	0–6–0ST	56	RS	2254	1875	—	—	1889r	
13	2–4–0	C	Dübs	858	1875	—	—	1912	13A in 1912
14	2–4–0	C	Dübs	859	1875	—	—	1919	14A in 1912
15	2–4–0	C	Dübs	860	1875	—	—	1906	
67	0–6–0	E	Stoke		1875	2340	8662	1928	
68	0–6–0	E	Stoke		1875	2341	8663	1928	
72	0–6–0	E	Stoke		1876	—	—	1919	
66	0–6–0	E	Stoke		1877	2342	8664	1930	
6	2–4–0T	A	Stoke		1878	—	—	1910	
8	2–4–0T	A	Stoke		1878	—	—	1914	8A in 1911
31	2–4–0T	A	Stoke		1879	—	—	1921	31A in 1914
52	2–4–0T	A	Stoke		1879	1454	—	1932	Reb 2–4–2T 1898
51	2–4–0T	A	Stoke		1880	—	—	1914	51A in 1913
53	2–4–0T	A	Stoke		1880	—	—	1921	53A in 1914
59	0–6–0ST	ST	Stoke		1880	1601	—	1930	59A in 1902
58	0–6–0ST	ST	Stoke		1881	1600	—	1927	58A in 1899
35	2–4–0T	A	Stoke		1881	1455	—	1932	Reb 2–4–2T 1898
40	2–4–0T	A	Stoke		1881	1456	—	1932	Reb 2–4–2T 1898

NSR No.	*Type*	*Class*	*Maker's No*	*Built*	*LMS Nos 1923*	*1928*	*With-drawn*	*Remarks*
4	2–4–0T	B	Stoke	1881	—	—	1921	4A in 1915
5	2–4–0T	B	Stoke	1881	—	—	1922	5A in 1915
30	2–4–0T	B	Stoke	1881	—	—	1920	30A in 1914
17	2–4–0T	B	Stoke	1882	1440	—	1928	17A in 1920
18	2–4–0T	B	Stoke	1882	1441	—	1933	18A in 1921
21	2–4–0T	B	Stoke	1882	1457	—	1932	Reb 2–4–2T 1901
22	2–4–0T	B	Stoke	1882	1442	—	1932	22A in 1921
25	2–4–0T	B	Stoke	1882	—	—	1921	25A in 1921
26	2–4–0T	B	Stoke	1882	—	—	1921	
28	2–4–0T	B	Stoke	1882	—	—	1922	
54	2–4–0	C	Stoke	1882	—	—	1906	*John Bramley Moore*
55	2–4–0	C	Stoke	1882	—	—	1911	*Colin Minton Campbell*
3	0–6–0T	D	Stoke	1883	1550	—	1930	
20	0–6–0T	D	Stoke	1883	1551	—	1931	
27	2–4–0T	B	Stoke	1883	1443	—	1925	27A in 1922
29	2–4–0T	B	Stoke	1883	1444	—	1932	29A in 1921
33	0–6–0T	D	Stoke	1883	1552	—	1929	
36	0–6–0T	D	Stoke	1883	1553	—	1935	
37	0–6–0T	D	Stoke	1883	1554	—	1931	
43	0–6–0T	D	Stoke	1883	1555	—	1931	
44	0–6–0T	D	Stoke	1883	1556	—	1931	
16	0–6–0T	D	Stoke	1884	1557	—	1936	
32	0–6–0T	D	Stoke	1884	1558	—	1929	
34	0–6–0T	D	Stoke	1884	1559	—	1930	
45	2–4–0	C	Stoke	1884	—	—	1911	
46	2–4–0	C	Stoke	1884	—	—	1911	
60	0–6–0T	D	Stoke	1884	1560	—	1928	
63	0–6–0T	D	Stoke	1884	1561	—	1929	
49	0–6–0T	D	Stoke	1885	1562	—	1931	
62	0–6–0T	D	Stoke	1885	1563	—	1929	
124	0–6–0T	D	Stoke	1885	1564	—	1932	124A in 1904
125	0–6–0T	D	Stoke	1885	1565	—	1928	125A in 1904
126	0–6–0T	D	Stoke	1886	1566	—	1931	
127	0–6–0T	D	Stoke	1886	1567	—	1937	
23	2–4–0T	B	Stoke	1886	1445	—	1928	23A in 1922
24	2–4–0T	B	Stoke	1886	1458	—	1934	Reb 2–4–2T 1901
48	2–4–0T	B	Stoke	1887	1446	—	1929	48A in 1923
61	2–4–0T	B	Stoke	1887	1459	—	1934	Reb 2–4–2T 1900
128	0–6–0T	D	Stoke	1887	1568	—	1928	
129	0–6–0T	D	Stoke	1887	1569	—	1931	
57	0–6–0T	D	Stoke	1888	1570	—	1937	
73	0–6–0T	D	Stoke	1888	1571	—	1929	
50	0–6–0T	D	Stoke	1889	1572	—	1931	
56	0–6–0T	D	Stoke	1889	1573	—	1929	
47	0–6–0T	D	Stoke	1890	1574	—	1929	
2	2–4–0T	B	Stoke	1890	1447	—	1930	2A in 1923
1	2–4–0T	B	Stoke	1891	1448	—	1930	1A in 1923
130	0–6–0T	D	Stoke	1891	1575	—	1929	
131	0–6–0T	D	Stoke	1891	1576	—	1936	
132	0–6–0T	D	Stoke	1891	1577	—	1929	
133	0–6–0T	D	Stoke	1892	1578	—	1930	
134	0–6–0T	D	Stoke	1892	1579	—	1934	
135	0–6–0T	D	Stoke	1892	1580	—	1931	
136	0–6–0T	D	Stoke	1892	1581	—	1928	
137	0–6–0T	D	Stoke	1893	1582	—	1929	
138	0–6–0T	D	Stoke	1893	1583	—	1936	
139	0–6–0T	D	Stoke	1893	1584	—	1934	
140	0–6–0T	D	Stoke	1893	1585	—	1930	

NSR No.	*Type*	*Class*	*Maker's No*		*Built*	*LMS Nos 1923*	*1928*	*With-drawn*	*Remarks*
141	0–6–0T	D	Stoke		1894	1586	—	1931	
142	0–6–0T	D	Stoke		1894	1587	—	1929	
10	2–4–0T	B	Stoke		1894	1449	—	1928	10A in 1923
71	2–4–0T	B	Stoke		1894	1450	—	1933	
7	2–4–0T	B	Stoke		1895	1451	—	1928	
143	0–6–0T	D	Stoke		1895	1588	—	1927	
144	0–6–0T	D	Stoke		1895	1589	—	1935	
145	0–6–0T	D	Stoke		1895	1590	—	1930	
146	0–6–0T	D	Stoke		1895	1591	—	1932	
147	0–6–0T	D	Stoke		1896	1592	—	1931	
148	0–6–0T	D	Stoke		1896	1593	—	1931	
100	0–6–0	100	Stoke		1896	2347	8669	1931	
101	0–6–0	100	Stoke		1897	2348	8670	1928	
102	0–6–0	100	Stoke		1897	2349	8671	1929	
149	0–6–0T	D	Stoke		1897	1594	—	1930	
150	0–6–0T	D	Stoke		1897	1595	—	1932	
151	0–6–0T	D	Stoke		1898	1596	—	1932	
152	0–6–0T	D	Stoke		1898	1597	—	1936	
103	0–6–0	100	Stoke		1698	2350	8672	1928	
79	0–6–0	100	Stoke		1898	2343	8665	1929	
78	0–6–0	100	Stoke		1899	2344	8666	1929	
81	0–6–0	100	Stoke		1899	2345	8667	1931	
153	0–6–0T	D	Stoke		1899	1598	—	1929	
58	0–6–2T	DX	Stoke		1899	2234	—	1929	
154	0–6–2T	DX	Stoke		1900	2235	—	1929	
155	0–6–2T	DX	Stoke		1900	2236	—	1929	
80	0–6–0	100	Stoke		1900	2346	8668	1931	
114A	0–6–0	114A	Crewe		1861	—	—	by1916	Aq. 1900 ex-LNW 65
115A	0–6–0	114A	Crewe	1261	1869	—	—	by1916	Aq. 1900 ex-LNW1740
116A	0–6–0	114A	Crewe	431	1860	—	—	by1916	Aq. 1900 ex-LNW 423
117A	0–6–0	114A	Crewe	569	1862	—	—	by1916	Aq. 1900 ex-LNW 744
159	0–6–0	159	NW	588	1900	2351	8673	1936	
160	0–6–0	159	NW	589	1900	2352	8674	1933	
161	0–6–0	159	NW	590	1900	2353	8675	1936	
162	0–6–0	159	NW	591	1900	2354	8676	1929	
163	0–6–0	159	NW	592	1900	2355	8677	1936	
164	0–6–0	159	NW	593	1900	2356	8678	1934	
156	0–6–2T	DX	Stoke		1902	2238	—	1931	76 in 1902
157	0–6–2T	DX	Stoke		1902	2237	—	1929	59 in 1902
158	0–6–2T	DX	Stoke		1902	2239	—	1927	77 in 1902
165	0–6–2T	L	VF	1891	1903	2242	—	1935	
166	0–6–2T	L	VF	1892	1903	2243	—	1933	
167	0–6–2T	L	VF	1893	1903	2244	—	1935	
168	0–6–2T	L	VF	1894	1903	2245	—	1934	
169	0–6–2T	L	VF	1895	1903	2241	—	1936	125 in 1905
170	0–6–2T	L	VF	1896	1903	2240	—	1935	124 in 1904
1	0–2–2T		BP	4643	1905	—	—	1927	Sold Rail-motor
2	0–2–2T		BP	4644	1905	—	—	1927	Sold Rail-motor
3	0–2–2T		BP	4793	1905	—	—	1927	Sold Rail-motor
15	2–4–0	19	Stoke		1906	—	—	1920	
54	2–4–0	19	Stoke		1906	—	—	1920	
82	0–6–0	New 100	Stoke		1907	2357	8679	1929	
83	0–6–0	New 100	Stoke		1907	2358	8680	1928	
9	0–4–4T	M	Stoke		1907	1431	—	1936	
11	0–4–4T	M	Stoke		1907	1432	—	1935	
12	0–4–4T	M	Stoke		1908	1433	—	1935	
41	0–4–4T	M	Stoke		1908	1434	—	1939	
42	0–4–4T	M	Stoke		1908	1435	—	1930	

NSR						*LMS Nos*		*With-*	
No.	*Type*	*Class*	*Maker's*	*No*	*Built*	*1923*	*1928*	*drawn*	*Remarks*
98	0–6–2T	New L	Stoke		1908	2246	—	1936	
99	0–6–2T	New L	Stoke		1908	2247	—	1928	
156	0–6–2T	New L	Stoke		1908	2248	—	1937	
157	0–6–2T	New L	Stoke		1908	2249	—	1936	
93	0–6–2T	New L	Stoke		1909	2250	—	1934	
94	0–6–2T	New L	Stoke		1909	2251	—	1936	
95	0–6–2T	New L	Stoke		1909	2252	—	1934	
158	0–6–2T	New L	Stoke		1909	2253	—	1936	Sold
84	0–6–0	H	Stoke		1909	2359	8681	1930	
85	0–6–0	H	Stoke		1909	2360	8682	1929	
88	0–6–0	H	Stoke		1909	2361	8683	1928	
169	0–6–0	H	Stoke		1909	2362	8684	1928	
6	0–6–0	H	Stoke		1910	2363	8685	1929	Belp.
90	0–6–0	H	Stoke		1910	2364	8686	1929	Belp.
86	4–4–0	G	Stoke		1910	595	5410	1929	Belp.
87	4–4–0	G	Stoke		1910	596	5411	1929	Belp.
170	4–4–0	G	Stoke		1910	597	5412	1928	Belp.
171	4–4–0	G	Stoke		1910	598	5413	1933	Belp.
91	0–6–0	H	Stoke		1911	2365	8687	1930	Belp.
92	0–6–0	H	Stoke		1911	2366	8688	1930	Belp.
8	4–4–2T	K	Stoke		1911	2180	—	1933	Sup. Belp.
45	4–4–2T	K	Stoke		1911	2181	—	1934	Sup. Belp.
46	4–4–2T	K	Stoke		1911	2182	—	1934	Sup. Belp.
55	4–4–2T	K	Stoke		1911	2183	—	1933	Sup. Belp.
13	4–4–2T	K	Stoke		1912	2184	—	1935	Sup. Belp.
14	4–4–2T	K	Stoke		1912	2185	—	1933	Sup. Belp.
38	4–4–0	KT	Stoke		1912	599	5414	1928	Sup. Belp.
39	4–4–2T	K	Stoke		1912	2186	—	1933	Sup. Belp.
51	0–6–2T	New L	Stoke		1913	2254	—	1934	Belp.
64	0–6–2T	New L	Stoke		1913	2255	—	1936	Belp.
65	0–6–2T	New L	Stoke		1913	2256	—	1935	Belp.
69	0–6–2T	New L	Stoke		1913	2257	—	1937	Sold Belp.
89	0–6–2T	New L	Stoke		1913	2258	—	1934	Belp.
96	0–6–2T	New L	Stoke		1913	2259	—	1936	Belp.
97	0–6–2T	New L	Stoke		1913	2260	—	1934	Belp.
172	0–6–2T	New L	Stoke		1913	2261	—	1937	Belp.
30	0–6–4T	New C	Stoke		1914	2040	—	1934	Sup. Belp.
31	0–6–4T	New C	Stoke		1914	2041	—	1935	Sup. Belp.
53	0–6–4T	New C	Stoke		1914	2042	—	1935	Sup. Belp.
70	0–6–4T	New C	Stoke		1914	2043	—	1935	Sup. Belp.
173	0–6–4T	New C	Stoke		1914	2044	—	1936	Sup. Belp.
174	0–6–4T	New C	Stoke		1914	2045	—	1934	Sup. Belp.
4	0–6–4T	New C	Stoke		1915	2046	—	1937	Sup. Belp.
5	0–6–4T	New C	Stoke		1915	2047	—	1934	Sup. Belp.
114	0–6–4T	F	Stoke		1916	2048	—	1934	Sup. Belp.
115	0–6–4T	F	Stoke		1916	2049	—	1934	Sup. Belp.
116	0–6–4T	F	Stoke		1916	2050	—	1935	Sup. Belp.
117	0–6–4T	F	Stoke		1916	2051	—	1935	Sup. Belp.
1	0–4–0BE		Stoke		1917	Bel2	—	1963	Battery loco
118	0–6–4T	F	Stoke		1918	2052	—	1936	Sup. Belp.
119	0–6–4T	F	Stoke		1918	2053	—	1935	Sup. Belp.
120	0–6–4T	F	Stoke		1918	2054	—	1936	Sup. Belp.
121	0–6–4T	F	Stoke		1919	2055	—	1934	Sup. Belp.
74	0–6–0T	KS	KS	4079	1919	1602	—	1932	
75	0–6–0T	KS	KS	4080	1919	1603	—	1933	Sold
15	0–4–4T	New M	Stoke		1920	1436	—	1939	
17	0–4–4T	New M	Stoke		1920	1437	—	1935	
19	0–4–4T	New M	Stoke		1920	1438	—	1936	

NSR No.	Type	Class	Maker's No		Built	LMS Nos 1923	1928	With-drawn	Remarks
54	0–4–4T	New M	Stoke		1920	1439	—	1931	
72	0–6–2T	New L	Stoke		1920	2262	—	1937	Sold Belp.
18	0–6–2T	New L	Stoke		1921	2263	—	1936	Belp. Sup. 1922
22	0–6–2T	New L	Stoke		1921	2264	—	1936	Sold Belp. Sup. 1922
25	0–6–2T	New L	Stoke		1921	2265	—	1936	Sup. Belp.
26	0–6–2T	New L	Stoke		1921	2266	—	1936	Belp.
29	0–6–2T	New L	Stoke		1921	2267	—	1935	Belp. Sup. by LMS
23	0–6–0T	4 cylr D	Stoke		1922	2367	8689	1928	Reb 0–6–0 1924 Sup.
27	0–6–2T	New L	Stoke		1922	2268	—	1936	Belp. Sup by LMS
28	0–6–2T	New L	Stoke		1922	2269	—	1934	Belp.
1	0–6–2T	New L	Stoke		1923	2270	—	1937	Sold Sup. Belp.
2	0–6–2T	New L	Stoke		1923	2271	—	1937	Sold Sup. Belp.
10	0–6–2T	New L	Stoke		1923	2272	—	1935	Sup. Belp.
48	0–6–2T	New L	Stoke		1923	2273	—	1937	Sup. Belp.
3ft. 6in. gauge locomotives:									
—	0–4–0ST		HH		1877	—	—	1936	*Frog*
—	0–4–0ST		HH		1877	—	—	1936	*Toad*
—	0–4–0ST		1634		1901	—	—	1936	*Bobs*
2ft. 6 in. gauge locomotives:									
1	2–6–4T		K	4258	1904	1	—	1936	*E. R. Calthrop*
2	2–6–4T		K	4259	1904	2	—	1935	*J. B. Earle*

Abbreviations:

BP	Beyer Peacock & Co.	SB	Sharp Bros.
HCR	Hudswell, Clarke & Rogers	SS	Sharp, Stewart & Co.
HH	Henry Hughes	VF	Vulcan Foundry
JP	Jones & Potts	WE	Worcester Engine Co.
K	Kitson & Co.	WGB	W. G. Bagnal & Co.
KS	Kerr, Stuart & Co.	Aq.	Acquired
KTH	Kitson, Thompson & Hewitson	Belp.	Belpaire Firebox
N	Neilson & Co.	c	*circa* (about)
NW	Nasmyth, Wilson & Co.	Reb.	Rebuilt
RS	Robert Stephenson & Co.	Sup.	Superheated

Nos. 10, 18, 22 and 25 had their superheaters replaced by the LMS.

Two NSR locomotives are preserved in their old colours at the Museum of Staffordshire Life, Shugborough Hall, near Colwich:

No 1 0–4–0 Battery electric built 1917
No 2 0–6–2T Class 'New L' built 1923

6: DIMENSIONS OF LOCOMOTIVES

For the older classes these are given as rebuilt

Class	Type	Driving Wheels ft.	Driving Wheels in.	Cylinders in.	Boiler Diam ft.	Boiler Diam in.	Boiler Length ft.	Boiler Length in.	Firebox Length ft.	Firebox Length in.	Grate Area sq. ft.	Steam Pressure lb. sq. in.
KS	0–6–0T	3	9	15 ×20	3	8	8	11	5	9½	18	160
9	2–4–0T	5	6	16½×24	4	0	10	4¼	4	11⅞	15½	140
9 conv.	2–4–2T	5	6	16½×24	4	0	10	4¼	4	11⅞	15½	140
F	0–6–0	5	0	17 ×24	4	0	10	4¼	4	11⅞	15½	140
E	0–6–0	5	0	17 ×24	4	2	10	1½	4	11⅞	15½	150
69	0–6–0	4	6	17 ×24	4	2	10	4¼	4	11⅞	15½	150
A	2–4–0T	4	6	17 ×24	4	2	10	4¼	4	11⅞	15½	150
A mod.	2–4–0T	5	1	17 ×24	4	2	10	4¼	4	11⅞	15½	150
A conv.	2–4–2T	5	1	17 ×24	4	2	10	4¼	4	11⅞	15½	150
B	2–4–0T	5	6	17 ×24	4	2	10	4¼	4	11⅞	15½	150
B conv.	2–4–2T	5	6	17 ×24	4	2	10	4¼	4	11⅞	15½	150
D	0–6–0T	4	6	17 ×24	4	2	10	4¼	4	11⅞	15½	150
ST	0–6–0ST	4	0	17 ×24	4	2	10	4¼	4	11⅞	15½	150
100	0–6–0	4	6	17 ×24	4	2	10	4¼	4	11⅞	15½	150
New 100	0–6–0	4	6	17 ×24	4	2	10	4¼	4	11⅞	15½	160
C	2–4–0	6	0	17 ×24	4	2½	10	4¼	4	11⅞	15½	150
DX	0–6–2T	4	6	18 ×24	4	2	10	4¼	5	7⅞	17	150
15	2–4–0	6	6	18 ×24	4	4	10	8	4	11⅞	15½	160
159	0–6–0	5	0	18½×26	4	4	10	6	6	5	20½	150
L	0–6–2T	5	0	18½×26	4	7	10	9	6	0	18	175
M, New M	0–4–4T	5	6	18½×26	4	7	10	9	6	0	18	175
H	0–6–0	5	0	18½×26	4	7	10	9	6	0	18	175
4 Cylr. D	0–6–0T	4	6	(4)14 ×24	4	7	10	9	6	0	17½	175

Class	*Type*	*Driving Wheels*		*Cylinders*	*Boiler*				*Firebox Length*		*Grate Area*	*Steam Pressure*
					Diam		*Length*					
		ft.	*in.*	*in.*	*ft.*	*in.*	*ft.*	*in.*	*ft.*	*in.*	*sq. ft.*	*lb. sq. in.*
New L	0–6–2T	5	0	18½×26	4	9	10	9	6	6	19½	175
H belpaire	0–6–0	5	0	18½×26	4	9	10	9	6	6	19½	175
G	4–4–0	6	0	18½×26	4	9	10	10	7	0	21	175
New C	0–6–4T	5	0	20 ×26	4	9	10	10	7	0	21	170
New F	0–6–4T	5	6	20 ×26	4	9	10	10	7	0	21	170
K	4–4–2T	6	0	20 ×26	4	9	10	10	7	0	21	170
KT	4–4–0	6	0	20× 26	4	9	10	10	7	0	21	170
L & M	2–6–4T	2	6	11½×16	2	11¼	9	6	3	8	9	150

7: LOCOMOTIVE POWER CLASSIFICATIONS

		NSR *power class*	*1923 power class*	*1928 power class*
A, B	2-4-0T		1	1P
A, B	2-4-2T		1	1P
C	0-6-4T	1	5	5F
D	0-6-0T	4	2	2F
4 cylr D	0-6-0		3	
DX	0-6-2T	3	2	2F
E	0-6-0	5	1	1F
F	0-6-4T	2	4	4P
G, KT	4-4-0		3	3P
H	0-6-0	2	3	3F
K	4-4-2T		3	3P
KS, ST	0-6-0T	5	1	1F
L	0-6-2T	2	3	3F
M	0-4-4T		3	3P
69, 100, 159	0-6-0	3	2	2F

8: ALLOCATION OF LOCOMOTIVES TO ALSAGER, MACCLESFIELD, STOKE AND UTTOXETER 30 DECEMBER 1950

Class	BR *numbers*	*Total*
2-6-2T Stanier	40086/103/22/6/8/44/56/7	9
2-6-4T Fairburn	42061-3/233-6/675/6/83	10
2-6-4T Fowler	42319/23/43/4/9/55-7/60/2-4/9/75/6	
	42381/2/6	18
2-6-4T Stanier	42431/40/3/5/7/9/58/68/71/9/94/543/67	
	42584/603/5/9/11/63-5/7/8/70-2	26
0-6-0 MR	43915	1
0-6-0 LMS	44063/7/8/77/9/93/118/20/6/307-10/41-4	
	44353/8/9/63/9/73/5/7-80/3/8/91/3/6	
	44448/50/3/5/78/84/9/96/8-500/2-4/7/8	
	44513/48/96	52
4-6-0 Stanier	45114/257/78/324-6/81	7
0-6-0T LMS	47281/338/70/80/445/587/95/6/9/602/9	
	47610/6/47/8/50	16
0-6-0 LNWR	58427	1
	Total locomotives:	140

9: LMS 1933 NUMBERS OF NSR CARRIAGE STOCK

1933 Nos	*Body length & wheels* ft	in		*Compartments*		*Built*
962-3	29	3	6w	OVOL	(a)	1896-1901
964-5	49	0	8w	POVOVOL	(c)	1909
966-7	"		"	LOVOOVOL	(c)	"
10601-3	"		"	111111	(c)	1913-21
15263-4	42	0	"	Third	(n)	1904
15265-6	49	0	"	33333333	(a)	1906-7
15267-8	"		"	"	(c)	1910-20
17771	"		"	3331133	(c)	1913
17772-5	"		"	2211122	(a)	1907
17776-9	"		"	"	(c)	1910
17780-2	"		"	111113	(c)	1912-14
18195-7	"		"	111L111	(c)	1914-20
18908-11	"		"	222L2222	(b)	1908
18912-20	"		"	"	(c)	1909-20
19919-22	"		"	22L11L22	(a)	1906-7
19923-6	"		"	"	(c)	1909-11
19927-9	"		"	1111L33	(c)	1919
24093-6	"		"	33B	(b)	1908
24097-105	"		"	"	(c)	1909-20
24106-7	"		"	3333B	(e)	1906-7
24108-9	"		"	"	(f)	1908
24110-19	"		"	"	(g)	1910-14
24120-9	"		"	"	(h)	1914-20
24130-3	"		"	33333B	(a)	1907
24134-7	"		"	333333B	(a)	"
24766-7	42	0	"	Compo brake	(n)	1904
24670-1	49	0	"	3333LB	(a)	1906-7
24672	"		"	"	(c)	1910
25941-2	"		"	333L2L1B	(b)	1908
25943-5	"		"	333L1L1B	(a)	1907
26594-625	29	3	6w	33333	(a)	1894-1907
26626-35	35	6	"	333333	(a)	1899-1905
27213-9	29	3	"	2112	(a)	1895-1907
27220-4	35	6	"	31113	(a)	1891-1905
27225-6	29	3	"	31P13	(a)	1904
27400	35	6	"	2L11L2	(a)	1896

1933 Nos	*Body length & wheel*			*Compartments*		*Built*
	ft	*in*				
24449-52	35	6	6w	3P1L13	(d)	1891-1905
24453-5	,,		,,	2L11L2	(a)	1900-5
27762-74	29	3	,,	33B	(a)	1899-1907
27775-91	35	6	,,	333B	(a)	1891-1905
27975-6	29	3	,,	P2L33	(a)	1895
34172-84	,,		,,	Brake van		1897-1907
37150-3	22	6	4w	Covered carriage truck		1905
38636-40	20	0	,,	Milk van		1897-1908
38641-68	28	11	6w	,,		1896-1911
38669-93	35	7	,,	,,		1912-21
41862-4	15	0	4w	Open carriage truck		1907
41865-72	22	0	,,	,,		1910-21
43694-733	21	6	,,	Horsebox		1900-14
43995	22	0	,,	Prize cattle van		1906

Total number of vehicles: 358

Compartment classification:

1—first class; 2—second class; 3—third class; B—brake; L—lavatory; O—open unclassed saloon; P—parcels and luggage; V—vestibule

(a)—arc roof, single mouldings between adjacent third compartments and double mouldings between firsts and/or seconds

(b)—arc roof, double mouldings between thirds, treble between firsts and/or seconds

(c)—as (b) but with elliptical roof

(d)—as (a) with lavatories for adjacent first compartments only. Other lavatory coaches had access for all compartments

(e)—as (a) with single pair of luggage doors each side

(f)—as (e) with double mouldings

(g)—as (f) with elliptical roof

(h)—as (g) but with double pair of luggage doors each side

(n)—narrow gauge saloon for the Leek & Manifold line

Note: from 1911 all second class compartments became third class except for carriages Nos 25941-2, 27400 where they became first class.

10: CHIEF OFFICERS

Chairmen:

John Lewis Ricardo	1846-62
Thomas Broderick	1862-65
Lt Col Charles Pearson	1865-74
Colin Minton Campbell	1874-83
Sir Thomas Salt	1883-1904
Tonman Mosley (Lord Anslow from 1916)	1904-22

Secretaries:

Joseph Samuda	1846-76
Percy Morris	1876-94
R. E. Pearce	1894-1922

General Managers:

Samuel Parker Bidder	1848-53
John Curphey Forsyth	1853-63
Percy Morris	1863-76
Martin Smith	1876-82
William Douglas Phillipps	1882-1919
F. A. L. Barnwell	1919-22

Locomotive Superintendents:*

Robert N. Angus	1847-75
C. Clare	1875-82
Luke Longbottom	1882-1902
John Henry Adams	1902-15
J. A. Hookham	1915-22

Engineers:

S. P. Bidder	1846-48
J. C. Forsyth	1848-65
James Johnson	1865-70
Thomas Weatherburn Dodds	1870-74
T. W. Horn	1874-77
William H. Stubbs	1877-86
G. T. Crosbie-Dawson	1886-1914
F. A. L. Barnwell	1914-20
C. G. Rose	1921-22

* Designated Locomotive Foreman until 1874

Bibliography

Beside the books mentioned in the text and notes of reference, a number of other works were consulted generally, including:

Ahrons, E. L. *Locomotive and Train Working in the Latter Part of the Nineteenth Century*. Volume two

Bradshaw's *Railway Manual, Shareholders' Guide & Directory*. Various years

British Railways. *Your New Railway* (April 1966)

Clinker, C. R. *Register of Closed Passenger Stations & Goods Depots in England, Scotland & Wales* 1923-1962

Clinker, C. R. *Railways of the West Midlands. A Chronology* 1808-1954

Essery, R. J., Rowland, D. P. and Steel, W.O. *British Goods Wagons* (1970)

Greville, M. D. *Chronological List of the railways of Cheshire 1837-1939*

Harrison, William. *History of the Manchester Railways* 1882 (Reprinted 1967)

Jones, Kevin P. *Steam Locomotive Development: An Analytical Guide to Literature on British Steam Locomotive Development 1923-62*

'Manifold'. *The Leek & Manifold Light Railway* (1965)

Nixon, F. *The Industrial Archaeology of Derbyshire* (1969)

Ottley, G. *Bibliography of British Railway History* (1965)

Railway Year Book. Various years

Savage, C. I. *An Economic History of Transport*

Schneider, A. & Mase, A. *Railway Accidents of Great Britain & Europe* 1970

Stephenson Locomotive Society *Railway Progress 1909-59*

Journals of the Historical Model Railway Society, Railway & Canal Historical Society, Railway Correspondence & Travel Society, Stephenson Locomotive Society.

Magazines: *Modern Railways, The Railway Magazine, Railway World, Trains Illustrated*

Acknowledgements

Telling this story would have been so much harder but for the enthusiasm and practical help of many people. Much of the original material came from the company records at the British Transport Historical Records Office and we are grateful to the archivist, E. H. Fowkes, his predecessor, E. Atkinson, and their staff. We have greatly valued the friendship and help of Dr J. R. Hollick of Ashbourne, who placed at our disposal the voluminous material of the 'Manifold' collection and his private papers, and read the manuscript before it was 'signalled through' to the publishers.

Our task has been lightened by the help of railway officials: F. R. L. Barnwell, chief civil engineer, Western Region, whose father was the last general manager of the NSR; D. S. M. Barrie, chairman Eastern Region; C. F. G. Chappell, chief accountant, London Midland Region; Jeffrey Dentith, area maintenance engineer, Chester; John Edgington, Frank Young, divisional manager, Stoke; Harold Forster, station manager, Manchester Piccadilly; G. Oldham, works manager, Crewe; Ron Owen, public relations, Stoke; Jeffrey Williams, Public Relations Officer, Birmingham.

Peter Cheeseman, artistic director of the Victoria Theatre, Stoke, has kindly let us use quotations (at the head of Chapters) from the musical documentary *The Knotty*. The editor of the *Times Literary Supplement* published a call for information which brought response from America.

We have greatly valued the assistance of the staff at Cheshire Record Office, Derby Public Library, the John Rylands Library, Manchester, Lancashire County Library, Whitefield, Manchester Central Reference Library; members of the Historical Model Railway Society; Industrial Locomotive Society; Manchester Locomotive Society; Railway & Canal Historical Society; Messrs C. A. Appleton, J. H. Barratt, Stafford county planning and development officer; J. M. Boyes, D. E. Bick, H. D. Bowtell, A. W. Brackenbury, N. Goodwin, J. Groom, K. D. Holt, G. Marquisse (New York), C. A. Moreton, B. Roberts, A. G. Thelwall, O. Veltom, G. D. Whitworth.

Dr E. G. Ashton and Dr I. Scrimgeour (Canada), both provided photographs as well as notes and the photographic material has been enriched by help from Park Pictures (Manchester) Limited, and by offers by M. G. Fell, George W. Hall of Gloucester (who spared no effort to find photographs taken by his father, Thomas Grainger Hall, when he was an apprentice at Stoke); H. B. Oliver, R. E. G. Read, Ron Rushton and J. Walker, who placed at our disposal the collection of his late cousin and photographs taken by J. Lowndes. Mr Walker, incidentally, lives at Whiston alongside the 1802 Caldon tramway route in a house designed by Pugin and built by the NSR for the Caldon Quarry manager.

Whitefield,
Manchester,
October 1970

Rex Christiansen and
R. W. Miller

Index

Illustrations are indicated by **bold** type